Primitive Views
of the World

Edited by
STANLEY DIAMOND

COLUMB

Ne

Note.—Joseph Campbell's contribution to this volume, "Primitive Man as Metaphysician," appears in somewhat altered form in his book *The Masks of God: Primitive Mythology* (New York, The Viking Press, 1959; London, Secker and Warburg, 1960).

First published as chapters in *Culture in History: Essays in Honor of Paul Radin* (Columbia University Press, 1960)

ISBN 0-231-08552-4
Printed in the United States of America
10 9 8 7 6 5 4 3

CONTENTS

INTRODUCTION: THE USES OF THE PRIMITIVE   V
   Stanley Diamond

CONCERNING THE CONCEPT OF "PRIMITIVITY"   1
   Kurt Goldstein

PRIMITIVE MAN AS METAPHYSICIAN   20
   Joseph Campbell

THINKER AND INTELLECTUAL IN PRIMITIVE SOCIETY   33
   Robert Redfield

OJIBWA ONTOLOGY, BEHAVIOR, AND WORLD VIEW   49
   A. Irving Hallowell

THE WORLD OF THE KERESAN PUEBLO INDIANS   83
   Leslie A. White

NAVAHO CATEGORIES   95
   Clyde Kluckhohn

THE GOTR CEREMONY OF THE BORO GADABA   129
   Karl Gustav Izikowitz

REFLECTIONS ON THE ONTOLOGY OF RICE   151
   Jane Richardson Hanks

THE PRIMITIVE PRESENCE IN PRE-CLASSICAL GREECE   155
   Thalia Phillies Howe

PLATO AND THE DEFINITION OF THE PRIMITIVE   170
   Stanley Diamond

ANTHROPOLOGICAL PERSPECTIVES ON THE MODERN
COMMUNITY   194
   Maurice Stein

To the Unknown African
who, because of his primal and poetic humanity,
was regarded by white men as a "thing" to be
bought, sold, and used as an instrument of pro-
duction; and who, alone in the forests of West Africa,
created a vision of life so simple as to be terrifying,
yet a vision that was irreducibly human . . .

Richard Wright, *Black Power* (New York, Harper, 1954)

INTRODUCTION: THE USES OF THE PRIMITIVE

THE IDEA OF THE primitive is as old as civilization because civilized men have, always and everywhere, been compelled by the conditions of their existence to try to understand their roots and human possibilities. But the converse does not hold. Primitive societies, so far as I know, have not generated any systematic notion or idea, certainly not any vision, of civilization. This I believe to be an odd and revealing circumstance. How are we to explain it? May we say that primitive people have no conception of progress or development, nor any sense of history, and thus no basis for projecting an image of civilization? I think not. In the first place, primitive peoples have strong canons and perceptions of personal growth or progress, as the individual journeys through society, moving from experience to experience, crisis to crisis, ritual to ritual, on what the Winnebago call "the road of life and death." The concrete *idea* of personal development saturates primitive society. Second, primitive cosmologies are often developmental in the broadest, metaphorical sense. Primitives do not lack a general capacity to conceptualize development or change in form over time; their perceptions are not static. Nor do they ignore simple chronologies, or event sequences; the memories of primitive people are, in the absence of writing, unusually efficient. But history to them is the recital of sacred meanings within a cyclic, as opposed to a lineal, perception of time. The merely pragmatic event, uninvolved with the sacred cycle, falls, as it were, outside history, because it is of no importance in maintaining or revitalizing the traditional forms of society. So it is true, I believe, to state that primitives have no *secular* sense of history, and no lineal *idea*, and hence no prophetic *ideal*, of social progress. Moreover, progress as an abstraction has no meaning for them.

This is, obviously, not the result of a lack of imagination but of a lack of need. Primitive myths, folk tales, legends, oral traditions generally, abound in the most vivid and trenchant symbolic comments on the human condition, but their content, in no case of which I am aware, foreshadows that level of social structure and quality of cultural being which we call civilization. The civilized human condition, it would seem, is *inconceivable* to primitive peoples. It is not even imagined as a mythological alternative, since civilized behavior is so critically different, in actuality, from primitive behavior, as different, let us say, as the differences between the sexes. Nor is this the result of a lack of contact between any given primitive people and civilization. For example, no American Indian tribe, moving on the expanding margins of civilization, fighting for the room to breathe, proved willing or eager to "civilize" itself after the model of the Europeans.

In fact, acculturation has always been a matter of conquest. Either civilization directly shatters a primitive culture which happens to stand in its historical right of way or a primitive social economy, in the grip of a civilized market, becomes so attenuated and weakened that it can no longer contain the traditional culture. In both cases, refugees from the foundering groups may adopt the standards of the more potent society in order to survive as individuals. But these are conscripts of civilization, not volunteers. Thus, the idea of civilization is, among primitives, determined after the fact of contact and, then, the conceptions seem negative, fragmented, uncommitted to any grandiose notion of civilization as such, and they are often uncomfortable caricatures of our cheapest desires. Pertinently, among the more significant political leaders of the emerging ex-Colonial states in areas where primitive cultural characteristics still remotely exist, one gets no sense of any deracinated and secular belief in progress. Rather, there is always the conception of a *return* to the communal ethos and disciplined expressiveness, of the primitive community, achieved through a new technology and more broadly based social forms. As we shall see, this was a typical Enlightenment attitude. Strangely enough, as the last phase of the French Revolution reaches Africa, the leadership looks to the spirit of the past of its own people, to those "savage tribes" that caught the fancy of certain *philosophes,* and which they used to exemplify certain truths, as a guide and catchword for the future. If Old Europe and the New World, which it spawned, are to survive their own hardening civilization, it may be to those "savage tribes" now emerging that we must look. Torn by the Western world, still free of our vested interests and archaic capital equipment, more disordered but not so civilized and sick as we are, they may, if granted their fair share of the world's technology, yet prove the case for the Enlightenment, which is also our case. That, at any rate, is what their best leaders, speaking in the idiom of our eighteenth-century forefathers, imply. But their polities are no longer primitive; they trade on memories and on the inherited richness of the apolitical human associations in the localities. No primitive society has gone to civilization as to a greater good—in the emerging areas it is simply a question of using whatever primitive resources remain.

The fact (startling as it may seem to a civilized mentality) is that the majority of men for the greater portion of human history and prehistory have found primitive societies economically, socially, and spiritually (or, as we would say, ideologically) *viable*. The absence of revolutions and reform movements, the nativistic opposition that arises when primitive cultures are under assault, with doctrines that turn the unacculturated state into an Eden and chiefs into prophets, preaching that civilization is but the wrath of God which may be exorcised by penance and right living, the spontaneous, marked distaste (despite the selective borrowing of potent instruments) when the primitive culture retains a base from which to view civilization, and the absence of any alternative mode of life as a systematic element in primitive oral tradition are all symptomatic of the human adequacy of primitive institutions. The passionate notion of death and rebirth through ritual, the linking of the deceased to the living and the unborn, the projected kinship of the society with nature and the person with society, in creative correlation with traditional subsistence techniques, set primitive perceptions against the idea of progress. Even when a relatively integrated and defiant primitive society borrows from civilization a superior tool for a specific purpose, the effort is made to incorporate the new element into the preexistent structure of belief and action. It is not imagined that the tool may have other consequences. How often primitive persons have lost their way in civilization because they could not anticipate, and therefore never learned or learned too late, the responses expected of them in a novel environment! How often they have misconstrued intention,

misread sign or symbol, or looked for brothers where only strangers lived! To mistake the city for a compound, the European for
an elder or a peer, or money in the hand for the capacity to live
alone—such little soul-destroying errors need only be committed
once.

The cyclic sense of time in accord with natural and human
rhythms and the absence of the idea of progress and of any vision
of civilization are, of course, related phenomena; they are further
correlated with the nature of primitive as opposed to civilized
technology. When we examine archaic civilizations (Egypt, Baby-
lonia, Greece, China, Rome) or contemporary commercial-indus-
trial civilizations, we find that the life pace set by the demands of
the market, the civil authority, or the machine increasingly dis-
place human and natural rhythms. In both slave- and machine-
based societies, the expressive, musical movements of the primitive,
communal work group have been abandoned. The primitive work
group is traditional and multifunctional; labor is, of course, utilitarian but it is also sacred—a sport, a dance, a celebration, a thing
in itself. In civilization, group labor becomes a compulsive means.
In an archaic society, slaves may work under overseers, in large,
uniform groups, constructing, by brute labor, public utilities; or
they may work under extreme pressure, using rationalized, mechanical motions, to produce as many agricultural or commercial
products as possible within a given period of time, in order to
maximize profit to masters.

In machine-based societies, the machine has incorporated the
demands of the civil power or of the market, and the whole life
of society, of all classes and grades, must adjust to its rhythms.
Time becomes lineal, secularized, "precious"; it is reduced to an
extension in space that must be filled up, and sacred time disap-
pears. The secretary must adjust to the speed of her electric type-
writer; the stenographer to the stenotype machine; the factory
worker to the line or lathe; the executive to the schedule of the train
or plane and the practically instantaneous transmission of the
telephone; the chauffer to the superhighways; the reader to the
endless stream of printed matter from high-speed presses; even
the schoolboy to the precise periodization of his day and to the

watch on his wrist; the person "at leisure" to a mechanized domestic environment and the flow of efficiently scheduled entertainment. The machines seem to run us, crystallizing, in their mechanical or electronic pulses, the means of our desires. The collapse of time to an extension in space, calibrated by machines, has bowdlerized our natural and human rhythms and helped dissociate us from ourselves. Even now, we hardly love the earth or see with eyes or listen any longer with our ears, and we scarcely feel our hearts beat before they break in protest. Even now, so faithful and exact are the machines as servants that they seem an alien force, persuading us at every turn to fulfill our intentions which we have built into them and which they represent—in much the same way that the perfect body servant routinizes and, finally, trivializes his master.

Of such things, actual or possible, primitive societies have no conception. Such things are literally beyond their wildest dreams, beyond their idea of alienation from village or family or the earth itself, beyond their conception of death, which does not estrange them from society or nature but completes the arc of life. There is only one rough analogy. The fear of excommunication from the kinship unit, from the personal nexus that joins man, society, and nature in an endless round of growth, in short, the sense of being isolated and depersonalized and, therefore, at the mercy of demonic forces—a punishment and a fear widespread among primitive peoples—may be taken as an indication of how they would react to the technically alienating processes of civilization if they were to understand them. That is, by comprehending the attitude of primitive people about excommunication from the web of social and natural kinship we can, by analogy, understand their repugnance and fear of civilization.

Primitive society may be regarded as a system in equilibrium, spinning kaleidoscopically on its axis, but at a relatively fixed point. Civilization may be regarded as a system in internal disequilibrium; technology or ideology or social organization are always out of joint with each other—that is what propels the system along a given track. Our sense of movement, of *incompleteness,* contributes to the idea of progress. Hence, the idea of progress is

generic to civilization. And our idea of primitive society as existing in a state of dynamic equilibrium and as expressive of human
and natural rhythms is a logical projection of civilized societies,
in opposition to the latter's actual state. But it also coincides with
the *real* historical condition of primitive societies. The longing for
a primitive mode of existence is no mere fantasy or sentimental
whim; it is consonant with fundamental human needs, the fulfillment of which (although in different form) is, as we have discovered in the milieus of civilization, a precondition for our more
elaborate lives. Even the skeptical and civilized Samuel Johnson,
who derided Boswell for his intellectual affair with Rousseau, had
written:

when man began to desire private property then entered violence,
and fraud, and theft, and rapine. Soon after, pride and envy broke out
in the world and brought with them a new standard of wealth, for man,
who till then, thought themselves rich, when they wanted nothing, now
rated their demands, not by the calls of nature, but by the plenty of
others; and began to consider themselves poor, when they beheld their
own possessions exceeded by those of their neighbors.

This may be inadequate ethnology, but it was the *cri de coeur* of
a civilized man for a surcease from mere consumption and acquisitiveness, and, so interpreted, it assumes something about primitive
societies that is true, namely, predatory property, production for
profit, as we know it, does not exist among them.

The search for the primitive is, then, as old as civilization. It is
the search for the utopia of the past, projected into the future; it
is paradise lost and paradise regained, with civilization being the
middle term. It is birth, death, and transcendent rebirth, the passion called Christian, the trial of Job, the oedipal transition, the
triadic metaphor of human growth, felt also in the vaster pulse of
history. And this search for the primitive is inseparable from the
vision of civilization. No prophet or philosopher of any consequence has spelled out the imperatives of his version of a superior
civilization without assuming certain constants in human nature
and elements of a primitive condition, without, in short, engaging
in the anthropological enterprise. A utopia detached from these

twin pillars—a sense of human nature and a sense of the pre-civilized past—becomes a nightmare. For humanity must then be conceived to be infinitely adaptable and thus incapable of historic understanding or self-amendment. Even Plato's utopia presumes, at least, a good if no longer viable prior state, erroneously conceived as primitive by the refined Greek when it was merely rustic; and the *Republic* was, after all, founded on a theory of human nature that was certainly wrong. Nevertheless it was a saving grace, for Plato believed that his perfectly civilized society would *realize* human possibilities, not merely manipulate them.

Even the most brilliant and fearful utopian projections have been compelled to solve the problem of the human response, usually with some direct or allegorical reference to a prior or primitive level of functioning. In Zamiatin's *We,* a satirical work of great beauty, the collective society of the future is based on, and has become a maleficent version of, Plato's *Republic;* the people have been reduced to abstract ciphers, their emotions being controlled and centralized (as in the *Republic,* mathematics is the most sublime language, but it is not a means of human communication, only an abstract dialogue with God), and history has ceased to exist. Zamiatin documents the growth of the internal rebel who is gradually educated in the experience of love. When the revolt against the State of Happiness occurs, the civil power uses two ultimate weapons: one is a method of instantaneously disintegrating the enemy; since the enemy is legion, the other method is the salvation of the person, as an eternal civil servant, through a quick, efficient operation on the brain that results in a permanent dissociation of intellect and emotion without impairing technical intelligence. Zamiatin's description of the rebel rendered affectless, lucidly describing the changes on his beloved coconspirator's face, and feeling nothing, as she dies, anticipates Camus and transmits in its terrifying, poignant flatness a psychological truth about our time that have become a dreadful cliché. In other words, Zamiatin informs us that such a materialist, secularized, and impersonal utopia can function only by altering human nature itself. And, of course, outside the glass wall of that utopian city which had arisen out of the ruin of the "final" war between the country and the city is a green wilderness in which primitive rebels living off the land, alive to their humanity, seek to free the ultimately urbanized brother within.

The point is, and it applies equally to the lesser works of Huxley, Orwell, and others, that where the utopian projection is conceived as a nightmare, that is, as a mere extension of the shape of contemporary industrial society, and where the intent is to protest rather than to create a vision of a more viable future, even in such cases the author finds himself rediscovering the flaw in the monolith—human nature—and the necessity of a more existential realization through a more primitive expression.

Contemporary civilization everywhere tends toward collectivization, whether upon a "public" or "private" basis; it is not the devil of any particular system. Thus, contemporary states forge or ignore history; political myths are created which propagate the official version of human nature and an inevitable past that wholly justifies the present. The capacity to create primitive myths that explore the ambivalence of man, the plains and precipices of the spirit in which we are privileged to wander by the mere fact of our humanity, and the incessant struggle for a common human identity simply withers like an unused human muscle.

In the face of these civil compulsions, the Soviet authors Mayakovsky, poet, and Olesha, novelist, conceive a "conspiracy" of *ambivalent* emotions, which holds all society in ransom for the chance at social expression. In *The Bedbug,* Mayakovsky resurrects, in a more perfectly collective future, a "vodka-soaked, guitar-strumming vulgarian of a party member, with a proletarian ancestry." He is displayed in a glass case as a zoological curiosity with certain superficial similarities to man. At the close of the play, this "insect" shouts: "Citizens! Brothers! My own people! Darlings! How did you get here? So many of you! When were you unfrozen? Why am I alone in the cage? Darlings, friends, come and join me! Why am I suffering? Citizens! . . ." But this vulgarian of the late twenties, who, Mayakovsky prophesied, would be a hero of human feeling before the century was out, is led back to his cage by an armed guard. In his "Letter from Paris to Comrade Kostrov on the Nature of Love," Mayakovsky instructs a literary bureaucrat in the complex meaning of that emotion: "Love has inflicted/ on me/ a lasting wound . . . / Love will always hum—love/ human and simple. Hurricane/ fire/ water/ surge forward, rumbling. Who/ can/ control this? Can you?/ Try it. . . ." Similarly, in "Conversation with a Tax Collector about Poetry," he ridicules the Philistine standards of the state: "Your form/ has a mass of questions:/ 'Have you traveled on business/ or not?'/ But suppose/ I have/ ridden to death a hundred Pegasi/ in the last/ 15 years?/ And here you have—/ imagine my feelings!—/ something/ about servants/ and assets./ But what if I am/ simultaneously/ a leader/ and a servant/ of the people/ . . . Citizen tax collector/ I'll cross out/ all the zeros/ after the five/ and pay the rest. I demand/ as my right/ an inch of ground/ among/ the poorest/ workers and peasants."

With their roots in a more tragic view of life than our own, and confronted with a blunter, more clearly demarcated style of collectivism, the Russian literary conspiracy against utopia merges with a critique of the modern industrial state that is universal.

The idea of the primitive is, then, as old as civilization, because civilization creates it in the search for human identity. This was already evident in the works of Herodotus, Tacitus, Ovid, Horace, Hesiod, and other poets and scholars of Western classical antiquity; they tried to grasp the nature of their own ancestry and conceptualize the barbarian strangers who thronged the borders of their archaic states. I say "conceptualize," not merely "describe," because any act of historical understanding is a reading of systematic meaning into the behavior of others. In seeking to understand the primitive world from which they descended and which echoed all around them, these early chroniclers, themselves the product of political societies, also had to sound the depths of their own actual or potential experience. That is, the task was not only conceptual in the abstract but demanded that quality of introspective imagination that moved Terence to write, *Home sum: humani nil a me alienum puto,* "I am a man. I consider nothing alien to me." It is a remark that any historian and any anthropologist (for anthropology is in the field of history) must be able to make, or they should remain silent. Yet such a conviction cannot be empirically validated. No anthropologist has had experience in more than a few societies; no historian can live in the time about which he tells us.

The point is that the absolute prerequisite of historical consciousness is an unrelenting exploration of the self as it does exist and may be imagined to exist. The facts of other cultures, the artifacts, mentifacts, and sociofacts, are the external phenomena, the indirect evidence which must be tracked down to their human sources. The conceptualization of another culture or of another period in history (the problem is the same) is the result of the interaction of the sense of self with the artifacts of another time and place. The idea of the primitive is, then, a construct. But this is merely to acknowledge that all historical thinking is "constructive," which does not render historical knowledge merely subjective. Rather, the assumption is that, as members of the same species, human beings are capable of interpreting the inwardness of the acts of others. Historical knowledge is, therefore, a form of *communication,* analogous to immediate human transaction in vivo. Both share an a priori component. When communicating with other people, we assume that they are as we are. That is, we feel sure that common meanings can be understood and expressed through an unexpressed consensus about the meaning of the symbols involved. This process includes the idiosyncratic and highly personal use of symbols, as, for example, when one reads and understands a novel or a poem, whose language may be symbolically richer and subtler than that of ordinary communication. But the author of the novel or poem, or the person with whom we communicate directly, is no more accessible to us than is an actor in another time or place. We interpret his consciousness on the basis of symbolic acts. *What the other is,* if that makes any sense at all, is otherwise inaccessible; his acts speak for him. The paradigm of historical knowledge, then, is in direct human communication: we approach an understanding of people of the past or of other cultures through an appreciation of the meaning of their emotions as expressed in signs, which constitute direct physical evidence, or symbols. It is our consciousness, as a species, that enables us to empathize with what we do not directly share. The authentic historian may thus be said to have attained, by training and talent, a very high pitch of speciational consciousness. He approaches other societies in other times with the confidence that his humanity is equal to the task of registering *differences*. And that, though not the only element, is the *critical* one in all human communication.

The anthropologist must be such a historian. In conceptualizing a primitive society, he interprets signs and symbols by exchanging places with the actors in the system under study. The mere cataloguing or even systematic linking of institutions and artifacts is meaningless unless the effort to reproduce the social consciousness, the cultural being of the people who live and produce in their modality, is made. Every technique available must, of course, be used in these efforts, but the techniques may not become ends in themselves. If we detach the social forms and tools from persons and arrange and rearrange them typologically in the service of this or that method or as abstract, deductive models, we lose touch with concrete social reality, with the imprecisions of human behavior, and with its actual meaning at a particular time. The merely logical elaboration of kinship systems that we may impose upon a people does not necessarily reflect the consciousness of the actors, and may, in fact, lead to a grotesque notion of behavior if translated into behavioral equivalents. The abstract concern with the evolution of the forms of energy, which represents no encountered historical sequence, is similarly irrelevant, as opposed, for example, to a description of what it means to make and use and control a primitive tool in contrast to pushing a button on an automatic lathe or working in a coal mine. The study of cultural apparatus finds its basic meaning in the attempt to understand the social consciousness that it both reflects and creates. Otherwise the study of man is not the study of man but the study of social, ideological, economic, or technical forms, a sort of cultural physics. The end, however, does not lie in technique but in the effort to understand those who are different, by virtue of what they have created, from ourselves, responding as we know we would in their circumstances. As a young sociologist wrote recently in criticizing Parsonian and related systematics: "They failed to touch upon an entire vast realm of the industrial experience, horror; they failed to comprehend either the collective horrors or the personal horrors which certain features of industrial society almost necessarily involve. What may be needed is a 'sociology of horror' in which social science tries to be honest with the industrial world and with itself."

The possibilities of conceptualizing a primitive society (indeed any society anywhere) are inexhaustible. The intent and position of the observer are constant variables. Their portraits may differ in emphasis, but if they are faithful to the data they examine and if their purposes are clear they will not be contradictory but complementary. For example, nineteenth-century anthropology hardly deals with the problem of war, whereas, in the last decade, we have become increasingly fixed on the nature, definition, and extent of war and, thus, of human conflict generally. This is surely correlated with the fact that the nineteenth century, although marked by a few civil and colonial struggles, was, relatively speaking, an era of international amity in the Euro-American purview. The critical problem of the twentieth century has further directed our attention, as anthropologists, to primitive warfare, and the conclusion presently in the air (although Malinowski had made the point a generation ago) seems to be that it is qualitatively distinct from the modern species, that is, abstract, ideological conflicts and mass secular means of extermination are unknown in primitive society. Primitive war consists in heavily ritualized skirmishes (Malinowski refused to define them as "war"), except where the life of a culture is at stake. It seems clear that, as human society develops, the intricacy and pertinence of our images of past societies increase rather than decrease. The distinctions in these images of primitive society are, in the broader sense, instrumental; we describe the system with a continuous redefinition and refinement of problems as they exist in our own time. Of course, incompetence and dishonesty can assume the guise of historical knowledge, but the reference here is to serious work, by students who possess no more than the usual complement of human foibles.

There is, then, no final or static or exclusively objective picture of primitive society. *We* snap the portrait, using film of different sensitivity for different purposes. Moreover, there is no really sophisticated portrait of primitive society that can be transmitted to us by an actor from within the system, precisely because it is our experience of civilization that leads to questions that the primitive person is not likely to ask about his culture and to recognize problems or even see virtue where he perceives routine. The difficulties, for example, that beset human communication in contemporary, industrial society are foreign to primitive cultures. Lacking experience in civilization, they are probably beyond primitive conception. Therefore, it is only a representative of our civilization who can, in adequate detail, document the differences and help create an idea of the primitive, which would not ordinarily be constructed by primitives themselves. We *need* such ideas of the primitive, but that does not make them any the less "objective" or valid. The complementarity of systems, the possibility of different yet independently consistent, purposive interpretations, faithful to the data, is in the very nature of historical knowledge. Indeed, as Neils Bohr indicates, it is in the very nature of our knowledge of physical systems.

The more immediate, modern origin of the idea of the primitive is in the European Enlightenment. Two complexly connected traditions, which have since polarized the thinking of anthropologists yet never completely divided it and which can therefore be described as ambivalent, began to emerge clearly in the eighteenth century, notably in France but throughout Western Europe. Rousseau, above all, as well as Monboddo, the early Herder, Schiller, and others represent the *retrospective* tradition, that is, the conscious search in history for a more "deeply expressive, permanent, human nature and cultural structure," in contrast to the nascent modern realities that were being generated by the revolutionary bourgeoisie. The preceding Age of Discovery had introduced the West to the primitive world, and this became the fulcrum for the effort to understand the contemporary scene in a Europe that had been growing increasingly civilized and enlightened, through the late Renaissance and the Reformation, even before the Enlightenment itself. The Age of Discovery held a constant image of another aspect of humanity before the Europe that was beginning to break out of medievalism and look outward in space and, freed of medieval cosmology, back to its own roots in time.

Montaigne and Camoëns in the sixteenth century, later Dryden, and then Pope had responded with a more or less sentimental, more or less sophisticated but always arresting primitivism. More systematic and balanced formulations were to succeed theirs. The direction and the purpose were clearly marked by Rousseau, who in questioning the credentials of missionaries as chroniclers of savage tribes ("for the study of man there are requisite gifts which are not always the portions of the saints") called upon "the scientific academies to send expeditions composed of trained and genuinely philosophical observers to all savage countries, that they might compose at leisure, a natural, moral, and political history of what they have seen. By such a study a new world would be disclosed and by means of it, we should learn to understand our own."

The Age of Discovery provided the opportunity for direct scrutiny of radically different peoples, the forerunner of field work and participant observation. This latter technique, the basic methodological contribution of anthropology, is an extension of the notion of the Romantic historians that sympathy with "the object of study" was essential to historical understanding. The majority of subsequent historians of any stature, whether or not technically associated with the Romantic tradition, itself an aspect of the German Enlightenment, have accepted this principle as a necessary prerequisite of historical knowledge. As Marc Bloch put it: "Behind the features of landscape, behind tools or machinery, behind what appear to be the most formalized documents, and behind institutions, which seem almost entirely detached from their founders, there are men, and it is men that history seeks to grasp."

The mere pursuit of forms obscures, also, our understanding of functional equivalents, to which diverse forms may be assimilated. Hence, our broader sense of historical levels suffers, and we fail to report, for example, in our formal work, *what it is like* to move in a human and natural world of kinship as opposed to a technical stratum of civilized society. The study of the fantastic array of irreducible cultural forms that men have invented is, of course, worthwhile in itself; they are the reason for the existence of museums and the occasion for aesthetic contemplation, but they do not substitute for the functional sense from within.

Despite their formal and structural preoccupations, the majority of anthropologists continue to record, with the left hand, deep affection and respect for their primitive informants. Claude Lévi-Strauss, for example, who has been concerned with some of the most abstract problems in the field of social structure, is, at the same time, capable of writing a book that is proudly in the Rousseauan tradition. In *In the Company of Man* a number of anthropologists, representing a broad spectrum of areal and topical interests, converge to a single opinion about the extraordinary character of their informants; they are portrayed as expressive, insightful, brave, dignified, deeply individuated, and so on. In other works, Colin Turnbull, Elizabeth Marshall, Laura Bohannan, Monica Wilson, Knut Rasmussen, and Peter Freuchen, to name a few, revel in the complex humanity of primitive peoples. Frequently, as noted, this is in sharp contrast to the more technical aspects of such work. That is, the forms of the society studied are not integrated with the state of cultural being described in more personal statements.

In undertaking participant observation, anthropologists are, then, in the Romantic tradition of historical knowledge, in turn based upon the retrospective tradition of the Enlightenment, which found its living laboratory in the Age of Discovery. The eagerness with which most anthropologists have accepted the canons of participant observation in small communities testifies to something beyond pride of technique. It is, I believe, the symptom of an attitude that anthropologists, as civilized individuals, share about the inadequacy of civilized human associations. The anthropological temperament is, after all, marginal. It is historical; we take the deep past seriously; we speak for societies that cannot speak for themselves, and we cherish the things men make; we are preservers, not destroyers. We are specialists in tradition in an age that is growing traditionless. We are still largely self-selected to study people off the mainstream of contemporary civilization. We think enough of such people to live among them, to learn from and to respect them, and in their light examine ourselves and our society. We come close to being real citizens of the world, not merely adherents of an abstract and legal concept of world government. In this final phase of the era of nation-states, not necessarily of nationalities, that can be a dangerous frame of mind. We are, in other words, marginal in temperament; if not quite Kierkegaard's double agents, we are, at least, sharply aware of the narrowing chances of cultural variation in the modern world, of the loss of customs and languages. We worry about such matters, and we are not easily taken in by political propaganda or advertisements for progress. I think that we are repelled by such slogans as "Progress is our *only* product," and most of us would probably associate our selves with Lévi-Strauss when he wrote: "Civilization manufactures monoculture like sugar beet."

When anthropologists or people in related disciplines, who learned the technique from anthropologists, undertake participant observation in their own societies, we may interpret this as both a professional and a personal effort to create human ties that are highly restricted, attenuated, or specialized in contemporary industrial milieus. The very *need* for field work among people of our own society is, of course, a symptom of dissociation and not merely an imperative of social complexity, since field work among the middle class is done, for example, by middle-class intellectuals. More often than not they are shocked by what they learn, as were Seeley, Sims, and Loosely in their investigation of Crestwood Heights. This implies a degree of social and human ignorance about ourselves (I do not mean that pejoratively; we all share it) that is unimaginable among primitive persons. The proliferation of psychological counselors of every conceivable type not shamans, not dramatists, not creators of meaning, but adjusters, those fragile safety valves for the emotional underground of our rationalizing civilization, is a parallel symptom of the hardening and formalization of human associations. Rousseau, the parent of our retrospective tendency, had already complained of this, as Lovejoy indicated, when he spoke of "the elaborate structure of pretense and accommodation, the keeping up of appearances, the tribute which the vanity of one leads him to pay to the vanity of another, in order that he may receive a return in kind," that mark the emotional life and behavior of civilized men. The "savage," wrote Rosseau, "has his life within himself; civilized man, in the opinion of others." We may reformulate this more sophisticatedly as follows: In contemporary civilization, the person tends to dissolve into the status or role; among primitives, new statures are assimilated to the person, who grows to encompass them through crisis rites, ritual dramas that may be psychologically and physically painful but give him a series of brilliant moments in a living drama on a social stage in a chorus of kinsmen. Henry James understood the modern situation also. In *The Private Life,* he dissects a character who, "though a master of all the social graces, had *no* private life; he ceased to exist altogether when not in society—when no longer an object of the admiring attention of others."

Participant observation is, in our society, an effort to get behind this infinite regression of social masks that hypercivilized sociologists, lost in a reified maze of role and status studies, mistake for personal reality and a sort of eternal human truth. Just as anthropologists, as representatives of civilization, have a need to construct an idea of the primitive, so they participate in primitive societies in order to tell us what it is like to abandon oneself to a human encounter and, when engaging in field work in our own society, what it means simply to seek a human encounter.

The Enlightenment generated a mature version of the primitive (as distinct from the earlier "primitivism"), defined by Rousseau and necessarily related to his severe criticism of nascent, modern culture; correlatively, it initiated a modern vision of an evolving secular civilization. Reinforced by the new techniques that seemed to be at hand for the control of the natural environment and flushed by the possibilities of a new science, rooted in Newton, Bacon, and Locke, the English forerunners of the Enlightenment, the Encyclopedists in general sought an empirically derived, rational, and logical periodization of the laws of nature and society and the revelation of a new man, freed from all past superstitions and prejudice. This *prospective* trend in Enlightenment thinking, this evolutionary thrust into the future, was related to its apparent opposite: the retrospective concern with a more permanent definition of the nature of the species and of the realization of human needs in an appropriate social environment. As I have pointed out in the instance of the fictional utopias, Enlightenment thought plunged into the past to develop a more viable sense of the future. However, Enlightenment thinkers tended to move in one or another of its major streams. Rousseau, alienated by the rising bourgeoisie, the new urbanism, the pervading commercialism and acquisitiveness, the droning bureaucracies, and the estrangement of men from natural and human rhythms, devoted most of his energies to the retrospective search for the means of uniting technical education and a more fully human socialization; and he addressed himself to the role of human volition in the formation and acceptance of government. But it is important to recall that this was a matter of emphasis; despite the epigrammatic Voltaire, Rousseau never counseled a return to any historically specific "state of nature," as he put it, "that was a deduction in the manner of his adversaries," and such a return he dismissed as impossible; although he did wonder that men should have abandoned that relatively creative life which we would probably designate as early neolithic. But he answers his question with surprising adequacy, foreshadowing in general outline the work of the evolutionary prehistorians, Gordon Childe, Graham Clark, and others. There is no doubt that the *Discourse on the Origins of Equality* is the earliest systematic modern effort of any consequence to build a grand theory of human and cultural evolution; and it is the first outline of a general text in anthropology.

Rousseau spoke consistently of the "perfectability" of man; he believed in the possibility and necessity of progress. But he recognized that certain human possibilities had been creatively realized in an *inimitable* way in the viable societies of primitive people. In contrast, Condorcet, Quesnay, and most of their fellow *philosophes* were primarily in the prospective mode—Condorcet wrote his *Sketch for a Historical Picture of the Progress of the Human Mind* while in hiding from the Terror, and probably committed suicide in Robespierre's prison; he was not progressive *enough,* having fought against the death penalty for the deposed King. Did any major *philosophe* ever wholly lose the dialectic sense of return that renders the future livable and is the hallmark of the authentic historian?

Modern anthropology, then, is the natural heir of the Enlightenment, the axial age of contemporary civilization. Our basic concern with primitives springs from the use to which Rousseau and others wished to put the Age of Discovery. Participant observation, that further refinement of field work, is rooted in the sense of history, in the effort to penetrate the consciousness of past actors, to evaluate our social being against theirs. Our progressive, evolutionary, lawful, materialistic, and secular interpretations of human development tie us to the prospective Encyclopedists. Our wrestling with the *problem* of human nature, with its variety and unity, our appreciation of cultural variation, distrust of civilization, and preoccupation with the contrasting values of primitive society place us in the retrospective tradition.

But there is one Enlightenment inheritance that we have lost: the theoretical-instrumental unity of thought and action. No Enlightenment thinker felt that he was talking into the wind; they all spun out their ideas in an experimental, dangerous, and changing environment. For better or worse, a sheltered scholasticism was conceived as the medieval antagonist. The thinkers of the Enlightenment spoke to the ordinary citizen on the one hand (the Encyclopedia had a wide popular sale in France proportionate, of course, to the extent of literacy—the papers of the American Revolution were breakfast reading) and worked as revolutionaries, ministers of state, teachers, but independent teachers, of kings, on the other. No Enlightenment thinker could have concluded with Ralph Linton that:

the signs are plain that this era of freedom is [also] drawing to a close, and there can be little doubt that the study of culture and society will be the first victim of the new order. The totalitarian State has no place for it. In fact, for men to take an interest in such matters is in itself a criticism of the existing order, an indication that they doubt its perfection. Unless all history is at fault, the social scientist will go the way of the Greek philosopher. However . . . [he] will leave a heritage of technique for investigation and *of discerned but unsolved problems;* a new frontier from which free minds will sometime press forward again into the unknown. When this time comes, perhaps after centuries of darkness and stagnation, men will look back to us as we look back to the Greeks.

Here, then, is an anthropologist expressing his frustration at being socially and politically impotent and thus acknowledging his desire to be otherwise, to be in the Enlightenment mode. The only practical echo of the Enlightenment imperative to action is in the ambiguous milieu of applied or action anthropology, which has no force in the formative social decisions of our time but, rather, reflects them.

As with their major Enlightenment ancestors, no contemporary anthropologist is wholly committed to the retrospective or prospective undertaking. The profession looks backward and forward at the same time, while uncomfortably straddling the breach between knowledge and action. But there are relatively distinct types. Radin, Redfield, Sapir, and more recently Lévi-Strauss are significant figures in the retrospective tradition. We may take Sapir as characteristic. His distinction between genuine and spurious, that is, authentic and inauthentic cultures, readily transforms itself into a primitive-civilized historical sequence. The affective-cognitive-instrumental unity of many primitive activities serves as a basis for Sapir's critique of civilization (see, for example, his analysis of the affective isolation of the telephone operator); yet Sapir's whole approach is a plea for an understanding and an amendment of the modern condition.

Typical ambivalence is expressed by Redfield and Lévi-Strauss. In concluding his *Primitive World and Its Transformations,* Redfield finds it necessary to become prospective. He tries to define progress objectively, more or less following Kroeber's problematical criteria, although Kroeber had been skeptical about the subjective validity of the notion of progress as such. There is no need to examine Redfield's indexes of progress (he was a brilliant retrospectivist at heart), for they are not impressive; the important thing is to note the ambivalent and unresolved Enlightenment inheritance.

Lévi-Strauss, in his summary of his life thus far as an anthropologist, concludes that all human efforts can be reduced to the arrangement and rearrangement of elements, forming transient structures; eventually man and his works will sink back without a trace into the flux of matter. This is as close as Lévi-Strauss gets to a *prospective* statement, and it is linked to, even if it is a rather negative version of the ideas of, the physiocrats, particularly those of Baron d'Holbach. However, we can understand this view logically, not only historically, if we recall that Lévi-Strauss is a structuralist with a deep respect for primitive society, in the Rousseauan tradition. Since the primitive is beyond recall and since Lévi-Strauss is profoundly skeptical of the possibilities of civilization, the disintegration of human effort in the future, as in the past, is all that we can anticipate, unless we accept the great Frenchman's deism, which is also an Enlightenment inheritance.

Julian Steward, Leslie White, Gordon Childe, and one of their great progenitors, Tylor, are primarily *prospectivists*. Yet Tylor, for example, refers to the fact that "among the lessons learnt from the lives of rude tribes is how society can go on without the policeman to keep order." White, despite his mechanical materialism (which is adumbrated among the physiocrats), assumes that a primitive level of integration is a historical reality; he has always refrained from an enthusiastic assessment of the present condition of civilization, and he has written empathically of a primitive world view. Steward's evolutionism has been similarly tempered, and at one time in his career he documented the position of the clown in primitive societies, thus implying an essential difference with civilization—the way in which socially ambiguous and personally ambivalent attitudes are structured in primitive cultures.

Most anthropologists are, however, less consciously committed to either Enlightenment tradition. Kroeber, Benedict, Boas, and Linton, among others, indicate more randomly both retrospective and prospective tendencies. Benedict's relativism is particularly interesting in this context. It seems, on the one hand, to have been motivated by the desire to reflect the state of social consciousness signaled by the structure of a culture, in accord with the Romantic notion of historical knowledge. On the other hand, by trying to reveal the multifarious human expressions in primitive society, it, in effect, denies the inhumanity of primitive peoples and the irrelevance of studying them. Perhaps we can reformulate Benedict's mission as the effort to establish the value of studying primitive societies by a close scrutiny of their *values*. But despite obvious criticisms, which need not be discussed here, it seems to me that the most striking thing about Benedict is her use of anthropology as a weapon for *culturally criticizing modern civilization*. Her work is a metaphorical critique of her own time—of the position of women, of our acquisitiveness, our popular culture, ethnic prejudices, the inadequacy of our educational system, our misconceptions of liberty, and so on—all done with high style and verve. This variety of relativism must be seen, then, as an attempt to educate a chaotic and narrowing society to a more spacious view of human possibilities, and for that reason alone it is likely to outlive more orthodox work. Benedict came to the study of culture with a sense of problem; but that, of course, is only the *first* step in the construction of faithful and significant histories.

There are other indications of the traditional ties of this middle group. Kroeber writes very sensitively of the values of folk culture, contrasting them with civilization, and reprimands the Soviets for being among the most ardent proponents of a universal, progressive, industrial state, and thus of an alienating collectivism, in contrast to the communal values, the personalism, and the full participation of the person in folk society. Linton proposes that the decay of the local group in contemporary society, that is, of the sense and reality of community, is the fundamental problem of modern man—since it is through the local group that people learn to realize their humanity. This is a critical anthropological concept, and it is drawn from experience in the primitive locality, composed of reciprocating persons, growing from within, as opposed to the imposed, technically estranging, modern collective. Lowie found it appropriate to write a book entitled *Are We Civilized,* and his portrait of the Crow world view is deeply sensitive and respectful. Boas constructs objective criteria of progress, roughly anticipating Kroeber's, but throughout his work, particularly in the area of art, runs an appreciation of the achievements of primitive peoples and also an explicit effort to understand their varieties of aesthetic consciousness, which he believes to be more intense than is ordinarily the case in civilization. His active concern with the condition of modern civilization hardly needs documentation. Malinowski shared that concern and drew up a kind of model of primitive social functioning—which he characterized as protodemocratic and nonexploitative—in order to illuminate, by contrast, the nature of, and express his opposition generally to, the nation-state and, more specifically, to modern totalitarianism. Can we doubt that his "functionalism" is the reflection of that circular, institutionally integrated (but not conflict-free) process that binds economic, social, and ideological aspects of behavior into single irreducible acts in primitive society? Functionalism is a synthetic rather than analytic concept—it does not segregate causes and effects but deals with self-sustaining systems—in which the idea of progress is irrelevant because institutional disequilibrium is never severe enough to generate dramatic types of internal change. Functionalism may be a sophisticated outsiders' view of the primitive system from within, a system to which Malinowski paid the highest tribute. Malinowski's initial error, if we may call it that, was in assuming that functionalism was a tool of general social analysis rather than a theory based on human experience on a particular level of history. Later, he realized that his functionalist attitudes, which took the legitimacy and human adequacy of primitive societies for granted, could not be mechanically applied to civilized, increasingly totalitarian states; that is, the latter were not necessarily good or viable merely because they seemed to function. Hence, his last book, *Freedom and Civilization*. More recently, most of the prominent British social anthropologists have indicated, in a series of published popular lectures, their respect for the institutions of primitive society and the ordinary values of primitive life, about which they generalize.

It is clear, then, that most anthropologists somehow manage to combine both Enlightenment perspectives in their attitudes and, to a lesser degree, in their work—even if without resolution. These teachers of ours were critics in the Enlightenment mode. But conscious efforts at synthesis, at the confrontation and transcendence of our historically derived ambivalence are rare. Lewis Henry Morgan is almost unique in this respect. His hand in Rousseau's, he concludes *Ancient Society* as follows:

Since the advent of civilization, the outgrowth of property has been so immense, its forms so diversified, its uses so expanding, and its management so intelligent in the interests of its owners, that it has become, on the part of the people, an unmanageable power. The human mind stands bewildered in the presence of its own creation. The time will come, nevertheless, when human intelligence will rise to the mastery over property, and define the relations of the state to the property it protects, as well as the obligations and the limits of the rights of its owners. The interests of society are paramount to individual interests, and the two musƒ be brought into just and harmonious relations. A mere property career is not the final destiny of Mankind, if progress is to be the law of the future, as it has been of the past. The time that has passed away since civilization began is but a fragment of the past duration of Man's existence, and but a fragment of the ages yet to come. The dissolution of Society bids fair to become the termination of a career of which property is the end and aim—because such a career contains the elements of self-destruction. Democracy in Government, brotherhood in society, equality in rights and privileges, and universal education foreshadow the next higher plane of society to which experience, intelligence, and knowledge are steadily tending. It will be a revival, in a higher form, of the liberty, equality, and fraternity of the ancient Gentes.

This is the most effective summary statement in Morgan, deriving logically from his view of the Iroquois and his conception of the rise of civilization traced through the early phases of the Greek and Roman states. The statement is libertarian in intent and, interestingly enough, dialectic in form, thus sharing a common Enlightenment ancestry with the German Romantic culture historians, climaxed, in a Platonic mode, by Hegel. The classical Marxists, who were intellectual cousins of Morgan and involved, if less centrally, with anthropological problems, similarly tried to resolve the Enlightenment ambivalence by prophesying a future in which the state apparatus would wither away and the new technology would be wedded to the principles, in higher form of the primitive commune, thus looking backward with Rousseau and forward with Condorcet and company. Marx found Morgan's work congenial because each had reached a complementary conclusion in working over parallel materials with commonly inherited cultural tools.

Morgan's effort to synthesize our split Enlightenment inheritance was significant, but we need superior efforts. I believe it is necessary for us to develop a more precise and subtle idea, an inductive model of primitive society, informed by the problems of civilization —as Morgan was concerned with the problem of property, and Malinowski with war and totalitarianism—resulting in complementary conceptions of primitive society that place, in critical perspective, critical aspects of *our* civilization. In seeking to speak for man, not for nation-states and not for systems, anthropology will have to assume a comprehensively critical role, based on our respect for and knowledge of human nature, and the "irreducibly" human, I would say the primitive, past.

The following articles reassembled here, originally published as a tribute to Paul Radin, and still in that spirit, need no specific introduction from me. Ranging widely in time and space and tackling a variety of theoretical problems, they speak strongly for themselves. In one way or another, the authors are engaged with primitive views of the world. The sequence of essays should be obvious: from general definitions of primitive processes to specific interpretive descriptions of primitive societies, concluding with critiques of civilization in anthropological, that is, primitive, perspective.

STANLEY DIAMOND

Syracuse, New York
December, 1963

CONCERNING THE CONCEPT OF "PRIMITIVITY"

By Kurt Goldstein

THE USE of the word "primitive" in the literature about human behavior is very confusing. Its application to the ways of "uncivilized" people, at face value so different from those of civilized man, originated in the popular assumption that these ways were expressions of an inferior mentality. This opinion seemed to find scientific confirmation, particularly in the results of the research of Levy-Bruhl, who spoke of a prelogical mentality of primitive people whose life is supposed to be determined by the law of participation, a concept which he had taken over from Durkheim. The members of these societies do not experience themselves as separate individuals; they and the objects in their world appear to them sometimes as the same, sometimes as others.

Paul Radin has, on the basis of unbiased consideration of reported phenomena, taken a definite critical stand against the correctness of Levy-Bruhl's interpretation, so that it may seem no longer necessary to mention the latter in our discussion of the problem of primitivity—this the less as Levy-Bruhl later abandoned some of his concepts. However, we are induced to refer to his concepts because they had and still have a great influence on the interpretation of a number of abnormal mental phenomena of cultured and "uncultured" people, as, for instance, the behavior of children or of patients with mental diseases, of dreams, and the like. This situation demands our consideration not only because the assumption that these and other phenomena are experiences of a similar "primitive" mental state was one of the main origins of the confusion concerning the term primitive, but also because, as we shall see, it is based on a wrong interpretation of the mentioned phenomena. To illustrate the role Levy-Bruhl's ideas still play in this field, I would like to quote some remarks by a scientist who plays a considerable role in spreading the concept of the so-called prelogical mind and the similarity between the inferior mentality of primitive people and the other conditions I pointed to. He writes:

"The paleologician expresses himself in egocentric speech habits, for his thinking is predicative, and he has regressed to the egocentric speech of the child" (Domarus, 1944, p. 112). "We know that the child's speech has some elements of the speech of the primitive people . . . . . Therefore we are once more driven to the conclusion that the specific paleological thought and speech processes of the schizophrenics are in essence those of primitive people . . . the specific laws of language in schizophrenics show that they are the same as those of primitive people or even those of higher animals."

Another author tells us that if we accept this concept of paleological thinking it means that from the evolutionary point of view in biology, and correspondingly a comparative developmental approach in psychology, we also have to assume "the notion that intermediary stages once existed between some apes or ape-like species and the races of man who live today. Presumably these intermediary races of man thought paleologically" (Arieti, 1955, p. 269).

Heinz Werner has tried (Werner and Kaplan, 1956) to bring order into the chaos concerning the concept of primitivity by clarifying the various conditions to which the term has been applied. He wishes to reserve it—in relation to his concept of developmental psychology—for the lower level of behavior in the increasing differentiation and hierarchic integration characteristic for development. He writes: "It is empirically true that the processes emerging in the actual time sequence frequently conform to the developmental sequence; what occurs earlier in time often involves a greater lack of differentiation than what occurs later." Indeed, he does not want to be misunderstood as assuming that "primitive" means simply that which chronologically comes first. "The empirical relationship does not entail the proposition that temporal order of emergence and developmental sequence are of the same logical character." If I understand his reservation correctly, he wishes to avoid giving the impression that he believes in the generally relinquished "biogenetic *Grundgesetz*" of Haeckel. What he wants, it seems to me, is merely to state that the various behavior forms in different stages represent observable facts which can be considered similar or different expressions of degrees of differentiation. Indeed it seems to me doubtful whether, from this point of view, findings in the ontogenetic development of human beings could be compared with those in phylogenetic sequences; it seems particularly doubtful that childhood phenomena could be put parallel to those in "primitive" people. I have the impression that his studies have the intention of making such comparisons. I may or may not be correct on this, but I I do think that Werner did not pay enough attention in this comparison to *an aspect* which seems to me of essential significance for any comparison of phenomena observed in different organisms or in different stages of development: we should never consider phenomena isolatedly, and we should never compare phenomena observed in isolation. What we observe is *embedded in the activity of the total organism,* and all its activity is an expression of the coming to terms of the particular organism with the outer world in its tendency to realize its nature as much as possible (Goldstein, 1939). Any phenomenon can be correctly interpreted only if one at least considers it from this point of view too.

Developmental psychology considers phenomena in isolation insofar as it is interested in their formal structure; thus it often neglects the contents as unimportant. But when we want to understand a phenomenon, i.e., interpret it as a means for the organism's self-realization, we must also take the contents into consideration. Particularly is this the case when we want to decide whether we are dealing in a phenomenon with the effect of one definite capacity or the lack of another —in our example the lack of a higher mental activity. Or, when we want to know whether the organism possesses a capacity but it does not become effective in a definite situation—that is, in a definite relationship between organism and world—because the intention of the organism's activity can be fulfilled equally or even better without it.

It is not my intention to discuss concepts of the so-called primitive mind critically. Rather I prefer to analyze some phenomena often considered primitive which I have studied intensively, and to see whether this analysis gives us possibly a better interpretation of the behavior of "primitive" people than the assumption of prelogical thinking—an interpretation which, as I would like to show, is in principle in accordance with the results of the studies of Paul Radin.

It was particularly experiences with patients which taught me what erroneous interpretations of behavior one can arrive at when the conclusion is based on consideration of isolated phenomena, and how wrong one's results can be if one compares them with others which appear similar, even equal, at face value (Goldstein, 1946).

Before describing the behavior of certain patients with greater or lesser damage of the higher mental functions, I want to make some remarks concerning the concept of the organization of the human mind to which I came through studies of personalities with such damage.

We can distinguish in the behavior of normal human beings two kinds of approach to the world; we call these *concrete* behavior and *abstract* behavior (Goldstein and Gelb, 1925). Before I characterize both in more detail, I would like to illustrate the difference of the two approaches by a simple example. When we enter a darkened bedroom and switch on the light we act concretely, often without being aware of what we are doing; we experience only a desire to have light. The reaction is based on the aftereffect of previous equal situations. One can say we are given over somewhat passively to the world and bound to the immediate experience of the very things or the situation.

If, however, we reflect that by switching on the light we might awaken someone sleeping in the room and therefore do not switch it on, we approach the situation abstractly. We transcend the immediately given specific aspect of sense impressions; we detach ourselves from them and consider the situation from a conceptual point of view and react accordingly.

The two approaches are specific for all behavior organization of the human being (Goldstein and Scheerer, 1941) but one should not consider them as the effect of two different, separate capacities; they are rather two levels of the capacity of the human being. Each approach constitutes one definite behavioral range of performance, but they are always effective together as a unit which determines the organization of the performance. The participation of one or the other approach in a performance differs according to the different significance of one or the other approach for the fulfillment of the task.

All performances of the organism have the structure of a *figure-ground organization,* i.e., we have to distinguish in the unitary activity which every performance presents that one part which fulfills the task directly from another one which represents the activity in the "background" on which the correct performance is based (Goldstein, 1946, p. 109). We call the first activity the figure, the other one the ground. What is meant by figure and ground becomes immediately obvious in visual experiences, for instance, in the difference between a picture and the ground on which it is presented; here one can also see that figure and ground are *dependent on each other* and that the phenomena in one influence the other. Like visual performances, all other performances of the organism show the same figure-ground organization, all motor actions, feelings, thinking, speaking, and the like.

Which capacity level becomes figure and which ground depends upon the way in which the task can best be fulfilled. In some tasks this will be by virtue of one level of activity, in others by the other level. It is very important to be aware that the *starting* of any performance *presupposes the abstract attitude*. Also, in performances which have to be executed in concrete behavior, for instance motor automatisms, the situation has to be prearranged in such a way that concrete behavior is set in motion; the ground has to be prepared so that it can run smoothly, independently. To achieve that, the abstract attitude is necessary. Furthermore, if for any reason anything goes wrong in the concrete activity, we need the abstract attitude to correct the mistake and to induce the continuation of the interrupted task.

In many situations of normal life the ground is prepared for concrete behavior in general, so that concrete behavior can be elicited immediately. That is the case in the organization for special work activity in industry, similarly in social life by organization according to customs.

In such situations we may be inclined to assume that the concrete approach *alone* is determining behavior. Patients with impairment of abstract attitude may not appear to deviate grossly from normal persons in everyday behavior because many routine tasks do not require the abstract attitude once activity has been set in motion and the situation in which it must occur is given. But otherwise they show definite failures, we can say, in all situations to which one can come to terms only by the abstract approach.

From an analysis of the behavior of a great number of such patients in various situations in everyday life and in special test situations, we learned, on the one hand, the different modes of behavior in which the abstract attitude is necessary, and on the other hand, what characterizes the structure of concrete behavior. I would like to mention some of the modes of behavior where the patient *fails:* when it is necessary to give an account to himself for acts and thoughts; when he has to keep in mind various aspects of a task or any presentation simultaneously; therefore the same object may appear as something different when considered by chance from another aspect or in another situation. The patient cannot break up a given whole into parts to isolate and so synthesize them. He cannot form concepts, symbols, and does not understand them; therefore his language has lost the character of being used in a symbolic way (Goldstein and Scheerer, 1941; Goldstein, 1948). The patient is not able to detach the ego from the outer world or from inner experiences; the relationship between different objects, different events, persons, words, may be determined by their accidentally appearing in the same place or at the same time. Syllogisms may be based on the similarity of parts of the premises—or, better said, on what appears so to the patient. Under certain conditions the predicate may determine the conclusion while under normal conditions it is determined by the subject. But, under other conditions, experience of similarity of other parts of the two sentences which the premises represent determines this. One has to be aware that the patient is not even able to realize what is demanded of him; he is unable to understand the structure of a syllogism and the procedure to solve the problem.

The concrete behavior does not imply conscious activity in the sense of reasoning. We surrender to experiences of an unreflected character; we are confined to the immediate apprehension of a given thing or situation in its particular uniqueness, which is never mediated by discursive reasoning. Our thinking and acting are directed by the claims which one particular object or an aspect of it or a situation makes. I want to stress that the concrete attitude exists also in respect to ideas, thoughts, and feelings.

The concrete behavior of the patient with defect of abstraction shows *characteristic differences from concrete behavior of normals*. The normal person is induced to behave concretely in special situations, but his reaction does not occur passively—there is some intention to do it. The individual is not forced to perform it. Even when some reaction runs automatically, we have in the background the feeling of its significance, embedded in a wider, more or less aware realm of experiences. When we make a mistake we are able to correct it by switching to the abstract attitude which, one could say, is always hovering around. The patient is forced to react to the object, to the situation. His doing is not an activity of himself as a person; one should rather speak of a reaction of an apparatus to a stimulus to which it is bound. The object is a "sign," by which the reaction is elicited. But not even that is fully correct. Not everything can become a sign; the sign has always some relation to the subject who can use it. For the patient everything can become a "sign"—a stimulus, a word, an object, a situation, a feeling—which for any reason comes to the fore and becomes connected with something else, for instance, when it occurs at the same time or place or otherwise. This connection becomes determining for future activities. What is connected remains so until some other "stronger" stimulation takes place. Everything that occurs gets the character of "evidence."

The patient cannot easily detach himself from definite objects and the like; it is difficult, sometimes impossible, for him to realize other potential functions of the same object. He appears fixed, rigid. On the other hand, he may be particularly suggestible to any connections which are induced to him by other people, if they are presented in such a way that he can grasp them with the concrete behavior. He may not be able to evoke images voluntarily, but they may come passively to the fore and even overwhelm him in such a way that he cannot get rid of them. He may not be able to distinguish them from real experiences.

Because of the difficulty of producing reasonable relations, often what is normally on the "fringes" of our experience but usually is eliminated from use in our reactions may become effective and produce connections difficult to understand, but understandable from this point of view.

We have till now referred to the phenomena in concrete behavior in everyday life, in practical work. But there are other normal reactions and experiences which belong to concrete behavior: physiognomic experiences, emotions, religious experiences and activities in different forms, from the rites, mythical experiences and activities, to the highest forms—the rituals in the "highest" religions.

Where these behavior forms appear in primitive people they are often considered as a special expression of an inferior mind. They represent, in opposition to the experience mediated by the intellectual approach, a more *immediate concrete relationship* between the individual and the world, especially the world of living beings, but also what we call the physical world: landscapes, mountains, the ocean, the sky, the sun, the stars, clouds, thunder, and the like. These play a considerable role in the life of man. The same phenomenon which can be experienced as an object in the ordered outer world in which things are going on, and in which we act on the basis of abstract attitude or in concrete activity, appears from this point of view something totally different. These experiences are the basis of people's awe, admiration, devotion; conversely, of the feeling of helplessness and anxiety. They are the cause of a great number of activities which are strictly in opposition to rational understanding but have for them reality and influence the people.

Even highly educated people cannot escape from these influences. As much as one tries to eliminate these "disturbing" experiences which we have in all man's different realms, to eliminate them by interpreting the phenomena as illusions, they appear again and again, sometimes in very complex systematic forms in cosmic theories, religious interpretations, myths, social customs, individual habits. These immediate experiences in relation to other human beings give rise particularly to assumptions about what is going on in the experiences of the "other." They are the basis of mutual understanding among human beings. The thinking underlying these experiences does not follow the laws of logical thinking. It shows similarity with the organization of concrete behavior.

I have come to the conclusion that man always lives in two spheres of experience: the sphere in which the subject and object are experienced as separate and only secondarily related, and another one in which he experiences oneness with the world (Goldstein, 1958).

Because we observe these experiences in normal human beings, we must say they and the world in which they appear belong to man's nature. When we then see that they cannot be understood by logic, we are inclined to consider them as aberrations, i.e., pathological phenomena or manifestations of an inferior mentality. It is particularly these phenomena which induced the assumption that the primitive has a prelogical mind.

Are we right to make such an evaluation? One may think so if one neglects the differences between normal and pathological concreteness. Here particularly the *isolatedness* of the experiences and actions of the pathological person is in opposition to the relatedness of the normal concrete behavior to the individual in its totality and the general condition in which it occurs. What is described as prelogical is more like the pathological than the normal concreteness. Is not the case the same concerning the mentality of the primitive people? Is their mentality not more similar to our normal concreteness than to the concreteness of the patients? The study of patients with missing abstract attitude who can use only the concrete capacity level shows that they can live in an ordered way if their *fellow men prepare the conditions* (by their abstract behavior) in such a way that the patient can do justice to demands in a concrete way. The positive result of their activities is therefore the effect of the influence of both capacity levels in cooperation. The same is the case when normal individuals are involved in concrete activities. The difference is that the latter can *prepare the conditions themselves* (with their own abstract capacity) in an appropriate way.

From my experience with the behavior of patients, I guessed that the *people in primitive societies may not be inferior, but that their behavior may correspond to what we have characterized as concrete behavior.* If that can be assumed, we come to the further question: *how can these people exist with their concrete level of behavior alone?* and I pondered whether their *existence may not be guaranteed by the abstract attitude of fellow men.*

Authors who assume that the behavior of primitive people shows inferior mentality, that it is an expression of a prelogical state of mind came to the conclusion that people with this mentality could not survive, for example, the "ape-like ancestors of man" who possessed only this capacity. Arieti asked "how these primitive races were able to survive or evolve into others ["higher" ones] if their actions were determined by a system of thinking which is so unrealistic . . .," and he comes to the conclusion that "eventually the races which could not sufficiently overcome this type of thinking perished" (1955, p. 272). I could agree with him that human beings with such an inferior mentality could not survive—but only if one assumes that they were really human beings. If they were not that, why should living beings of another kind not have other conditions of existence? Now it is really only a hypothesis that these "predecessors" of man have lived. Arieti is interested in this problem of the possibility of the existence of a prelogical individual because he ascribes the same mentality to the living "primitive" men. He attempts to explain their existence by assuming that it is made possible through the "support of the authority" (the tribe); "therefore they may be able to indulge in the ritual with a certain facility" (1955, p. 227).

But how does this *support of the authority originate?* Does this not presuppose the existence of people of another, "higher" mentality in the society than the "primitive" man? I think that such an assumption would be necessary, not only as an explanation of the "concern" of the "authority" with their fellow men but particularly as explanation of the insight into the reason why the primitive man is not able to handle the difficulties of the world. Only then could the support occur in the correct way. If one assumes that the authority consists not of men but of rules of organization which guarantee the life of the tribe, then the problem is: *How could these rules grow out of a society of such inferior mentality?* I think only if one assumes that the inherited regulations were created by *men of higher mentality.* But that would mean that such men existed at least sometimes in the tribe. If that was the case, why not assume that one may have overlooked the fact that they exist also in present primitive society? Anyway it must induce us to study whether this may not be the case. This seems not improbable because rules can only be transmitted in history and remain effective later if there are men behind them who understand them and make them work.

With that, the not very plausible assumption of the existence of ape men as predecessors of men who perished would not be necessary. One would only have to assume that men with the higher mental capacity have always existed and may exist now in primitive tribes, although the great number of these people may live on a lower level of capacity, or, as I prefer to say, do behave concretely. When we speak later about Radin's concept of primitive societies, we shall see that this *seems really to be the case.* Such an assumption would make it unnecessary to explain how from the prelogical being the logical man "evolved." Without discussing this very delicate problem, I would like to say that I personally believe that there is no proof that such a development took place, and I do not see how it would be possible. How could (which it would mean) the symbolic function—so characteristic for man—develop from a capacity level which gives only the possibility for thinking and acting in "sign" relations?

Returning to the problem of how people who possess only concrete behavior can exist, again the observation of patients has brought us important information. As an example I would like to refer to the condition of the brain-damaged individuals we talked about before. We saw that patients with severe impairment of the abstract capacity level are not able to fulfill those tasks which we mentioned as depending on the use of this capacity. Therefore in the first period after the injury they are not able to come to terms with many demands of our —their previous—world and they therefore come easily into catastrophes and anxiety. Because of the disturbing aftereffects of the catastrophes, they are not even able to actualize fully their preserved concrete capacity. We could show that after a certain time mechanisms develop which protect them against the anxiety. How this occurs I cannot discuss here, but it is certainly not within their consciousness (Goldstein, 1939, pp. 42 ff.). But by these protections their life becomes more ordered, if even more restricted. They would have to live in a very reduced condition if they did not have the help of the people around them. *What does this help consist of?* What we observe is that after a certain time the patients come into better relations with the environment and are more able to use concretely what they had previously learned. One can easily get the impression that they are improved in respect to their defect. Examination of their capacities, however, shows that the defect exists as before. They can very easily come into catastrophes if confronted with tasks which cannot be fulfilled in concrete behavior. What brought the "improvement" was the organization of an environment from which such tasks do not, or only rarely, arise. Now they can live without difficulties in the way they are alone able to live, i.e., in an absolutely concrete form of behavior. This organization is the effect of the use of the abstract attitude of the people around them. Their behavior can be understood only as an effect of the *interaction of the abstract behavior of their fellow men and their own concrete behavior*. In this way their existence is guaranteed in spite of their being able only to behave concretely.

With that we came to the conclusion that living with the *concrete behavior alone is not possible*; human existence presupposes the influence of both capacity levels.

Another example which illustrates our viewpoint is the existence of the infant in the first year of life. The infant comes into the world as a very imperfect, very helpless organism, particularly because his abstract capacity is not yet developed. He escapes the immediate danger of death by the operation of some inborn mechanisms which immediately come into action. But as important as that is for survival, he would come again and again into disorder and dangerous catastrophes, he would not even be able to use his inborn capacities to come to terms with the world or to develop if he were not protected against these states of disorder by the people around, the prototype of whom is represented by the mother.

This protection consists in building up an *environment corresponding to the state of the infant's maturation.* Organization of this adequate "world" presupposes insight into the physical and psychological needs of the infantile organism and its changes during maturation. This insight and the tendency to use it in the interest of the infant is an effect of the application of abstract behavior. Certainly the mother does not always invent the adequate organization of the environment; she takes over many old customs she has learned from her mother or other people. But it cannot be said that her activities grow out of so-called instincts; they are the result of the abstract attitude of the mother and of the ancestors.

At about the end of the first year of the infant's life, the first signs of the development of abstract attitude become visible. Now more and more, but in very slow development, the behavior of the child shows the influence of the unity of the concrete/abstract capacity levels. The mother's influence has to change correspondingly. There is a time when the cooperation of the mother's abstract attitude with the not fully developed capacity of abstraction of the child represents a very complex problem, which is not always correctly solved by the mother and so may have an ill effect on the further development of the child. In this relationship between mother and child, the capacity of the mother to understand also the psychological needs of the child is of greatest significance. Because the concrete behavior of the child prevails for a long time, the structure of his behavior may show similarities with other conditions where concrete behavior is in the foreground—with the behavior of patients and primitive people. Therefore a comparison may be easily at hand. But the differences should warn us against assuming equal states of "development" in the various conditions. What for us at the moment is important is that the development of the behavior of the child shows clearly that it is the effect of *abstract and concrete behavior,* that the existence and development of the infant is guaranteed by the effect of the capacity of abstraction in the behavior of others until he has developed his own abstract attitude.

From my analysis of the behavior of persons lacking the use of the abstract attitude and showing correspondingly abnormal concreteness, I was inclined to assume that the people living in "primitive" societies may not have an inferior mentality but that they possess, like all human beings, the concrete-abstract unity of the human mental capacity. The impression of an inferior mentality might have arisen from the predominance of the concrete level in their behavior, by which they come to terms with the demands of the special world in which they live. I further assumed that they could exist only if their life was guaranteed by other people of the tribe, who have organized the world in such a way that people can come to terms with it with the concrete attitude. This in turn would make it necessary to assume that there are in the tribe people who have and use the abstract capacity. If that were true, then we would find here the same organization of their behavior as in our patients and in infants, insofar as it would represent the effect of the activity of themselves and of other people too. If this could be proved for primitive societies, then the question would arise: Do not the "primitive" people in these societies show under some conditions signs of abstract capacity also? It is not probable that a society consists of two groups of people mentally so different.

I was very much pleased when I realized that my conjecture seemed to be in agreement with the analysis of the mentality of "primitive" people by Paul Radin, and that his conclusions enforced my concept of the organization of human behavior in general.

I would like in this respect to refer to some statements by Radin in his book *Die religiöse Erfahrung der Naturvölker,* and to some of the reports by which he documents his conclusions. Radin stresses that the assumption of an inferior mentality of primitive people originated, on the one hand, from a generalization of the experiences with single or very few individuals. If a greater number had been investigated, it would have been realized that primitive people are not so passive, not such rigidly acting persons, but individuals; further—what is of particular significance—their individualities differ considerably. One can distinguish in all primitive societies two types of people, those who live strictly in accord with the rules of the society, whom he calls the "nonthinkers," and those who think, the "thinkers." The number of thinkers may be small but they play a great role in the tribe; they are the people who formulate the concepts and organize them in systems, which are then taken over—generally without criticism—by the nonthinkers. When one wants to understand the many peculiarities of the customs, rituals and the like, one must further pay attention to the fact that average people frequently misunderstand the formulations of the thinkers and distort them. There is another point in his remarks which is important, namely, that it is self-understood for these societies that the thinkers are so closely connected with community life that they also more or less participate in the certainly nonrational activities of the groups. This may give the impression that their mentality also is "primitive." Radin adds here that the same is the case also in civilized societies. He concludes: "Primitive societies differ in many respects essentially from ours, but not in that they have not the capacity of reasoning or in that they are not individuals." I would like to point out concerning his documentation for this opinion particularly the reports about conversations which Rasmussen had with the Eskimos. The comparison of the two reports given in detail leaves no doubt about the difference of the people in respect to thinking and not thinking, and about the existence of people with high mental capacity in the tribe, not essentially different from those in civilized societies. The latter makes it understandable, according to Radin, that the religious experiences of the primitive people show exactly the same differences that we find in the historical high religions—we find mystics, rationalists, conformists, revolutionaries, pragmatists.

When we read (Radin, 1950, p. 23) the remarks of the old Iglulik Eskimo, Ana—an Eskimo of the nonthinking type—in relation to the difficult life of the Eskimos, we recognize the realistic and concrete attitude toward the world; but the man seems not to be satisfied with simply pointing to the many difficulties and dangers of the life of the Eskimos but adds repeatedly the question: "Why is it so?" Further, "Why must there be storms which hinder us in looking for meat for ourselves and our beloved ones?" Why must the women he mentions suffer from pain and sickness without any guilt? Why must human beings suffer at all? And he adds to Rasmussen: "You also cannot answer our question—why is life as it is? And so it must be. We have no explanation." He adds then some remarks that are of particular significance in relation to the discussion of our problem about the capacity level of primitive people in comparison to our own. "We have anxiety . . . therefore our fathers tried, as their forebears taught them, to protect themselves by all those instructions and customs which grew out of experiences and the knowledge of generations. We do not know how and why. But we follow them so that we can live in peace. And with all our angacoqs and their secret knowledge, we know so little that we fear everything."

The report of Rasmussen concerning this Eskimo has, as Radin mentioned, induced Levy-Bruhl to assume the inferior mentality of the people. For him, Radin continues, the man's remark, "We have no explanation," represents the characteristic mental attitude of all primitive people, of each individual in every tribe. Is it justified to assume that such a man has a *prelogical* mind"? In this respect I would like to stress that his behavior *is not like the behavior of our patients.* It does not show the deviations, the compulsiveness, by which the patients differ from normal concrete people. The remarks of the man show definitely a relationship of his activities and experiences to his total personality; this corresponds to the *concreteness of normal civilized people* but is in *opposition to the behavior of the patients,* who have *no "personality," no "world,"* only more or less isolated *experiences.*

What might have brought the people of the primitive societies to this kind of organization of their culture to which concrete behavior is adequate? I cannot enter into a discussion of this problem. I do not feel at all competent for such a task. But I would like to say something about the role which *anxiety* plays in this respect. There is no doubt—again according to the remarks of the mentioned Eskimo—that the people know what anxiety is. On the other hand, they seem to have little anxiety. Radin says that Ana does not show in his behavior that he is in an emotional state when he speaks about the misery of their life and about their fear—at least not as if he experienced much anxiety. He mentioned that they live peacefully. If they were to be stricken by much anxiety that would not be possible, because as people living concretely they would not have the ability to escape anxiety. We know in general that anxiety cannot be overcome by concrete behavior. Thus the absence of anxiety must have another reason. *It is not eliminated; it does not occur,* because they live in a condition—due to their following the rules of the society—in which conflicts and anxiety usually do not arise. One could say also that they have no anxiety because they have the possibility of living in proportion with the demands on them.

This may not be so for the thinking people. To build up this adequate culture they must be aware of the anxiety and its danger and think about the way to avoid it. That would correspond again to the description of these people by Radin. They are aware of the difficulties of their own psychic disequilibrium and try to escape this by building up religious concepts and behavior. Their primary problem is to avoid anxiety and suffering and restore a normal psychic state of their own. With the awareness of this goal is connected another one, namely, to help the others to be able to live in physical and psychic health. It seems that this activity is based on altruistic feeling, even if other tendencies may be effective—the desire for power, reputation and wealth (Radin, 1950, p. 40). Be that as it may, *this goal would explain why they organize the society in such a way that physical and psychic health can also be reached by the nonthinking people.*

So it would be quite correct to say that people escape anxiety, but even better to speak of avoidance of the occurrence of conflict and anxiety by the structure of their culture. The nonthinking people may in their activity not be aware that the culture lets them avoid anxiety; in the same way as in civilized life, people who act concretely when menaced with anxiety are not aware that they are avoiding anxiety by acting concretely. The *nonthinking primitive people have no anxiety, because in the structure of their culture they are induced to act concretely and so do not come into conditions where anxiety could arise.* They know that there is anxiety; better, they are afraid of a great number of events. The thinker knows the reason for the occurrence of anxiety—as Radin has so clearly described in his discussion of the origin of their religion and organization of the rites to overcome their psychic disagreeableness—and so organized the culture in this way. This lack of much conflict and anxiety—also of guilt feelings—may explain why primitive people do not seem to suffer from compulsive neuroses. I think it is meaningless to say, as has been said, that the individuals have no compulsive neuroses, rather the whole culture is compulsive. There are mental states reported which look at face value like catatonia. What they represent is unclear. I would guess they represent severe shock reactions.

When the nonthinking Eskimo speaks of the significance of their culture as means to avoid anxiety, he may not be referring to his own experience of anxiety, but he is trying to explain how, by means of their culture, anxiety is avoided. That would show again how he is able to use his reasoning under certain conditions. When in his usual life in doing and thinking that is not the case, this would be explainable because it is not necessary. He behaves concretely because thereby he is able to achieve the best result. The application of abstract attitude may even disturb his successful concrete activities in the same way that the abstract attitude generally interferes in an activity which could be performed best in concrete behavior. The nonthinking man would then come into physical, particularly mental, disequilibrium which he would not be able to handle as the thinking man does and he would experience anxiety.

The concrete behavior of the primitive man consists particularly in the rituals, so-called magical experiences and religious and mythical activities. When we look at them isolated from the whole structure of the primitive culture, they may appear abstruse, irrational. They do not originate in the nonthinking people but are the produce of the religious concepts of the "thinking" religious man. They are the expression of the religious man's attempts to fulfill his needs, to find order in his life, particularly in respect to psychological difficulties, by assuming the existence of something outside himself which is more powerful than he and determines what is valuable in man's life and restores his psychic equilibrium (Radin, 1950, p. 28). What we observe in the nonthinking man are those parts of these concepts which can be grasped in a concrete way and may be modified, even distorted, by misunderstanding; but they play in the totality of his life the same role as for the thinking man, i.e., they stabilize his psychic life. They belong to the second sphere in which man lives in relation to the world, to which I have directed attention before (Goldstein, 1958). These phenomena may play a greater role in primitive life, but they are not essentially different from what we observe in the "thinking" man and the "nonthinking" man in civilized societies.

So we would come to the conclusion, in both civilized and primitive societies, acting and thinking are not the result of the concrete behavior alone. The abstract attitude is always effective in the organization of the "world" by the thinkers in such a way that the people can fulfill the task in a concrete way. This participation of the abstract attitude finds its expression in primitive society in the formation of a permanent structure of the society, in civilized life in certain formations under special conditions. This may give the impression that the abstract capacity of the individual is in the latter always somewhat in action—not so in the activities of primitive people. If one then overlooks the difference between normal concrete behavior and the behavior of patients with defect of abstraction, one may get the impression that the primitive people have an inferior mind, particularly because the "primitive" person appears more unfree, compulsive, which is the effect of the greater regularity of his life. Indeed, they are hardly comparable to the patients; they are much more able to shift from one activity to another when the situation demands it.

I know only too well that my little essay, which touches upon so many controversial problems, is not at all sufficient to clarify the concept of primitivity. However, it may stimulate consideration of the factors underlying the assumption of an inferior human mind, and may make us hesitate in comparing the behavior of children and patients with that of preliterate people. I hope the peculiarity of these people may come to be characterized by a more adequate term.

Paul Radin has said: "No progress in ethnology will be achieved until scholars rid themselves once and for all of the curious notion that everything possesses history, until they realize that certain ideas and concepts are ultimate for man." That is the same idea which grew out of my studies of the behavior of brain-damaged individuals in my attempt to acquire from these observations a concept of the nature of man.

REFERENCES

Arieti, S. 1955. Interpretation of Schizophrenia. New York, Brunner.

Cassirer, E. 1953. Philosophy of Symbolic Forms. New Haven, Yale Univ. Press.

Domarus, E. 1944. "The Specific Laws of Logic in Schizophrenia," in *Language and Thought in Schizophrenia,* ed. by J. S. Kasanin. Chicago, Univ. of Chicago Press.

Goldstein, K. 1939. The Organism. New York, American Book Co.

———— 1943. "The Significance of Psychological Research in Schizophrenia," *Journal of Nervous and Mental Diseases*, 97:261.

———— 1946. "Naming and Pseudonaming," *Word*, Vol. 2.

———— 1948. Language and Language Disturbances. New York, Grune & Stratton.

———— 1951. Human Nature in the Light of Psychopathology. Cambridge, Harvard Univ. Press.

———— 1958. "The Smiling of the Infant and the Problem of Understanding the 'Other'," *Journal of Psychology*, 44:115-91.

Goldstein, K. Gelb. 1920. Psychologische Analysen hirnpathologischer, Fälle I. Leipzig, Barth.

———— 1925. "Uber Farbennamenamnesie," *Psychologische Forschung*, 6:127-86.

Goldstein, K., and M. Scheerer. 1941. Abstract and Concrete Behavior: An Experimental Study. Psychology Monographs, Vol. 53.

Radin, Paul. 1950. Die religiöse Erfahrung der Naturvölker. Zurich, Rhein-Verlag.

Rasmussen, K. 1915. The Intellectual Culture of the Iglulik Eskimo. Copenhagen.

Werner, H., and B. Kaplan. 1956. "The Developmental Approach to Cognition: Its Relevance to the Psychological Interpretation of Anthropological and Ethnolinguistic Data, *American Anthropologist*, 58:No. 5.

PRIMITIVE MAN AS METAPHYSICIAN

By Joseph Campbell

"The name of the song is called 'Haddocks' Eyes.'"
"Oh, that's the name of the song, is it?" Alice said,
trying to feel interested. "No, you don't understand,"
the Knight said, looking a little vexed. "That's what
the name is called."

LEWIS CARROLL

"THE METAPHYSICAL NOTIONS of man may be reduced to a few types which are of universal distribution," Franz Boas declared in the first edition of *The Mind of Primitive Man* (New York, 1911, p. 156); in the second edition, prepared a quarter of a century later (1938), this observation did not appear. In American anthropology a tendency to emphasize the differentiating traits of primitive societies had meanwhile developed to such a degree that any mention by an author of common traits simply meant that he had not kept up with the fashion. Recently, however, the tide has turned. In the encyclopedic inventory of problems and theories, prepared under the chairmanship of A. L. Kroeber and published as *Anthropology Today* (University of Chicago Press, 1953), we find a substantial article by Clyde Kluckhohn on "Universal Categories of Culture," as well as references by a number of the other authors to the present need for comparative evaluations. No one, however, appears to have brought forward again the idea developed by Paul Radin thirty years ago, when his work on *Primitive Man as Philosopher* offered a formula by which the two points of view successively represented by Boas might have been reconciled and brought together in a single general theory. His observation that among primitive as well as highly civilized peoples the two types of man are to be found that William James long ago characterized as the tough-minded and tender-minded [1]—and that the myths and symbols of all societies are interpreted in differing senses by these two—has apparently been forgotten by the representatives of a science, which, in the words of Boas himself, "does not deal with the exceptional man." [2]

"From the man of action's viewpoint," wrote Dr. Radin, describing the attitude of the tough-minded type, "a fact has no symbolic or static value. He predicates no unity beyond that of the certainty of continuous change and transformation. For him a double distortion is involved in investing the transitory and ceaselessly changing object with a symbolic, idealistic, or static significance." The thinker, on the other hand, the tender-minded type, "is impelled by his whole nature, by the innate orientation of his mind, to try to discover the reason why there is an effect, what is the nature of the relation between the ego and the world, and what part exactly the perceiving self plays therein. Like all philosophers, he is interested in the subject as such, the object as such, and the relations between them. . . . An original, moving, shapeless or undifferentiated world must be brought to rest and given stable form. . . . Philosophers have always given the same answer to this problem and predicated a unity behind these changing aspects and forms. Primitive philosophers are at one with their European and Asiatic brothers here." [3]

It appears to me that any science that takes into consideration only or even primarily the vulgar, tough-minded interpretation of symbols will inevitably be committed to a study largely of local differentiations, while, on the other hand, one addressed to the views of thinkers will find that the ultimate references of their cogitations are few and of universal distribution. Anthropologists, by and large (or, at least, those of the American variety) are notoriously tough-minded. (There is a Haitian proverb, I am told: "When the anthropologist arrives, the gods depart!") They have tended to give reductive interpretations to the symbols of primitive thought and to find their references only in the particularities of the local scene. In the following pages I should like to suggest an amplification of this view.

I

The first problem to be confronted by anyone wishing to deal with the metaphysical notions of mankind is that of distinguishing between symbols and their references—between what we may term the *vehicles* and their *tenor*. For example, the three or four instances of "metaphysical notions" enumerated by Dr. Boas in his chapter on "The Universality of Cultural Traits," are not metaphysical notions at all. They are simply images, symbols, or vehicles, which by a tough-minded individual might be interpreted physically, as references not to any metaphysical realization whatsoever, but to remote facts, realms or lands much like our own—whereas the term "metaphysical" refers to no place, no time, no thing, no fact: not even wonders of such stuff as dreams are made of. "Belief in a land of the souls of the deceased," for example,[4] "located in the west, and reached by crossing a river": this is not in itself a metaphysical notion, though it may be given a metaphysical reading. Nor can we call metaphysical "the idea of a multiplicity of worlds,—one or more spanned over us, others stretching under us, the central one the home of man; the upper or lower, the home of the gods and happy souls; the other, the home of the unhappy."[5]

Such images are not the final terms of our subject, if it is of metaphysics that we are treating. They have often served, indeed, as vehicles of metaphysical expression, and part of our problem, certainly, is to collect, compare, and classify them; but we miss our proper point if we rest with them as they stand. For an image may signify various things in various contexts and to various minds. Furthermore, where an image has disappeared, it need not follow that the tenor of its reference has disappeared: this may be lurking under another image entirely. Nor in cross-cultural comparisons can we safely assume that because the symbolic figures differ from culture to culture the tenors of their references must differ also.

Let us consider, therefore, a brief series of mythological images culled from a number of cultures, which may be discovered to be the vehicles of a single metaphysical tenor.

II

Natalie Curtis, in *The Indians' Book* (Harper and Brothers, 1907), years ago published a remarkable origin myth that was recounted to her by an aged Pima chief, Hovering Hawk:

In the beginning there was only darkness everywhere—darkness and water. And the darkness gathered thick in places, crowding together and then separating, crowding and separating until at last out of one of the places where the darkness had crowded there came forth a man. This man wandered through the darkness until he began to think; then he knew himself and that he was a man; he knew that he was there for some purpose.

He put his hand over his heart and drew forth a large stick. He used the stick to help him through the darkness, and when he was weary he rested upon it. Then he made for himself little ants; he brought them from his body and put them on the stick. Everything that he made he drew from his own body even as he had drawn the stick from his heart. The stick was of grease-wood, and of the gum of the wood the ants made a round ball upon the stick. Then the man took the ball from the stick and put it down in the darkness under his foot, and as he stood upon the ball he rolled it under his foot and sang:

> I make the world, and lo!
> The world is finished.
> Thus I make the world, and lo!
> The world is finished.

So he sang, calling himself the maker of the world. He sang slowly, and all the while the ball grew larger as he rolled it, till at the end of his song, behold, it was the world. Then he sang more quickly:

> Let it go, let it go,
> Let it go, start it forth!

So the world was made, and now the man brought from himself a rock and divided it into little pieces. Of these he made stars, and put them in the sky to light the darkness. But the stars were not bright enough.

So he made Tau-mik, the milky-way. Yet Tau-mik was not bright enough. Then he made the moon. All these he made of rocks drawn forth from himself. But even the moon was not bright enough. So he began to wonder what next he could do. He could bring nothing from himself that could lighten the darkness.

Then he thought. And from himself he made two large bowls, and he filled the one with water and covered it with the other. He sat and watched the bowls, and while he watched he wished that what he wanted to make in very truth would come to be. And it was even as he wished. For the water in the bowl turned into the sun and shone out in rays through the cracks where the bowls joined.

When the sun was made, the man lifted off the top bowl and took out the sun and threw it to the east. But the sun did not touch the ground; it stayed in the sky where he threw it and never moved. Then in the same way he threw the sun to the north and to the west and to the south. But each time it only stayed in the sky, motionless, for it never touched the ground. Then he threw it once more to the east, and this time it touched the ground and bounced and started upward. Since then the sun has never ceased to move. It goes around the world in a day, but every morning it must bounce anew in the east.[6]

It is impossible to read this story without thinking of the far flung Old World theme of the primordial giant out of whose body the universe proceeds, and who, until the end of time, remains within the forms of the universe as the "self of all."

"In the beginning, this universe was only the self, in a human form," we read in the Sanskrit *Brihadaranyaka Upanishad.*

He looked around and saw nothing but himself. Then, at the beginning, he cried out, "I am he!" Whence came the name, I. That is why, even today, when a person is addressed, he first declares, "It is I," and then announces the other name that he goes by.

He was afraid. That is why people are afraid to be alone. He thought, "But what am I afraid of? There is nothing but myself." Whereupon his fear was gone. . . .

He was unhappy. That is why people are not happy when they are alone. He wanted a mate. He became as big as a woman and man embracing. He divided this body, which was himself, in two parts. From that there came husband and wife. . . . Therefore this body [before one marries a wife] is like one of the halves of a split pea. . . . He united with her; and from that were born men.

She considered: "How can he unite with me after producing me from himself? Well then, let me hide myself." She became a cow; but he became a bull and united with her: from that were born cattle. She became a mare, he a stallion; she a she-ass, he a donkey and united with her; from that were born the one-hoofed animals. . . . She became a goat, he a buck; she a ewe, he a ram and united with her: from that were born goats and sheep. Thus did he project everything that exists in pairs, down to the ants.

Then he knew: "Indeed, I am myself the creation, for I have projected this entire world." Whence he was called Creation. . . ." [7]

Sometimes, as here, the projection of the world is pictured in Brahmanical mythology as voluntary; sometimes, as in the *Kalika Purana,* [8] where the gods spring spontaneously from the yogic contemplation of the demiurge, Brahma, the creation is a succession of surprises even to the creator. In the Icelandic Eddas, it will be recalled, the cosmic hermaphrodite, Ymir, gives off Rime-Giants from his living hands and feet, but is attacked during a later age by the young gods, Wotan, Wili, and We, to be cut up and transformed into the entire theater of the cosmos. [9] Comparably, in the celebrated Babylonian "Epic of Creation," the young god Marduk kills, cuts up, and fashions the universe from the body of the primal chaos monster Tiamat. Ovid, in the first chapter of his *Metamorphoses,* states that a god, in the beginning, brought order out of chaos. [10] And we learn from the ancient Egyptian Memphite theology that Egypt, the universe, and all the gods, came forth from Ptah, "The Great One," "Him-with-the-lovely-face." [11]

In the Indian metaphysical system of the Vedanta, which purports to be a translation of the metaphorical imagery of Brahmanical myths into abstract philosophical terms, the primordial entity out of which the universe proceeds is described as a fusion of Pure Consciousness (Brahman, vidya) and Ignorance (Maya, avidya), where Ignorance (Maya) is compared to the female of the mythological pair, furnishing at once the womb and the substance of creation. By virtue of her obscuring power she occludes the Absolute Brahman, and by virtue of her projecting power she refracts the radiance of that Absolute in the forms of the world mirage, somewhat as a prism breaks the white light of the sun into the seven colors of the rainbow—for, as Goethe has phrased the same concept in his *Faust:* "Am farbigen Abglanz haben wir das Leben." [12] In the fifteenth-century *Vedantasara,* this marriage of Ignorance and Consciousness, Illusion and Truth, Maya and Brahman, is described as at once the efficient and material cause of all things. "Consciousness associated with Ignorance (and the latter possessed of the two powers) is both the efficient cause and the material cause of the universe . . .; just as the spider, when considered from the standpoint of its own self, is the efficient cause of the web, and, when looked upon from the standpoint of its own body, is also the material cause of the web." [13]

Translated into Kantian terms, Ignorance as here interpreted corresponds to the *a priori* forms of sensibility (time and space), which are the inmost and outmost boundaries and the preconditions of all empirical experience: these *a priori* forms occlude the metaphysical realm of absolute reality and project the universe of phenomenality. But what the "true being" of the ultimate reality, dissociated from our modes of experience, might be, we shall never know; for, as the "great Chinaman of Königsberg" phrases it: "Was es für eine Bewandniss mit den Gegenständen an sich und abgesondert von aller dieser Receptivität unserer Sinnlichkeit haben möge, bleibt uns gänzlich unbekannt." [14]

Thus Hovering Hawk, the *Brihadaranyaka Upanishad,* the *Kalika Purana,* the Eddas, the Babylonian "Epic of Creation," Ovid, the Memphite theology, Vedantic philosophy, Kant, and Goethe, through varieties of metaphor, have stated and stated again a single thought—and what would appear to be an easy thought to state, namely: the One, by some sleight of hand or trick of the eye, has become the

Manifold. Yet, instead of stating this thought directly, they have employed allegorical vehicles, now of pictorial, now of abstract character, and, curiously, though each of the vehicles succeeds in conveying at least a hint of the tenor of the message, none actually elucidates it— none really explains, or even directly represents, the mystery of the coming of the Manifold out of the One. And in this respect Kant's formulation is no more satisfactory than Hovering Hawk's.

But the problem, again regarded, is seen to be not susceptible of outright elucidation; for it is a problem of the relationship of a known term (the universe) to an unknowable (its so-called source): that is to say, it is, strictly speaking, a metaphysical, not an empirical problem. Whether such a problem be presented for contemplation in the picture language of the myth or in the abstract of philosophy, it can only be presented, never elucidated. And since it is thus finally ineffable, no single metaphor, no combination of metaphors, can exhaust its implications. The slightest change of standpoint, and the entire conception undergoes kaleidoscopic transformation, as do likewise the correlative vehicles of imagery and communication. The primordial One, for instance, may be represented as masculine (as in the case of Brahma), feminine (as in the World Mother), hermaphrodite (as in the cases of 'I' and Ymir), anthropomorphic (as in most of the above presented examples), theriomorphic (as in the Persian myth of the dismembered World Ox), botanomorphic (as in the Eddic image of the World Ash, Yggdrasil), simply ovoid (as in the stories of the World Egg), geometrical (as in the Tantric yantras), vocal (as in the cases of the Vedic sacred syllable OM and the Kabbalistic Tetragrammaton), or absolutely transcendent (as in the cases of the Buddhistic Void and Kantian Ding an sich). But even the notion of the Oneness of the primordial is finally only a metaphor—referring past itself to an inconceivable term beyond all such pairs of opposites as the One and the Manifold, masculinity and feminity, existence and non-existence.

III

Kant, in his *Prolegomena zu einer jeden künftigen Metaphysik, die als Wissenschaft wird auftreten können,*[15] supplies an extraordinarily simple formula for the proper reading of a metaphysical symbol. What he offers is a four-term analogy (*A* is to *B* as *C* is to *X*), which points not to an incomplete resemblance of two things, but to a complete resemblance of two relationships between quite dissimilar things ("nicht etwa, eine unvollkommene Ähnlichkeit zweier Dinge, sondern eine vollkommene Ähnlichkeit zweier Verhältnisse zwischen ganz un-ähnlichen Dingen"): not "*A* somewhat resembles *B*," but "the relation-ship of *A* to *B* perfectly resembles that of *C* to *X*," where *X* represents a quantity that is not only unknown but absolutely unknowable—which is to say, metaphysical.

Kant demonstrates this formula in two examples:

1. As the promotion of the happiness of the children (*A*) is related to the parents' love (*B*), so is the welfare of the human race (*C*) to that unknown in God (*X*) which we call God's love.

2. The causality of the highest cause is precisely, in respect to the world, what human reason is in respect to the work of human art.

He then discusses the implication of the second of these examples, as follows: "Herewith the nature of the highest cause itself remains unknown to me; I only compare its known effect (namely, the consti-tution of the universe) and the rationality of this effect with the known effects of human reason, and therefore I call that highest cause a Reason, without thereby attributing to it as its proper quality, either the thing that I understand by this term in the case of man, or any other thing with which I am familiar."

Mythological, theological, metaphysical analogies, in other words, do not point indirectly to an only partially understood empirical term, but directly to a *relationship between two terms,* the one empirical, the other metaphysical; the latter being, absolutely and forever and from every conceivable human standpoint, unknowable.

If this be so then we shall have misread the series presented in section II, if we suppose that we have fully caught its tenor in the simple statement, "the One, by some sleight of hand, has become the Multiple." Such a statement furnishes, indeed, a terse summary of the vehicular aspect of the analogous metaphors but leaves unclarified their metaphysical tenor; that is to say, it summarizes only the first two terms of an implied four-term analogy, which would read, fully rendered, as follows: "As many (*A*) proceed from one (*B*), so does the universe (*C*) from God (*X*)." But the term *X*, it must be insisted, remains absolutely unknown and unknowable. Oneness can no more be a quality of this *X* than can Love or Reason. Hence, as Kant has

declared, it is only by analogy that we speak of Love or Reason as
of God.

X remaining unknown, then, the precise nature of its relationship to
C must likewise remain unknown. Magic, simple fissure, sexual pro-
creation, violent dismemberment, refraction, effusion, and delusion
are among the relationships suggested—suggested, not as proper to
the mystery of creation itself, but as vehicles to carry the analogy.
And there are no end of possible vehicular relationships; no end of
possible A terms and related B terms; for instance: as Earth Maker
(B^1) is related to the things drawn from his body (A^1); as All-father
(B^2) is related to the creatures that he has begotten (A^2); as meditating
Brahma (B^3) is related to the visions of his meditation (A^3); as occluded
light (B^4) to its refractions (A^4); the spider (B^5) to its web (A^5); etc.,
etc., etc., *ad infinitum* (B^n: A^n); so is God (X) related to creation (C).

IV

Unless the myths can be understood—or felt—to be true in some
such way as this, they lose their force, their magic, their charm for the
tender-minded and become mere archaeological curiosities, fit only
for some sort of reductive classification. And this, indeed, would appear to be the death that the heroes of the myths themselves most
fear. Continually, they are pointing past and through their phenomenal
to their universal, transcendental, aspect. "I and my Father in Heaven
are One," declares the Christ, for example. And Shri Krishna, in the
Bhagavad Gita, shows that all the forms of the world are rooted in his
metaphysical essence, just as that essence itself, reciprocally, is rooted
in all things:

Neither the hosts of gods, nor the great saints, know my origin, for in every
way I am the source of all the gods and great saints. He who knows Me,
birthless and beginningless, the great Lord of worlds—he, among mortals,
is undeluded, he is freed from all sins ... I am the Self existing in the
heart of all beings; I am the beginning, the middle, and also the end of all
beings. Of the gods, I am Vishnu; of luminaries, the radiant sun; ... of
bodies of water, I am the ocean; ... of measures, I am time; of beasts,
I am the lord of beasts; of birds, I am the lord of birds; ... of fishes, I am
the shark; of streams, I am the Ganges; ... I am the gambling of the
fraudulent; I am the power of the powerful; I am victory, I am effort,
I am the harmony of the harmonious; ... of punishers, I am the scepter;
of those who seek to conquer, I am the statesmanship; of things secret,
I am silence, and the knowledge of the knowers am I....[16]

Comparably, Killer-of-Enemies, the hero of the Jicarilla Apache tribe of New Mexico, declares, when he is about to depart from the people:

This earth is my body. The sky is my body. The seasons are my body. The water is my body too. . . . The world is just as big as my body. The world is as large as my word. And the world is as large as my prayers. The seasons are only as great as my body, my words, and my prayer. It is the same with the waters; my body, my words, my prayers are greater than the waters. Whoever believes me, whoever listens to what I say, will have long life. One who doesn't listen, who thinks in some evil way will have a short life. Don't think I am just in the east, south, west, or north. The earth is my body. I am there. I am all over. Don't think I stay only under the earth or up in the sky, or only in the seasons, or on the other side of the waters. These are all my body. It is the truth that the underworld, the sky, the waters, are all my body. I am all over. I have already given you that with which you have to make an offering to me. You have two kinds of pipe and you have the mountain tobacco.[17]

Or once again, in the words of Aeschylus:

Zeus is air, Zeus is earth, Zeus is heaven;
Zeus is all things and whatsoever is higher
than all things.[18]

"We should understand well," said an old Sioux medicine man, Black Elk, the Keeper of the Sacred Pipe, "that all things are the works of the Great Spirit. We should know that He is within all things: the trees, the grasses, the rivers, the mountains, and all the four-legged animals, and the winged peoples; and even more important, we should understand that He is also above all these things and peoples. When we do understand all this deeply in our hearts, then we will fear, and love, and know the great Spirit, and then we will be and act and live as He intends."[19]

Wherever myths still are living symbols, the mythologies are teeming dream worlds of such images. But wherever systematizing theologians have appeared and gained the day (the tough-minded in the gardens of the tender) the figures have become petrified into propositions. Mythology is misread then as direct history or science; symbol becomes fact, metaphor dogma, and the quarrels of the sects arise, each mistaking its own symbolic signs for the ultimate reality—the local vehicle for its timeless, ineffable tenor.

"But he who is called Krishna," said the nineteenth century Indian teacher, Ramakrishna, "is also called Shiva and bears the names Shakti, Jesus, and Allah as well—the one Rama with a thousand names. . . . The substance is one under different names and everyone is seeking the same substance; nothing but climate, temperament, and names vary."[20]

V

And so now we have to ask whether mythology can have originated in the camps of the tough-minded and only later have become sublimated and sophisticated into metaphysical poetry by the broodings of the tender-minded; or whether its course of development must not have been in precisely the opposite direction, from the poetical imagery of the tender-minded to the clumsy misreadings of the ungifted many. Dr. Boas appears to have been a champion of the former view. In his article already referred to, on "The Ethnological Significance of Esoteric Doctrines," he wrote:

It may be said that the exoteric doctrine is the more general ethnic phenomenon, the investigation of which is a necessary foundation for the study of the problems of esoteric teaching. It is, therefore, evident that we must not, in our study of Indian life, seek for the highest form of thought only, which is held by the priest, the chief, the leader. Interesting and attractive as this field of research may be, it is supplementary only to the study of the thoughts, emotional life, and ethical standards of the common people, whose interests center in other fields of thought and of whom the select class forms only a special type.[21]

Dr. R. R. Marett, on the other hand, in his article "Mana," in the *Encyclopaedia Britannica* (14th ed.), appears to take the opposite view. "By the very virtue of his profession," he writes, "the medicine man or the divine king must hold himself apart from those who by status or by choice are *noa,* laymen. The latter may live in brutish contentment; but to the end they lack enlightenment, participating in the highest mysteries at best from without. Every member of a primitive society is in some degree versed in experience of the occult, though for the most part some better qualified person is present to help him through it."

Whether primary or secondary in temporal terms—that is to say, in terms of "Which came first?"—the tender-minded, esoteric view is clearly the one that has played the chief role in the significant shaping of traditions, since it is everywhere the priests and shamans who have maintained and developed the general inheritance of myths and symbols. Dr. Radin, I observe, like Dr. Boas, regards the role of the intellectual as secondary in primitive societies.[22] He gives due recognition to the force of philosophical thought in the shaping of their cultural inheritance, however; and since we cannot go back, even hypothetically, to the moment when a metaphysical insight first dawned in a human mind, to learn whether myths, rituals, and symbols had already given shape to the society in which the first genius lived who thought like a philosopher, perhaps Dr. Radin's balanced recognition of the dialogue of the two types in the continuance and development of primitive traditions is about as far as we can go. "How are we ever to trace properly the development of thought and, more specifically, that of our fundamental philosophical notions," he asks, "if we begin with false premises? If it can be shown that the thinkers among primitive peoples envisage life in philosophical terms, that human experience and the world around them have become subjects for reflection, that these ponderings and searchings have become embodied in literature and ritual, then obviously our customary treatment of cultural history, not to mention that of philosophical speculation, must be completely revised."[23]

For myself, however, I believe that we owe both the imagery and the poetical insights of myth to the genius of the tender-minded; to the tough-minded only their reduction to religion. As far as I know, in the myths themselves the origins of their symbols and cults have always been attributed to individual visionaries—dreamers, shamans, spiritual heroes, prophets, and divine incarnations. Hovering Hawk, for example, when asked how his people made their songs, replied: "We dreamed them. When a man would go away by himself—off into solitude—then he would dream a song."[24]

In any case, the time has certainly come—as Paul Radin told us long ago—for the collectors and classifiers to regard the pretensions of their materials to a deep significance. From every corner of the globe they have gathered images, tales, and myths; yet the science of interpreting the materials can hardly be said to have broached even the first outposts of the psychology of man's approach to and experience of the metaphysical; for up to now the interest of the scholars has been almost exclusively ethnological and historical. They have analyzed from many points of view what may be termed the stylistic variations of the vehicles. Yet, what such stylistic variations signify it will certainly be impossible to say until the tenors of clusters of analogous metaphors have been established and understood. For the bed rock of the science of folklore and myth is not in the wisps and strays of metaphor, but in the ideas to which the metaphors refer.

NOTES

[1] *Pragmatism* (Longmans, Green and Company, New York, 1907), Lecture I, "The Present Dilemma in Philosophy."

[2] *Race, Language and Culture* (The Macmillan Company, New York, 1940): "The Ethnological Significance of Esoteric Doctrines" (1902), p. 314.

[3] Paul Radin, *Primitive Man as Philosopher* (D. Appleton and Company, New York and London, 1927), pp. 247-52.

[4] Boas, *Race, Language and Culture*, p. 156.

[5] *Ibid.*, p. 157.

[6] Natalie Curtis, *The Indians' Book*, pp. 315-16.

[7] *Brihadaranyaka Upanishad* I.iv, 1-5.

[8] *See also* Heinrich Zimmer, *The King and the Corpse* (Bollingen Series XI, Pantheon Books, New York, 1948; 2d. ed. with index, 1956), pp. 239 ff.

[9] *The Prose Edda*, Gylfaginning IV-VIII.

[10] Ovid, *Metamorphoses* I, 21.

[11] Cf. Henri Frankfort, *Kingship and the Gods* (University of Chicago Press, Chicago, 1948), pp. 25 and *passim;* see Index under "Ptah."

[12] Goethe, *Faust*, Part II, 1.1, last line.

[13] *Vedantasara* 55-56.

[14] Immanuel Kant, *Kritik der reinen Vernunft*, I.8.i.

[15] Immanuel Kant, *Prolegomena zu einer jeden künftigen Metaphysik die als Wissenschaft wird auftreten können*, paragraphs 57-58.

[16] *Bhagavad Gita*, chap. x abridged.

[17] Morris Edward Opler, "Myths and Tales of the Jicarilla Apache Indians," *Memoirs of the American Folklore Society*, XXXI (New York, 1938), 133-34.

[18] Aeschylus, *Heliades*, frag. 70.

[19] Foreword to Joseph Epes Brown, *The Sacred Pipe: Black Elk's Account of the Seven Rites of the Oglala Sioux* (University of Oklahoma Press, 1953), p. xx.

[20] *The Cultural Heritage of India* (Advaita Ashrama, Mayavati, India, 1936), II, 518-19.

[21] Boas, *Race, Language and Culture*, pp. 314-15.

[22] Radin, *Primitive Man as Philosopher*, pp. 211-12.

[23] *Ibid.*, p. 386.

[24] Curtis, *The Indians' Book*, p. 314.

THINKER AND INTELLECTUAL
IN PRIMITIVE SOCIETY

By Robert Redfield

AGAINST THE BACKGROUND of prevailing anthropological concentration upon cultures, groups, customs and institutions there stands out Paul Radin's long-maintained interest in *particular* individuals in primitive societies and especially in the intellectually creative productions of some of them. In two ways he has been a pioneer. Publication of "The Autobiography of a Winnebago Indian" stimulated the now widespread use of autobiographies in the study of cultures and of personalities in cultures. Both Clyde Kluckhohn[1] and Margaret Mead,[2] in discussing anthropological uses of extended documents recording first-person statements by informants, have given expression to a general recognition that it was *Crashing Thunder* which directed professional attention to the making of such documents and to their interpretation. Another door opened for us when Paul Radin found among primitive peoples certain individuals who were thinkers, persons with a vocation for things of the mind, who worked upon the ideas and images of their tradition to make them coherent and, maybe, abstract.[3] This discovery ran counter to notions at that time current as to the unreflective, custom-bound life of primitive peoples. It also contradicted those philosophers who found the origins of philosophy in the religious beliefs and rites of the unreflective many. John Dewey declared that if Dr. Radin's work was even approximately right, it required a thoroughgoing revision of prevailing ideas of the intellectual history of mankind.[4] In primitive society, Radin was saying, there are already philosophers. In commenting here on this second important contribution to anthropology I shall try to say just what type of being Radin discovered or asserted to exist, and to connect or compare this type with some others.

This human type, the thinker, is put forward as a kind of man or mind performing a kind of role or function. It is both a temperament and an

The late Dr. Redfield was Professor of Anthropology at the University of Chicago.

activity. Let us look first at the former aspect of this type. Radin makes no attempt to describe a total personality; he describes only certain qualities of mind. The thinkers are those who have "a marked capacity for articulating their ideas and for organizing them into coherent systems."[5] A thinker is "constrained to answer certain questions, to try to discover why there is an effect. . . ." He does not accept the world as a mere series of events "on the same level," he requires explanations; for him "some type of coordination is imperatively demanded."[6] These qualities may be, says Radin, "basic and inherent."[7] They appear in marked degree in only a few individuals in any society.

This type contrasts with its opposite, "the man of action," whose mind does not require integration of event and meaning into systems. Presumably these types are ideal, and in actual individuals are more or less purely represented. Radin's terms may not be the most felicitous that could be found; at least it may be said that some men who lack the special qualities of mind attributed to thinkers do not always act very conspicuously, but rather plod along in routine; and further it seems that there are many very thoughtful men who do not consider fundamental and comprehensive questions at length or integrate event and meaning into coherent wholes. The Mayan villager, Eustaquio Ceme, of whom I have written,[8] was a very thoughtful man in that he considered, persistingly and penetratingly, many questions—religious, moral, political. He would pause when a problem occurred to him and take it away to give it thought; later he would set out, in careful words, the opinions or conceptions or explanations to which his cogitation had brought him. But he was primarily a man of action in that he planned and executed courses of action; he was a leader of his people in a period of transition and crisis.

It might be simpler, at least in these paragraphs, to say that Radin showed us evidences of the activities of certain primitive minds in conceiving and articulating the nature of things as coherent, as coordinated by some principle or principles. This is a very special kind of thinking. Whether it corresponds to the thinking done by philosophers in civilized societies is a question. The nature of this special quality of mind is known to those who have read Isaiah Berlin's essay on Tolstoy. Berlin interprets a line of the Greek poet Archilochus to "mark one of the deepest differences which divide writers and thinkers, and, it, may be, human beings in general." The one type, "the fox," consists of men who live by ideas scattered and often unrelated to one another. But the man of the other type, "the hedgehog," relates "everything to a single central vision, one system more or less coherent or articulate . . . a single, universal, organizing principle . . . ." [9] Berlin is writing about great Western literature and sees Dante as a hedgehog and Shakespeare as a fox, but, I think, he is talking about qualities of mind similar to those which Radin has found in primitive "thinkers." Radin discovered the hedgehogs in primitive society.

How do we know that any particular human being has this quality of mind? If today we had him before us for testing, it is probable that we should use ink blots to find out. Dr. Mead made Rorshach tests of her best Arapesh informant, Unabelin. Dr. Klopfer, looking at the protocols and without other acquaintance with that Arapesh, declared that he had "no intellectual positive interest in organizing the material on one card into a concept . . ." and "no capacity for abstract organization of material . . . no theoretical mind whatever." [10] Unabelin was no hedgehog. I received the impression of his alert and curious foxiness just by reading the edited transcript of his interviews with Margaret Mead. He was interested in many things, but there was nothing philosophical about his interest. It is the exceptional human individual who has the quality of mind that Radin has made us recognize in primitive society.

By their works shall we know them. Radin presents to us contrasting texts of myths from the same society and asks us to accept his judgment that one was written by a thinker and the other by what he calls a man of action. I do not know if he knew personally the tellers of the two Winnebago myths he gives us, but I am almost sure he did not know the Maori or the Dakota whose tales he also offers as the products of thinkers. He recognizes the thinkers from the coherent and abstract organization of idea and symbol in the accounts that they gave to this or that anthropologist. In the texts Radin uses I too see this difference: texts that march along like a catalogue or a mere sequence of events, and texts that have an intellectual and often esthetic integrity. If we accept this kind of proof that the thinker-qualities existed in the tellers, we are using the text—speaking now broadly—as a projective test. The tradition provides the people of that society with elements of symbol and event, with mythic content;

there is a certain flexibility or ambiguity in these elements; they may be interpreted and articulated more or less particularly, more or less coherently and integrally.

When a native informant speaks to an anthropologist at length the document that results is more or less autobiographic, more or less "auto-ethnographic" (Kroeber's word).[11] It tells about the personal experiences and thoughts of the teller, or it describes the ways of life of his people. Many of the recently published personal documents from primitive people are primarily autobiographic; the informant was told to tell about himself and found it not too difficult to do so. *The Son of Old Man Hat*,[12] *Sun Chief*,[13] Du Bois's *Alorese*,[14] and most of the short Walapai narratives published under Kroeber's editorship,[15] are autobiographies. In the autobiography given Mead by her Arapesh there is much auto-ethnography also. The recent strong interest in personality and its formation has stressed the production of autobiographies and on the whole it has been the revelation of personality rather than of a native mind working on a tradition that has interested the anthropologist.

But the relative emphasis on autobiography or auto-ethnography depends also on the interests and the temperament of the informant. I repeat a twice-published observation when I say that when Kluckhohn asked the Navaho, Mr. Moustache, to tell everything about his life, he produced no autobiography but rather "a philosophic homily."[16] This happened because Mr. Moustache was by temperament suited to be a moralist, in later life had become one, and was quite conscious of his role in transmitting the moral tradition (as Kroeber's discussion of the case well shows).[17] Autobiographies tend to expose not only personality in culture as analyzed by the anthropologist and psychologist, but also the teller's self-conception; and this self-conception in not a few cases is a statement of how the teller's career seems to *him* to fulfill statuses and roles recognized by the society. Later, when these remarks come to deal with roles, this aspect of the autobiography will become relevant. But in discovering the hedgehog-thinker it is the auto-ethnography—the account of custom, the myth, the description of the universe and its meanings, the tale that expresses reflection and perhaps questioning—that is most useful to us. Even a philosophic individual, looking back on his life, sees much that is episodic, insubordinate to principle and unified meaning. We see a unified whole not so much in our experiences as in our thoughts about the meaning of life. So the thinker is to be found in his works of the mind and accounts of the origin or nature of things, rather than in the story of what happened to him.

It would be interesting to learn whether several judges, reading a group of texts of auto-ethnographies, would come to the same conclusion as to which of them are productions of "thinkers" and which are not. Further, it would help us along in identifying the thinkers and their works if we considered several versions of the same myth as told by different informants. Have we examined the collections of variant myths that we now have with this question in mind? Beyond this possible enquiry lie important and less accessible questions. Perhaps the text cannot be used as a test of the mental qualities of the teller. Does a given myth, coherent, integrated and abstract, reflect the mental qualities of the narrator or those of preceding thinkers whose production the present narrator is reproducing, as an unpoetical person might recite a poem? I do not read Dr. Radin as necessarily asserting that the Dakota or the Maori who told the myth was himself a thinker; Radin's first purpose is to show that *some* thinkers have worked upon the tradition. Further, how much originality, how much rearranging of the elements of a tradition, is accomplished by even the best thinkers in primitive societies? Is it not possible that the most impressive of these productions, such as the Polynesian accounts of the origin and development of things, have come to the forms in which we know them by small increments of elaboration and systematization taking place in a multitude of oral reproductions over a long period of time?

Such a very impressive production, a really astonishing system of ideas in a primitive or archaic society, has come to our knowledge through the work of the late Professor Griaule and his associates among the peoples of the French Sudan. The publications[18] about the Dogon include several versions of long and complicated origin myths, a study of a secret language, a study of the meanings of 266 graphic signs, and, of immediate interest here, a long report of thirty-three interviews Griaule had with one informant. This book, *Dieu d'Eau*,[19] was produced for a general public and is without the apparatus of scientific publication; it is presumably something less than a complete account of what went on in this series of interviews. I shall here take it, however, at its face value. In these interviews Ogontêmmeli, an old blind man, once a hunter, gave Griaule in logical sequence an account of the origin and the nature of all things. One cannot read it, I think, and fail to recognize it as a work of the mind. All things—plants, animals, tools, man's social life, his rituals and the divine beings—are linked together in an intricate system of related meanings. The linkage is both genetic and static: everything has some connection with events going back to creation; and everything is bound to a system of parallel forms, of symbols—as, for example, the village is a human body; this body is also the primordial body of the first god; the house represents man's pedigree back to the gods; even pots are images of the universe. Further, this primitive Great Design is a definition and justification of human conduct; the same elaborately integrated system of symbols defines the significances of human life. In *Dieu d'Eau* this immense and complex work is reproduced by one man, virtually un-assisted by other men and of course, in the darkness of his blindness, without immediate mnemonic aid. Reading it one sees that this is not a case of memorizing a chant or other ritual form. It is not the order and form of words that matter to Ogontêmmeli; he is not reciting; he is thinking about the right relations of ideas and things, and his mind sees the outlines of a unified structure. He is thinking as hedgehogs think; his mind demands that coordination of which Radin speaks; a multiple general principle, causal, developmental and analogical, holds together a great mass of detail. Of explicit abstraction there is not much, but occasionally Ogontêmmeli speaks as if formulating, out of his own cogitations, this or that comprehensive principle. At the twentieth interview he says that in all sacrifices "first one's self is nourished, one is strengthened, then by the Word the strength is given back to the people. As each one gives to all, each receives from all. Between men there is a continuous interchange, a ceaseless movement of invisible flow . . . ." And at the seventh interview, after recognizing the complementarity of water and fire, and describing the way in which the sun's rays draw up water which then descends as rain, he in effect generalizes: "Draw up and make descend, draw up and make descend, that is the life of the world."

Here, it seems, we have the record of a primitive philosopher at work. But further examination of the document suggests some doubts or qualifications. Ogontêmmeli is reproducing a vision of the universe, and it is plain that he wants to get it right. He thinks about where a detail belongs in the vast scheme; at a few points where he is not sure he suspends his account and goes and asks someone else about it. But I do not find evidence that he struggles with difficulties and inconsistencies to resolve them by a creative effort of his own powers of intellect. In one or two places he gives two versions of a mythical episode; he just gives the two versions and offers no judgment of choice or attempt at reconciliation. From time to time Professor Griaule puts questions to him. To most of them Ogontêmmeli gives no answers, or says something that is unresponsive. It seems to me that the more explicit effort to reflect upon this material and provide connections and principles is made by Griaule in his questioning of the old Dogon. There are some small exceptions, a few places in the record where Ogontêmmeli does answer Griaule directly. Griaule asks why it was the *seventh* Nommo who became Master of the World, and the Dogon answers, "Because seven is the greatest number." When Griaule asks why seven is the greatest number, the reply comes, "Because it is the sum of three and four," three being associated with maleness and four with femaleness (from the numbering of the genitalia). But evidences of original contributions from Ogontêmmeli are few. If to think long and deeply about the nature of the world and its origins as tradition has proposed explanations to one, is to be a philosopher, Ogontêmmeli is a philosopher. He is not, if a philosopher is one who struggles with intellectual problems in abstract terms and offers solutions of some originality.

This is not to say, of course, that among the many Dogon there may not be more philosophical minds than Ogontêmmeli's. In another publication[20] Griaule suggests that these Dogon who have attained to the highest level of cosmogonic learning do not feel over them a "ceiling of knowledge"; rather, they think that they can still advance their understanding. On the other hand, such developments of thought that in fact do occur result from the play of different natures on traditional knowledge and lead only to variant conclusions resting always on the same basic principles. And elsewhere[21] he tells us that it is very difficult to introduce any significant novelty into Dogon ideas—both because they find expression in an intricate and tightly interrelated system of symbols, and because any departure from tradition would run against the opinions of a large intellectual elite and the more diffuse conceptions of the less instructed mass. The question recurs: Are there nevertheless still taking place small and unnoticed changes such as may account for the development of this vast system over much time? Or is it that with complexity and unification, such systems of thought reach a more or less stable condition so that what is recorded by Griaule is a finished edifice on which no further construction can take place?

The foregoing remarks tend to the conclusion that in primitive societies some individuals have those qualities of mind attributed by Radin to his "thinker," and that some expositions as to the origin or nature of things written down by anthropologists show the effects of such minds upon the body of knowledge in their society, and that, presumably, the more comprehensive, coherent, extensive and esoteric formulations of tradition that we have in our literature have resulted, however slowly, largely from the intellectual activities and oral reproductions of individuals with such qualities of mind. I do not think we know very much about the contributions to these structures of thought made by particular individuals.

Presumably, other things being equal, individuals with these special qualities of temperament are drawn into the restating of a tradition; for the Dogon Griaule assures us that it is those who have the required intelligence and curiosity who attempt to learn the higher levels of knowledge.[22] But we do not always find esoteric knowledge lodged in the minds of men with intellectual curiosity and ability to integrate thought. I recall that interviews (unpublished) had by Alfonso Villa Rojas with eight or nine h-menob, priestly functionaries of the Yucatec Maya, suggest that many of these men were repositories of special knowledge of prayers and rites, but were without unusual qualities of intellect. A man can enter into professional life by accident or for reasons of temperament having nothing to do with capacity to provide intellectual integration.

I turn to the professionalization, in primitive and not quite so primitive societies, of the life of the mind. The interest now shifts to the ways in which the kind of intellectual activity discussed above is carried on in statuses and roles, in institutions and perhaps offices, that are parts of the social organization or structure of the society. I should like, if possible, to limit the topic to the institutionalization of thoughtful consideration and coherent, possibly abstract, formulation of the traditional understanding of the nature of things. Specialists who memorize knowledge unknown to others, and use the knowledge in magical or religious activity, as do many priests, sorcerers and diviners, are not by that fact exemplars of the life of the mind. To know something other people do not know, and to use this knowledge in ways recognized in that society is to perform a role, possibly to occupy an office, but it is not necessarily to be a thinker, in Radin's special sense. The specialists who carry on institutionalized thinking depend upon the existence of recognized traditional learning, of a body of ideas and symbols susceptible to thoughtful consideration. As Radin has used "thinker" for someone with a kind of temperament and intellectual capacity, we might use the familiar word "intellectual" for one who performs a role in cultivating the life of the mind; he has or is expected to have employed the thinker's capacity in the cultivation of learning; in many cases he is a thinker. Intellectuals have their functions and their roles; they are seen by their fellows as doing something characteristic in society. The intellectuals of the Europe of modern times are associated with their effects on social or political movements.[23] The *literati* of traditional China, many of them scholars or creative writers, constituted a ruling class.[24] So we might ask whether there are intellectuals in primitive societies and if so, what are their functions and their roles.

The answer is probably either "not quite," or "yes, in some degree." We see something fully recognizable in civilizations—law, foreign policy, originally creative artists—and, looking back at this or that isolated nonliterate society we see in one or another of them something that represents or at least foreshadows what in civilizations has greatly developed. So with learning and intellectuals. In this or that primitive society tradition has become complex; its transmission and perhaps its elaboration is the work of specialists; there is perhaps recognition of roles to be fulfilled in performing this work; there is a separation between the learning of the professional and that of other people in the society; and perhaps in the future the creative contribution of the individual thinker may become apparent to us.

In making some order among the proto-artists and proto-intellectuals one might begin by attending to two familiar and probably very widespread tendencies in even the simplest societies: the tendency to recognize wisdom in the experience accumulated by old people; and the tendency to vest special knowledge, often esoteric, in practitioners of the ritual arts of one kind or another. Tradition must be held in minds; there may be so much of it that only parts of it can be held in any one mind, that of chanter or priest, diviner or sorcerer. The Factors of personality presumably contribute to the recruitment of both the specialized memorizer and the generally thoughtful and usually elderly repository of tradition. Kroeber has shown us[25] one type of thoughtful old person (represented by Kuni, the Walapai, and Mr. Moustache, the Navaho): a personality responsible, conservative, pious, sober, disposed to accept established forms; a self-conception fulfilling a role as preserver of tradition. The recorded utterances of Mr. Moustache[26] are predominantly moral advice; he is one who tells people not so much about the nature of things as about what a man ought to do; he sees the good life as right conduct. Kroeber's suggestion that such a type, both of person and of role, may be quite widespread, is readily acceptable.

In other aspects of the cultivated tradition we see other kinds of specialists—neither moralists nor intellectuals—but rather artists and entertainers. The occasional individual who is recognized by his fellows as unusually good at telling traditional tales may have qualities of personality that we have not yet fully identified; they are surely qualities different from those conspicuous in Mr. Moustache and Kuni. This function is performed by occupiers of recognized statuses or offices in some societies where great social and practical importance is attached to a content of tradition that must be remembered and from time to time restated. One thinks of the genealogies of Polynesian peoples and of the bardic chanter who establishes the illustriousness of the lineage of his patron. This is an office, an art, and—one imagines—in cases a personality type. Skill in poetic composition and in certain styles of vocal utterance, as well as the memorizing of genealogies, composed the art of the Hawaiian *Haku-mele,* "Master of Song." [27] The bardic castes of India perform similar functions, and master similar arts of composition and voice.[28] This is a type of cultivator of tradition that has appeared more than once in human history and that continues into civilized society.[29]

Moralist and bardic chanter, types of specialists maintaining tradition and exercising upon material some degree of considered and individualized creative effort, are not, however, intellectuals. The intellectual's special activity is predominantly neither homiletic nor poetic; it consists of a disposition to conceive and present an integral view of all things. He too remembers and transmits tradition, but for him it is the comprehensive questions as to the origins and the nature of man and the universe that are to be understood and communicated. The documents that express this kind of thinking tell of how things came to be as they are or explain how it is that they are as they are. They are causal or genetic or symbolic explanations of the meaning of life. Do we have also integrated statements of moral judgment—primitive ethics? In such documents as are given us for the Navaho, the ethics is implied rather than explicated; it is reflected from assertions as to particular conduct, right or wrong, bad or good. But bodies of mythology, or explanation of things and customs, obedient to apparent unifying ideas, are common in anthropological literature.

The enquiring mind, attentive to questions of ritual, cosmology and the symbolic significance of acts and objects, is frequently shown to exist in one nonliterate group or another. It is clear that in primitive societies there occur disagreements as to details of ritual, the form of the act or its interpretation; that elements of myth or ritual may have different meanings for different people of the same group, or different meanings for the same individual at different times; that improvised explanations are sometimes made; that these matters become a subject of discussion; and that primitive people commonly recognize the superior knowledge in such matters of some members of their group as compared with others.[30] In seeking the beginnings of intellectualism more is to be asked: do we find the thinkers constituting an institutionalized group or class carrying on the perpetuation and consideration of world view in fulfillment of a role, or in occupation of an office to which recognized duties are attached?

Much could be assembled that would suggest if not display some beginnings, in one circumstance or another, of learning and the intellectual life. Some comments on one outstanding instance of organized learning among an African people—the Dogon—may suggest one direction for further enquiry and comparison.

The accounts of the Dogon that I have seen[31] show that the knowledge of these people is highly organized, systematically and in some respects theoretically arranged, formally taught to child, youth and older person, conceived as attainable progressively through increasingly abstruse degrees of understanding, and bound together by fundamental organizing ideas. It is, emphatically, knowledge about the nature of things; the justifications and directives it offers for human conduct are apparently implied rather than declared; the Dogon learns what we might feel to correspond roughly to our natural history, sociology, theology, history and metaphysics. The amount of this knowledge is enormous; it is clear that no one could grasp its every detail, although the older and the most advanced in instruction certainly comprehend the great design into which fit endless details. One sample of this learning,[32] having to do with insects (including some other small creatures not arthropods), shows the nature of the knowledge and the progressively arcane nature of learning. Children are told to collect insects; these are sorted out by the elders, who then teach the names, uses, taboos and mythology connected with each. We are told that insects, like many other classes of natural or artificial things, fall into twenty-two categories, and that the order in which the twenty-two categories of insects are taken up for instruction is not the same as the properly traditional order. This latter order is revealed to the young person only after initiation; it is among the more arcane matters having to do with insects, including the correspondences of the insect-categories with those classifying birds, quadrupeds, reptiles, plants and the twenty-two parts of the human body. Later, also, comes revelation of the conventional graphic signs—groupings of simple lines—associated with certain of these categories and their meaning. This instruction of the young with regard to insects is but a small part of all the knowledge about nature, the technical arts and their products, and the mythological beings and events, and of a series of instructions that begins with lessons given, at least ideally, by the old man who is familial head to "the male members of the family *lato sensu*," and continues through a series of instructions and initiations. Women have their own body of knowledge, in which the same design of all things appears through study of things, events and occupations characteristic of women; and specialists in crafts know more about the meanings connected with that craft than do other people.

Griaule was told of four degrees of understanding recognized by the adult Dogon, and expressed in certain graphic signs that were shown to him. The knowledge at the next higher degree is not knowledge about kinds of things different from that at the lower degree; it is deeper knowledge of the same kind of thing. As the student advances, his learning becomes more and more profound and the organizing ideas of the whole become more apparent. The fourth and most profound degree is thought of as a culmination; degrees one, two and three are respectively "in front," "on one side," and "behind," but the fourth is "clear knowledge"; it is knowledge in its ordered complexity. Truly the ways of the hedgehog are institutionalized for all Dogon!

Griaule was given the names of eighty men of one Dogon community who had reached "clear knowledge." These men constituted 5 or 6 percent of the total population of that community, or about 12 percent of the adult male population. Ogontêmmeli was not one of these advanced initiates; Griaule says that his account represents only levels two and three; of the "clear knowledge" we are given a sample in the monograph about Sirius and the calculation of the exact period (of about sixty years) between celebrations of a certain ceremony. So this society includes a recognized group of especially learned men, not moralists or artists, but men of advanced knowledge.

Are they intellectuals? One wishes one knew something of the discussions they carry on with one another—if they do—and as to how they conceive their role in society. It is a fair assumption that they well know their importance in preserving and communicating the higher learning and in regulating religious ceremony. They surely have something in common with learned Brahmins, elderly mandarins, and modern philosophers. On the other hand—although I may have missed something in these publications that I should have seen—there is lacking evidence of criticisms of tradition, of important original contributions by individuals, of notable reformulations. Knowledge is apparently conceived as substantially fixed, to be progressively revealed as one goes through life. And the thorough integration of the degrees of learning and of those who have attained to the various degrees, in one body of thought, in one society of people sharing a common life, becomes notable as one begins to think about intellectuals in the great civilizations. For in these there is a tendency for the life of the mind to be carried on at some distance from the life of ordinary people and in its own, now somewhat separate, stream of tradition. The learning of the Mayan priest-astronomer surely connected, at necessary points of thought and action, with the practices and ideas of the peasantlike people of the villages; yet the priest-astronomer thought and worked apart in the shrine center, presumably communicated with other priest-astronomers, and advanced his abstruse calculations to knowledge not easily connected with what the villager knew. The Brahmins maintained their separation through caste, and the most learned of them shared knowledge with others like himself across much of India but touched the villager's thoughts only at points, and imperfectly through people of intermediate learning. Where a society has become so large and complex as to move the intellectual away from other people, where the learned inhabit a temple, a city, or a monastery, where learning is communicated among learned people distant from one another, where perhaps writing is added to help these developments to take place and to encourage the restatement of learning in a form consultable over long periods—where these things happen the more civilized instances of institutionalized intellectualism are to be recognized. In the case of the Dogon, learning may seem to us (but apparently not to them) to be a single-stepped pyramid up which the qualified man way ascend. In the great civilizations the pyramidal form is less easily suggested; the degree of separation of the intellectuals from other people suggests parallel but interrelated structures of thought, two or more streams of tradition flowing into one another and yet cutting somewhat distinct channels. This compounding or dividing of traditional knowledge is one of the characteristics of civilized life.

What we are told about the Dogon is a presentation of a way of life as traditional ideas perpetuated and perhaps cultivated. This way of life, like others, might be conceived as a society, as characteristic relationships among kinds of people. That Griaule and his associates have not done so, but have instead made us see first the integrated body of thought that is Dogon learning, a learning that rules, that gives meaning to, institutions and activities, may in part be a consequence of the bent of interest of the investigators, but it is also brought about by the fact that with these Sudanese learning is indeed complex and is systematically conceived and studied. Social structure seems to follow from the Dogon view of the universe rather than world view to emerge from social structure. In the great civilizations of Asia this manner of thinking about ways of life is also invited. Where a tradition is thoughtfully reproduced and perhaps cultivated, and especially where the learned are markedly distinguished from the unlearned, we may think of that central entity of our consideration, culture-society, as a body of knowledge, more or less pyramidal, more or less multilineal.

NOTES

[1] Clyde Kluckhohn, "The Personal Document in Anthropological Science," in *The Use of Personal Documents in History, Anthropology and Sociology* (Bulletin No. 53, Social Science Research Council, 1945), pp. 79-175.

[2] Margaret Mead, "The Mountain Arapesh: V. The Record of Unabelin, with Rorshach Analysis," *Anthropological Papers of the American Museum of Natural History*, Vol. 41, part 3 (1949).

[3] Paul Radin, *Primitive Man as Philosopher* (New York and London: D. Appleton & Co., 1927); *The World of Primitive Man* (New York: Henry Schuman, 1953).

[4] Radin, *Primitive Man as Philosopher*, pp. xv-xvii.

[5] Radin, *The World of Primitive Man*, p. 171.

[6] *Ibid.*, p. 39.

[7] *Ibid.*, p. 37.

[8] Robert Redfield, with Alfonso Villa Rojas, *Chan Kom, a Maya Village* (Washington, D.C.: Carnegie Institution of Washington Publication No. 448, 1934); *A Village That Chose Progress* (Chicago: University of Chicago Press, 1950).

[9] Isaiah Berlin, *The Hedgehog and the Fox* (New York: Mentor Books, The New American Library, 1957), pp. 7-8.

[10] Mead, "The Mountain Arapesh," pp. 378, 383.

[11] A. L. Kroeber, "A Southwestern Personality Type," *Southwestern Journal of Anthropology*, III (1947), 109.

[12] Walter Dyk, *The Son of Old Man Hat* (New York: Harcourt, Brace and Company, 1938).

[13] Leo W. Simmons, ed., *Sun Chief* (New Haven: Yale University Press, 1942).

[14] Cora Du Bois, *The People of Alor* (Minneapolis: The University of Minnesota Press, 1942).

[15] Fred Kniffen and others, *Walapai Ethnography*, ed. by A. L. Kroeber (Memoirs of the American Anthropological Association, No. 42, 1935).

[16] Clyde Kluckhohn, "A Navaho Personal Document with a Brief Paretian Analysis," *Southwestern Journal of Anthropology*, I (1945), 273.

[17] Kroeber, "Southwestern Personality Type."

[18] I am indebted to M. Claude Tardits for helping me to some acquaintance with these publications.

[19] Marcel Griaule, *Dieu d'Eau* (Paris: Editions du Chêne, n.d.).

[20] Marcel Griaule, "Le Savoir des Dogon," *Journal de la Société des Africanistes*, Tome XXII (1952), Fascicles I and II.

[21] Marcel Griaule, "L'Enquête orale en ethnologie," *Revue Philosophique de la France et de l'Étranger*, CXLII (1952), 540.

[22] *Ibid.*, p. 33.

[23] Roberto Michels, "Intellectuals," *Encyclopaedia of the Social Sciences*, VII, 118.

[24] Max Weber, "The Chinese Literati," in *From Max Weber: Essays in Sociology*, trans. and ed. by H. H. Gerth and C. Wright Mills (New York: Oxford University Press, 1946). Following Toynbee's special use of *intelligentsia*, that word might be reserved for those who have learned enough of the ways of a society dominating their own to enable their own community to deal with the

invaders. These men may not be intellectuals at all. The anthropologist encounters intelligentsia in tribal or peasant societies undergoing acculturation.

[25] Kroeber, "Southwestern Personality Type."

[26] John Ladd, *The Structure of a Moral Code* (Cambridge, Mass.: Harvard University Press, 1957), pp. 335-406. Mr. Moustache was Ladd's principal informant in the course of his study of Navaho morality. See also Kluckhohn, "A Navaho Personal Document."

[27] Martha Beckwith, *The Kumulipo, A Hawaiian Creation Chant* (Chicago: University of Chicago Press, 1951), pp. 35-41.

[28] A. M. Shah, "The Vahivancha Barots of Gujerat." Unpublished MS.

[29] *Ibid.* In Gujerat there are still bardic chanters who retain in memory the substance of their verses, but their importance declines while similar castes that make use of written records—their professional secrets—have a larger place in the affairs of their society. Some of the "followers of the written tradition" also recite or compose bardic chants and tell stories.

[30] For example, Monica Wilson, *Rituals of Kinship Among the Nyakussa,* "Publication of the International African Institute" (London: Oxford University Press, 1957), pp. 48, 106, 240.

[31] Marcel Griaule, *Dieu d'Eau;* "Le Savoir des Dogon"; "L'Enquête orale en ethnologie." Marcel Griaule and Germaine Dieterlen, "La Harpe-luth des Dogon," *Journal de la Société des Africanistes,* XX (1950), 209-28; "Un Systeme soudanais de Sirius," *ibid.,* 273-94; "Signes graphiques soudanais," *L'Homme, cahiers d'ethnologie, de geographie, et de linguistique,* 3 (1951). I have not had access to G. Dieterlen, *Essai sur la religion bambara* (Paris: Presses Universitaires, 1951).

[32] Griaule, "Le Savoir des Dogon."

OJIBWA ONTOLOGY, BEHAVIOR, AND WORLD VIEW

By A. Irving Hallowell

> *It is, I believe, a fact that future investigations will thoroughly confirm, that the Indian does not make the separation into personal as contrasted with impersonal, corporeal with impersonal, in our sense at all. What he seems to be interested in is the question of existence, of reality; and everything that is perceived by the sense, thought of, felt and dreamt of, exists.*
>
> PAUL RADIN

Introduction

IT HAS BECOME increasingly apparent in recent years that the potential significance of the data collected by cultural anthropologists far transcends in interest the level of simple, objective, ethnographic description of the peoples they have studied. New perspectives have arisen; fresh interpretations of old data have been offered; investigation and analysis have been pointed in novel directions. The study of culture and personality, national character and the special attention now being paid to values are illustrations that come to mind. Robert Redfield's concept of world view, "that outlook upon the universe that is characteristic of a people," which emphasizes a perspective that is not equivalent to the study of religion in the conventional sense, is a further example.

"World view" [he says] differs from culture, ethos, mode of thought, and national character. It is the picture the members of a society have of the properties and characters upon their stage of action. While "national character" refers to the way these people look to the outsider looking in on them, "world view" refers to the way the world looks to that people looking out. Of all that is connoted by "culture," "world view" attends

---

The courtesy of the Stanford University Press is acknowledged for permission to use portions of a paper by the author which appeared in *Person Perception*, ed. by R. Tagiuri and L. Petrullo.

especially to the way a man, in a particular society, sees himself in relation to all else. It is the properties of existence as distinguished from and related to the self. It is, in short, a man's idea of the universe. It is that organization of ideas which answers to a man the questions: Where am I? Among what do I move? What are my relations to these things? ... Self is the axis of "world view." [1]

In an essay entitled "The Self and Its Behavioral Environment," I have pointed out that self-identification and culturally constituted notions of the nature of the self are essential to the operation of all human societies and that a functional corollary is the cognitive orientation of the self to a world of objects other than self. Since the nature of these objects is likewise culturally constituted, a unified phenomenal field of thought, values, and action which is integral with the kind of world view that characterizes a society is provided for its members. The behavioral environment of the self thus becomes structured in terms of a diversified world of objects other than self, "discriminated, classified, and conceptualized with respect to attributes which are culturally constituted and symbolically mediated through language. Object orientation likewise provides the ground for an intelligible interpretation of events in the behavioral environment on the basis of traditional assumptions regarding the nature and attributes of the objects involved and implicit or explicit dogmas regarding the 'causes' of events." [2] Human beings in whatever culture are provided with cognitive orientation in a cosmos; there is "order" and "reason" rather than chaos. There are basic premises and principles implied, even if these do not happen to be consciously formulated and articulated by the people themselves. We are confronted with the philosophical implications of their thought, the nature of the world of being as they conceive it. If we pursue the problem deeply enough we soon come face to face with a relatively unexplored territory—ethno-metaphysics. Can we penetrate this realm in other cultures? What kind of evidence is at our disposal? The forms of speech as Benjamin Whorf and the neo-Humboldtians have thought? [3] The manifest content of myth? Observed behavior and attitudes? And what order of reliability can our inferences have? The problem is a complex and difficult one, but this should not preclude its exploration.

In this paper I have assembled evidence, chiefly from my own field work on a branch of the Northern Ojibwa, [4] which supports the inference that in the metaphysics of being found among these Indians, the action of persons provides the major key to their world view.

While in all cultures "persons" comprise one of the major classes of objects to which the self must become oriented, this category of being is by no means limited to *human* beings. In Western culture, as in others, "supernatural" beings are recognized as "persons," although belonging, at the same time, to an other than human category.[5] But in the social sciences and psychology, "persons" and human beings are categorically identified. This identification is inherent in the concept of "society" and "social relations." In Warren's *Dictionary of Psychology* "person" is defined as "a human organism regarded as having distinctive characteristics and social relations." The same identification is implicit in the conceptualization and investigation of social organization by anthropologists. Yet this obviously involves a radical abstraction if, from the standpoint of the people being studied, the concept of "person" is not, in fact, synonymous with human being but transcends it. The significance of the abstraction only becomes apparent when we stop to consider the perspective adopted. The study of social organization, defined as human relations of a certain kind, is perfectly intelligible as an objective approach to the study of this subject in any culture. But if, in the world view of a people, "persons" as a class include entities other than human beings, then our objective approach is not adequate for presenting an accurate description of "the way a man, in a particular society, sees himself in relation to all else." A different perspective is required for this purpose. It may be argued, in fact, that a thoroughgoing "objective" approach to the study of cultures cannot be achieved solely by projecting upon those cultures categorical abstractions derived from Western thought. For, in a broad sense, the latter are a reflection of *our* cultural subjectivity. A higher order of objectivity may be sought by adopting a perspective which includes an analysis of the outlook of the people themselves as a complementary procedure. It is in a world view perspective, too, that we can likewise obtain the best insight into how cultures function as wholes.

The significance of these differences in perspective may be illustrated in the case of the Ojibwa by the manner in which the kinship term "grandfather" is used. It is not only applied to human persons but to spiritual beings who are persons of a category other than human. In fact, when the collective plural "our grandfathers" is used, the reference is primarily to persons of this latter class. Thus if we study Ojibwa social organization in the usual manner, we take account of only one set of "grandfathers." When we study their religion we discover other "grandfathers." But if we adopt a world view perspective no dichotomization appears. In this perspective "grandfather" is a term applicable to certain "person objects," without any distinction between human persons and those of an other-than-human class. Furthermore, both sets of grandfathers can be said to be functionally as well as terminologically equivalent in certain respects. The other-than-human grandfathers are sources of power to human beings through the "blessings" they bestow, i.e., a sharing of their power which enhances the "power" of human beings. A child is always given a name by an old man, i.e., a terminological grandfather. It is a matter of indifference whether he is a blood relative or not. This name carries with it a special blessing because it has reference to a dream of the human grandfather in which he obtained power from one or more of the other-than-human grandfathers. In other words, the relation between a human child and a human grandfather is functionally patterned in the same way as the relation between human beings and grandfathers of an other-than-human class. And, just as the latter type of grandfather may impose personal taboos as a condition of a blessing, in the same way a human grandfather may impose a taboo on a "grandchild" he has named.

Another direct linguistic clue to the inclusiveness of the "person" category in Ojibwa thinking is the term *windīgo*. Baraga defines it in his *Dictionary* as "fabulous giant that lives on human flesh; a man that eats human flesh, cannibal." From the Ojibwa standpoint all *windīgowak* are conceptually unified as terrifying, anthropomorphic beings who, since they threaten one's very existence, must be killed. The central theme of a rich body of anecdotal material shows how this threat was met in particular instances. It ranges from cases in which it was necessary to kill the closest of kin because it was thought an individual was becoming a *windīgo,* through accounts of heroic fights between human beings and these fabulous giant monsters, to a first-hand report of a personal encounter with one of them.[6]

The more deeply we penetrate the world view of the Ojibwa the more apparent it is that "social relations" between human beings (*ánícinábek*) and other-than-human "persons" are of cardinal significance. These relations are correlative with their more comprehensive categorization of "persons." Recognition must be given to the culturally constituted meaning of "social" and "social relations" if we are to understand the nature of the Ojibwa world and the living entities in it.[7]

Linguistic Categories and Cognitive Orientation

Any discussion of "persons" in the world view of the Ojibwa must take cognizance of the well known fact that the grammatical structure of the language of these people, like all their Algonkian relatives, formally expresses a distinction between "animate" and "inanimate" nouns. These particular labels, of course, were imposed upon Algonkian languages by Europeans;[8] it appeared to outsiders that the Algonkian differentiation of objects approximated the animate-inanimate dichotomy of Western thought. Superficially this seems to be the case. Yet a closer examination indicates that, as in the gender categories of other languages, the distinction in some cases appears to be arbitrary, if not extremely puzzling, from the standpoint of common sense or in a naturalistic frame of reference. Thus substantives for some, but not all—trees, sun-moon (*gízis*), thunder, stones, and objects of material culture like kettle and pipe—are classified as "animate."

If we wish to understand the cognitive orientation of the Ojibwa, there is an ethno-linguistic problem to be considered: What is the meaning of animate in Ojibwa thinking? Are such generic properties of objects as responsiveness to outer stimulation—sentience, mobility, self-movement, or even reproduction—primary characteristics attributed to all objects of the animate class irrespective of their categories as physical objects in our thinking? Is there evidence to substantiate such properties of objects independent of their formal linguistic classification? It must not be forgotten that no Ojibwa is consciously aware of, or can abstractly articulate the animate-inanimate category of his language, despite the fact that this dichotomy is implicit in his speech. Consequently, the grammatical distinction as such does not emerge as a subject for reflective thought or bear the kind of relation to individual thinking that would be present if there were some formulated dogma about the generic properties of these two classes of objects.

Commenting on the analogous grammatical categories of the Central Algonkian languages with reference to linguistic and nonlinguistic orders of meaning, Greenberg writes: "Since all persons and animals are in Class I (animate), we have at least one ethnoseme, but most of the other meanings can be defined only by a linguiseme." In Greenberg's opinion, "unless the actual behavior of Algonquian speakers shows some mode of conduct common to all these instances such that, given this information, we could predict the membership of Class I, we must resort to purely linguistic characterization." [9]

In the case of the Ojibwa, I believe that when evidence from beliefs, attitudes, conduct, and linguistic characterization are all considered together the psychological basis for their unified cognitive outlook can be appreciated, even when there is a radical departure from the framework of our thinking. In certain instances, behavioral predictions can be made. Behavior, however, is a function of a complex set of factors —including actual experience. More important than the linguistic classification of objects is the kind of vital functions attributed to them in the belief system and the conditions under which these functions are observed or tested in experience. This accounts, I think, for the fact that what we view as material, inanimate objects—such as shells and stones—are placed in an "animate" category along with "persons" which have no physical existence in our world view. The shells, for example, called *mígis* on account of the manner in which they function in the Midewiwin, could not be linguistically categorized as "inanimate." "Thunder," as we shall see, is not only reified as an "animate" entity, but has the attributes of a "person" and may be referred to as such. An "inanimate" categorization would be unthinkable from the Ojibwa point of view. When Greenberg refers to "persons" as clearly members of the animate grammatical category he is, by implication, identifying person and human being. Since in the Ojibwa universe there are many kinds of reified person-objects which are other than human but have the same ontological status, these, of course, fall into the same ethnoseme as human beings and into the "animate" linguistic class.

Since stones are grammatically animate, I once asked an old man: Are *all* the stones we see about us here alive? He reflected a long while and then replied, "No! But *some* are." This qualified answer made a lasting impression on me. And it is thoroughly consistent with other data that indicate that the Ojibwa are not animists in the sense that they dogmatically attribute living souls to inanimate objects such as stones. The hypothesis which suggests itself to me is that the allocation of stones to an animate grammatical category is part of a culturally constituted cognitive "set." It does not involve a consciously formulated theory about the nature of stones. It leaves a door open that our orientation on dogmatic grounds keeps shut tight. Whereas we should never expect a stone to manifest animate properties of any kind under any circumstances, the Ojibwa recognize, *a priori,* potentialities for animation in certain classes of objects under certain circumstances.[10] The Ojibwa do not perceive stones, in general, as animate, any more than we do. The crucial test is experience. Is there any personal testimony available? In answer to this question we can say that it is asserted by informants that stones have been seen to move, that some stones manifest other animate properties, and, as we shall see, Flint is represented as a living personage in their mythology.

The old man to whom I addressed the general question about the animate character of stones was the same informant who told me that during a Midewiwin ceremony, when his father was the leader of it, he had seen a "big round stone move." He said his father got up and walked around the path once or twice. Coming back to his place he began to sing. The stone began to move "following the trail of the old man around the tent, rolling over and over, I saw it happen several times and others saw it also."[11] The animate behavior of a stone under these circumstances was considered to be a demonstration of magic power on the part of the Midé. It was not a voluntary act initiated by the stone considered as a living entity. Associated with the Midewiwin in the past there were other types of large boulders with animate properties. My friend Chief Berens had one of these, but it no longer possessed these attributes. It had contours that suggested eyes and mouth. When Yellow Legs, Chief Berens's great-grandfather, was a leader of the Midewiwin he used to tap this stone with a new knife. It would then open its mouth, Yellow Legs would insert his fingers and take out a small leather sack with medicine in it. Mixing some of this medicine with water, he would pass the decoction around. A small sip was taken by those present.[12]

If, then, stones are not only grammatically animate, but, in particular cases, have been observed to manifest animate properties, such as movement in space and opening of a mouth, why should they not on occasion be conceived as possessing animate properties of a "higher" order? The actualization of this possibility is illustrated by the following anecdote:

A white trader, digging in his potato patch, unearthed a large stone similar to the one just referred to. He sent for John Duck, an Indian who was the leader of the *wábano*, a contemporary ceremony that is held in a structure something like that used for the Midewiwin. The trader called his attention to the stone, saying that it must belong to his pavilion. John Duck did not seem pleased at this. He bent down and spoke to the boulder in a low voice, inquiring whether it had ever been in his pavilion. According to John the stone replied in the negative.

It is obvious that John Duck spontaneously structured the situation in terms that are intelligible within the context of Ojibwa language and culture. Speaking to a stone dramatizes the depth of the categorical difference in cognitive orientation between the Ojibwa and ourselves. I regret that my field notes contain no information about the use of direct verbal address in the other cases mentioned. But it may well have taken place. In the anecdote describing John Duck's behavior, however, his use of speech as a mode of communication raises the animate status of the boulder to the level of social interaction common to human beings. Simply as a matter of observation we can say that the stone was treated *as if* it were a "person," not a "thing," without inferring that objects of this class are, for the Ojibwa, necessarily conceptualized as persons.

Further exploration might be made of the relations between Ojibwa thinking, observation, and behavior and their grammatical classification of objects but enough has been said, I hope, to indicate that not only animate properties but even "person" attributes may be projected upon objects which to us clearly belong to a physical inanimate category.

The "Persons" of Ojibwa Mythology

The Ojibwa distinguish two general types of traditional oral narratives: 1. "News or tidings" (*täbătcamowin*), i.e., anecdotes, or stories, referring to events in the lives of human beings (*änícinábek*). In content, narratives of this class range from everyday occurrences, through more exceptional experiences, to those which verge on the legendary. (The anecdotes already referred to, although informal, may be said to belong to this general class.) 2. Myths (*átíso'kanak*),[13] i.e., sacred stories, which are not only traditional and formalized; their narration is seasonally restricted and is somewhat ritualized. The significant thing about these stories is that the characters in them are regarded as living entities who have existed from time immemorial. While there is genesis through birth and temporary or permanent form-shifting through transformation, there is no outright creation. Whether human or animal in form or name, the major characters in the myths behave like people, though many of their activities are depicted in a spatio-temporal framework of cosmic, rather than mundane, dimensions. There is "social interaction" among them and between them and *ánícinábek*.

A striking fact furnishes a direct linguistic cue to the attitude of the Ojibwa towards these personages. When they use the term *átíso'kanak*, they are not referring to what I have called a "body of narratives." The term refers to what we would call the characters in these stories; to the Ojibwa they are living "persons" of an other-than-human class. As William Jones said many years ago, "Myths are thought of as conscious beings, with powers of thought and action."[14] A synonym for this class of persons is "our grandfathers."

The *átíso'kanak*, or "our grandfathers," are never "talked about" casually by the Ojibwa. But when the myths are narrated on long winter nights, the occasion is a kind of invocation: "Our grandfathers" like it and often come to listen to what is being said. In ancient times one of these entities (*Wisekedjak*) is reputed to have said to the others: "We'll try to make everything to suit the *ánícinábek* as long as any of them exist, so that they will never forget us and will always talk about us."

It is clear, therefore, that to the Ojibwa, their "talk" about these entities, although expressed in formal narrative, is not about fictitious characters. On the contrary, what we call myth is accepted by them as a true account of events in the past lives of living "persons."[15] It is for this reason that narratives of this class are significant for an understanding of the manner in which their phenomenal field is culturally structured and cognitively apprehended. As David Bidney has pointed out, "The concept of 'myth' is relative to one's accepted beliefs and convictions, so that what is gospel truth for the believer is sheer 'myth' and 'fiction' for the non-believer or skeptic. . . . Myths and magical tales and practices are accepted precisely because pre-scientific folk do not consider them as merely 'myths' or 'magic', since once the distinction between myth and science is consciously accepted, the acquired critical insight precludes the belief in and acceptance of magic and myth."[16] When taken at their face value, myths provide a reliable source of prime value for making inferences about Ojibwa world outlook. They offer basic data about unarticulated, unformalized, and unanalyzed concepts regarding which informants cannot be expected to generalize. From this point of view, myths are broadly analogous to the concrete material of the texts on which the linguist depends for his derivation, by analysis and abstraction, of the grammatical categories and principles of a language.

In formal definitions of myth (e.g., *Concise Oxford Dictionary* and Warren's *Dictionary of Psychology*) the subject matter of such narrative often has been said to involve not only fictitious characters but "supernatural persons." This latter appellation, if applied to the Ojibwa characters, is completely misleading, if for no other reason than the fact that the concept of "supernatural" presupposes a concept of the "natural." The latter is not present in Ojibwa thought. It is unfortunate that the natural-supernatural dichotomy has been so persistently invoked by many anthropologists in describing the outlook of peoples in cultures other than our own. Linguists learned long ago that it was impossible to write grammars of the languages of nonliterate peoples by using as a framework Indo-European speech forms. Lovejoy has pointed out that "The sacred word 'nature' is probably the most equivocal in the vocabulary of the European peoples . . ."[17] and the natural-supernatural antithesis has had its own complex history in Western thought.[18]

To the Ojibwa, for example, *gízis* (day luminary, the sun) is not a natural object in our sense at all. Not only does their conception differ; the sun is a "person" of the other-than-human class. But more important still is the absence of the notion of the ordered regularity in movement that is inherent in our scientific outlook. The Ojibwa entertain no reasonable certainty that, in accordance with natural law, the sun will "rise" day after day. In fact, *Tcakábec*, a mythical personage, once set a snare in the trail of the sun and caught it. Darkness continued until a mouse was sent by human beings to release the sun and provide daylight again. And in another story (not a myth) it is recounted how two old men at dawn vied with each other in influencing the sun's movements.

The first old man said to his companion: "It is about sunrise now and there is a clear sky. You tell the sun to rise at once." So the other old man said to the sun: "My grandfather, come up quickly." As soon as he had said this the sun came up into the sky like a shot. "Now you try something," he said to his companion. "See if you can send it down." So the other man said to the sun: "My grandfather, put your face down again." When he said this the sun went down again. "I have more power than you," he said to the other old man, "The sun never goes down once it comes up."

We may infer that, to the Ojibwa, any regularity in the movements of the sun is of the same order as the habitual activities of human beings. There are certain expectations, of course, but, on occasion, there may be temporary deviations in behavior "caused" by other persons. Above all, any concept of *impersonal* "natural" forces is totally foreign to Ojibwa thought.

Since their cognitive orientation is culturally constituted and thus given a psychological "set," we cannot assume that objects, like the sun, are perceived as natural objects in our sense. If this were so, the anecdote about the old men could not be accepted as an actual event involving a case of "social interaction" between human beings and an other-than-human person. Consequently, it would be an error to say that the Ojibwa "personify" natural objects. This would imply that, at some point, the sun was first perceived as an inanimate, material thing. There is, of course, no evidence for this. The same conclusion applies over the whole area of their cognitive orientation towards the objects of their world.

The Four Winds and Flint, for instance, are quintuplets. They were born of a mother (unnamed) who, while given human characteristics, lived in the very distant past. As will be more apparent later, this character, like others in the myths, may have anthropomorphic characteristics without being conceived as a human being. In the context she, like the others, is an *ätíso'kan*. The Winds were born first, then Flint "jumped out," tearing her to pieces. This, of course, is a direct allusion to his inanimate, stony properties. Later he was penalized for his hurried exit. He fought with *Misábos* (Great Hare) and pieces were chipped off his body and his size reduced. "Those pieces broken from your body may be of some use to human beings some day," *Misábos* said to him. "But you will not be any larger so long as the earth shall last. You'll never harm anyone again."

Against the background of this "historic" event, it would be strange indeed if flint were allocated to an inanimate grammatical category. There is a special term for each of the four winds that are differentiated, but no plural for "winds." They are all animate beings, whose "homes" define the four directions.

The conceptual reification of Flint, the Winds and the Sun as other-than-human persons exemplifies a world view in which a natural-supernatural dichotomy has no place. And the representation of these beings as characters in "true" stories reinforces their reality by means of a cultural device which at the same time depicts their vital roles in interaction with other persons as integral forces in the functioning of a unified cosmos.

Anthropomorphic Traits and Other-than-Human Persons

In action and motivations the characters in the myths are indistinguishable from human persons. In this respect, human and other-than-human persons may be set off, in life as well as in myth, from animate beings such as ordinary animals (*awésiak*, pl.) and objects belonging to the inanimate grammatical category. But, at the same time, it must be noted that "persons" of the other-than-human class do not always present a human appearance in the myths. Consequently, we may ask: What constant attributes do unify the concept of "person"? What is the essential meaningful core of the concept of person in Ojibwa thinking? It can be stated at once that anthropomorphic traits in outward appearance are not the crucial attributes.

It is true that some extremely prominent characters in the myths are given explicit human form. *Wísekedjak* and *Tcakábec* are examples. Besides this they have distinctive characteristics of their own. The former has an exceptionally long penis and the latter is very small in size, yet extremely powerful. There are no equivalent female figures. By comparison, Flint and the Winds have human attributes by implication; they were born of a "woman" as human beings are born; they speak, and so on. On the other hand, the High God of the Ojibwa, a very remote figure who does not appear in the mythology at all, but is spoken of as a "person," is not even given sexual characteristics. This is possible because there is no sex gender in Ojibwa speech.

Consequently an animate being of the person category may function in their thinking without having explicitly sexual or other anthropomorphic characteristics. Entities "seen" in dreams (*pawáganak*) are "persons"; whether they have anthropomorphic attributes or not is incidental. Other entities of the person category, whose anthropomorphic character is undefined or ambiguous, are what have been called the "masters" or "owners" of animals or plant species. Besides these, certain curing procedures and conjuring are said to have other-than-human personal entities as patrons.

If we now examine the cognitive orientation of the Ojibwa towards the Thunder Birds it will become apparent why anthropomorphism is not a constant feature of the Ojibwa concept of "person." These beings likewise demonstrate the autonomous nature of Ojibwa reification. For we find here a creative synthesis of objective "naturalistic" observation integrated with the subjectivity of dream experiences and traditional mythical narrative which, assuming the character of a living image, is neither the personification of a natural phenomenon nor an altogether animal-like or human-like being. Yet it is impossible to deny that, in the universe of the Ojibwa, Thunder Birds are "persons."

My Ojibwa friends, I discovered, were as puzzled by the white man's conception of thunder and lightning as natural phenomena as they were by the idea that the earth is round and not flat. I was pressed on more than one occasion to explain thunder and lightning, but I doubt whether my somewhat feeble efforts made much sense to them. Of one thing I am sure: My explanations left their own beliefs completely unshaken. This is not strange when we consider that, even in our naturalistic frame of reference, thunder and lightning as perceived do not exhibit the lifeless properties of inanimate objects. On the contrary, it has been said that thunder and lightning are among the natural phenomena which exhibit some of the properties of "person objects."[19] Underlying the Ojibwa view there may be a level of naïve perceptual experience that should be taken into account. But their actual construct departs from this level in a most explicit direction: Why is an avian image central in their conception of a being whose manifestations are thunder and lightning? Among the Ojibwa with whom I worked, the linguistic stem for bird is the same as that for Thunder Bird (*pinésī*; pl. *pinésīwak*). Besides this, the avian characteristics of Thunder Birds are still more explicit. Conceptually they are grouped with the hawks, of which there are several natural species in their habitat.

What is particularly interesting is that the avian nature of the Thunder Birds does not rest solely on an arbitrary image. Phenomenally, thunder does exhibit "behavioral" characteristics that are analogous to avian phenomena in this region.[20] According to meteorological observations, the average number of days with thunder begins with one in April, increases to a total of five in midsummer (July) and then declines to one in October. And if a bird calendar is consulted, the facts show that species wintering in the south begin to appear in April and disappear for the most part not later than October, being, of course, a familiar sight during the summer months. The avian character of the Thunder Birds can be rationalized to some degree with reference to natural facts and their observation.

But the evidence for the existence of Thunder Birds does not rest only on the association of the occurrence of thunder with the migration of the summer birds projected into an avian image. When I visited the Ojibwa an Indian was living who, when a boy of twelve or so, saw *pinésī* with his own eyes. During a severe thunderstorm he ran out of his tent and there on the rocks lay a strange bird. He ran back to call his parents, but when they arrived the bird had disappeared. He was sure it was a Thunder Bird, but his elders were skeptical because it is almost unheard of to see *pinésī* in such a fashion. But the matter was clinched and the boy's account accepted when a man who had *dreamed* of *pinésī* verified the boy's description. It will be apparent later why a dream experience was decisive. It should be added at this point, however, that many Indians say they have seen the nests of the Thunder Birds; these are usually described as collections of large stones in the form of shallow bowls located in high and inaccessible parts of the country.

If we now turn to the myths, we find that one of them deals in considerable detail with Thunder Birds. Ten unmarried brothers live together. The oldest is called *Mätcíkīwis*. A mysterious housekeeper cuts wood and builds a fire for them which they find burning when they return from a long day's hunt, but she never appears in person. One day the youngest brother discovers and marries her. *Mätcíkīwis* is jealous and kills her. She would have revived if her husband had not broken a taboo she imposed. It turns out, however, that she is not actually a human being but a Thunder Bird and, thus, one of the *ätíso'kanak* and immortal. She flies away to the land above this earth inhabited by the Thunder Birds. Her husband, after many difficulties, follows her there. He finds himself brother-in-law to beings who are the "masters" of the duck hawks, sparrow hawks, and other species of this category of birds he has known on earth. He cannot relish the food eaten, since what the Thunder Birds call "beaver" are to him like the frogs and snakes on this earth (a genuinely naturalistic touch since the sparrow hawk, for example, feeds on batrachians and reptiles). He goes hunting gigantic snakes with his male Thunder Bird relatives. Snakes of this class also exist on this earth, and the Thunder Birds are their inveterate enemies. (When there is lightning and thunder this is the prey the Thunder Birds are after.) One day the great Thunder Bird says to his son-in-law, "I know you are getting lonely; you must want to see your people. I'll let you go back to earth now. You have nine brothers at home and I have nine girls left. You can take them with you as wives for your brothers. I'll be related to the people on earth now and I'll be merciful towards them. I'll not hurt any of them if I can possibly help it." So he tells his daughters to get ready. There is a big dance that night and the next morning the whole party starts off. When they come to the edge of Thunder Bird land the lad's wife said to him, "Sit on my back. Hang on tight to my neck and keep your eyes shut." Then the thunder crashes and the young man knows that they are off through the air. Having reached this earth they make their way to the brothers' camp. The Thunder Bird women, who have become transformed into human form, are enthusiastically received. There is another celebration and the nine brothers marry the nine sisters of their youngest brother's wife.

This is the end of the myth but a few comments are necessary. It is obvious that the Thunder Birds are conceived to act like human beings. They hunt and talk and dance. But the analogy can be pressed further. Their social organization and kinship terminology are precisely the same as the Ojibwa. The marriage of a series of female siblings (classificatory or otherwise) to a series of male siblings often occurs among the Ojibwa themselves. This is, in fact, considered a kind of ideal pattern. In one case that I know of six blood brothers were married to a sorority of six sisters. There is a conceptual continuity, therefore, between the social life of human beings and that of the

Thunder Birds which is independent of the avian form given to the latter. But we must infer from the myth that this avian form is not constant. Appearance cannot then be taken as a permanent and distinguishable trait of the Thunder Birds. They are capable of metamorphosis, hence, the human attributes with which they are endowed transcend a human outward form. Their conceptualization as "persons" is not associated with a permanent human form any more than it is associated with a birdlike form. And the fact that they belong to the category of *ätíso'kanak* is no barrier to their descending to earth and mating with human beings. I was told of a woman who claimed that North Wind was the father of one of her children. My informant said he did not believe this; nevertheless, he thought it would have been accepted as a possibility in the past.[21] We can only infer that in the universe of the Ojibwa the conception of "person" as a living, functioning social being is not only one which transcends the notion of person in the naturalistic sense; it likewise transcends a human appearance as a constant attribute of this category of being.

The relevance of such a concept to actual behavior may be illustrated by one simple anecdote. An informant told me that many years before he was sitting in a tent one summer afternoon during a storm, together with an old man and his wife. There was one clap of thunder after another. Suddenly the old man turned to his wife and asked, "Did you hear what was said?" "No," she replied, "I didn't catch it." My informant, an acculturated Indian, told me he did not at first know what the old man and his wife referred to. It was, of course, the thunder. The old man thought that one of the Thunder Birds had said something to him. He was reacting to this sound in the same way as he would respond to a human being, whose words he did not understand. The casualness of the remark and even the trivial character of the anecdote demonstrate the psychological depth of the "social relations" with other-than-human beings that becomes explicit in the behavior of the Ojibwa as a consequence of the cognitive "set" induced by their culture.

Metamorphosis as an Attribute of Persons

The conceptualization in myth and belief of Thunder Birds as animate beings who, while maintaining their identity, may change their outward appearance and exhibit either an avian or a human form exemplifies an attribute of "persons" which, although unarticulated abstractly, is basic in the cognitive orientation of the Ojibwa.

Metamorphosis occurs with considerable frequency in the myths where other-than-human persons change their form. *Wísekedjak,* whose primary characteristics are anthropomorphic, becomes transformed and flies with the geese in one story, assumes the form of a snake in another, and once turns himself into a stump. Men marry "animal" wives who are not "really" animals. And *Míkínäk,* the Great Turtle, marries a human being. It is only by breaking a taboo that his wife discovers she is married to a being who is able to assume the form of a handsome young man.

The senselessness and ambiguities which may puzzle the outsider when reading these myths are resolved when it is understood that, to the Ojibwa, "persons" of this class are capable of metamorphosis by their very nature. Outward appearance is only an incidental attribute of being. And the names by which some of these entities are commonly known, even if they identify the character as an "animal," do not imply unchangeableness in form.

Stith Thompson has pointed out that the possibility of transformation is a "commonplace assumption in folk tales everywhere. Many of such motifs are frankly fictitious, but a large number represent persistent beliefs and living tradition."[22] The case of the Ojibwa is in the latter category. The world of myth is not categorically distinct from the world as experienced by human beings in everyday life. In the latter, as well as the former, no sharp lines can be drawn dividing living beings of the animate class because metamorphosis is possible. In outward manifestation neither animal nor human characteristics define categorical differences in the core of being. And, even aside from metamorphosis, we find that in everyday life interaction with nonhuman entities of the animate class are only intelligible on the assumption that they possess some of the attributes of "persons."

So far as animals are concerned, when bears were sought out in their dens in the spring they were addressed, asked to come out so that they could be killed, and an apology was offered to them.[23] The following encounter with a bear, related to me by a pagan Ojibwa named Birchstick, shows what happened in this case when an animal was treated as a person:

One spring when I was out hunting I went up a little creek where I knew suckers were spawning. Before I came to the rapids I saw fresh bear tracks. I walked along the edge of the creek and when I reached the rapids I saw a bear coming towards me, along the same trail I was following. I stepped behind a tree and when the animal was about thirty yards from me I fired. I missed and before I could reload the bear made straight for me. He seemed mad, so I never moved. I just waited there by the tree. As soon as he came close to me and rose up on his hind feet, I put the butt end of my gun against his heart and held him there. I remembered what my father used to tell me when I was a boy. He said that a bear always understands what you tell him. The bear began to bite the stock of the gun. He even put his paws upon it something like a man would do if he were going to shoot. Still holding him off as well as I could I said to the bear, "If you want to live, go away," and he let go the gun and walked off. I didn't bother the bear anymore.[24]

These instances suffice to demonstrate that, at the level of individual behavior, the interaction of the Ojibwa with certain kinds of plants and animals in everyday life is so structured culturally that individuals act as if they were dealing with "persons" who both understand what is being said to them and have volitional capacities as well. From the standpoint of perceptual experience if we only take account of autochthonous factors in Birchstick's encounter with the bear his behavior appears idiosyncratic and is not fully explained. On the other hand, if we invoke Ojibwa concepts of the nature of animate beings, his behavior becomes intelligible to us. We can understand the determining factors in his definition of the situation, and the functional relations between perception and conduct are meaningful. This Indian was not confronted with an animal with "objective" ursine properties, but rather with an animate being who had ursine attributes and *also* "person attributes." These, we may infer, were perceived as an integral whole. I am sure, however, that in narrating this episode to another Indian, he would not have referred to what his father had told him about bears. That was for my benefit!

Since bears, then, are assumed to possess "person attributes," it is not surprising to find that there is a very old, widespread, and persistent belief that sorcerers may become transformed into bears in order better to pursue their nefarious work.[25] Consequently some of the best documentation of the metamorphosis of human beings into animals comes from anecdotal material referring to cases of this sort. Even contemporary, acculturated Ojibwa have a term for this. They all know what a "bearwalk" is, and Dorson's recent collection of folk traditions, including those of the Indian populations of the Upper Peninsula of Michigan, bears the title *Bloodstoppers and Bearwalkers*. One of Dorson's informants gave him this account of what he had seen:

When I was a kid, 'bout seventeen, before they build the highway, there was just an old tote road from Bark River to Harris. There was three of us, one a couple years older, coming back from Bark River at nighttime. We saw a flash coming from behind us. The older fellow said, 'It's a bearwalk, let's get it. I'll stand on the other side of the road (it was just a wagon rut) and you stand on this side.' We stood there and waited. I saw it 'bout fifty feet away from us—close as your car is now. It looked like a bear, but every time he breathe you could see a fire gust. My chum he fall over in a faint. That brave feller on the other side, he faint. When the bear walk, all the ground wave, like when you walk on soft mud or on moss. He was goin' where he was goin'.[26]

It is clear from this example, and others that might be added, that the Indian and his companions did not perceive an ordinary bear. But in another anecdote given by Dorson, which is not told in the first person, it is said that an Indian "grabbed hold of the bear and it wasn't there—it was the old woman. She had buckskin bags all over her, tied on to her body, and she had a bearskin hide on."[27] I also have been told that the "bearwalk" is dressed up in a bearskin. All such statements, of course, imply a skeptical attitude towards metamorphosis. They are rationalizations advanced by individuals who are attempting to reconcile Ojibwa beliefs and observation with the disbelief encountered in their relations with the whites.

An old-fashioned informant of mine told me how he had once fallen sick, and, although he took various kinds of medicine these did him no good. Because of this, and for other reasons, he believed he had been bewitched by a certain man. Then he noticed that a bear kept coming to his camp almost every night after dark. This is most unusual because wild animals do not ordinarily come anywhere near a human habitation. Once the bear would have entered his wigwam if he had not been warned in a dream. His anxiety increased because he knew, of course, that sorcerers often transformed themselves into bears. So when the bear appeared one night he got up, went outdoors, and shouted to the animal that he knew what it was trying to do. He threatened retaliation in kind if the bear ever returned. The animal ran off and never came back.

In this case there are psychological parallels to Birchstick's encounter with a bear: In both cases the bear is directly addressed as a person might be, and it is only through a knowledge of the cultural background that it is possible fully to understand the behavior of the individuals involved. In the present case, however, we can definitely say that the "animal" was perceived as a human being in the form of a bear; the Indian was threatening a human person with retaliation, not an animal.

A question that I have discussed in *Culture and Experience* in connection with another "bearwalk" anecdote, also arises in this case.[28] Briefly, the Ojibwa believe that a human being consists of a vital part, or *soul,* which, under certain circumstances may become detached from the body, so that it is not necessary to assume that the body part, in all cases, literally undergoes transformation into an animal form. The body of the sorcerer may remain in his wigwam while his soul journeys elsewhere and appears to another person in the form of an animal.

This interpretation is supported by an account which an informant gave me of a visit his deceased grandchild had paid him. One day he was traveling in a canoe across a lake. He had put up an improvised mast and used a blanket for a sail. A little bird alighted on the mast. This was a most unusual thing for a bird to do. He was convinced that it was not a bird but his dead grandchild. The child, of course, had left her body behind in a grave, nevertheless she visited him in animal form.

Thus, both living and dead human beings may assume the form of animals. So far as appearance is concerned, there is no hard and fast line that can be drawn between an animal form and a human form because metamorphosis is possible. In perceptual experience what looks like a bear may sometimes *be* an animal and, on other occasions, a human being. What persists and gives continuity to being is the vital part, or soul. Dorson goes to the heart of the matter when he stresses the fact that the whole socialization process in Ojibwa culture "impresses the young with the concepts of transformation and of 'power', malign or benevolent, human or demonic. These concepts underlie the entire Indian mythology, and make sensible the otherwise childish stories of culture heroes, animal husbands, friendly thunders, and malicious serpents. The bearwalk idea fits at once into this dream world— literally a dream world, for Ojibwa go to school in dreams."[29]

We must conclude, I believe, that the capacity for metamorphosis is one of the features which links human beings with the other-than-human persons in their behavioral environment. It is one of the generic properties manifested by beings of the person class. But is it a ubiquitous capacity of all members of this class equally? I do not think so. Metamorphosis to the Ojibwa mind is an earmark of "power." Within the category of persons there is a graduation of power. Other-than-human persons occupy the top rank in the power hierarchy of animate being. Human beings do not differ from them in kind, but in power. Hence, it is taken for granted that all the *ätíso'kanak* can assume a variety of forms. In the case of human beings, while the potentiality for metamorphosis exists and may even be experienced, any outward manifestation is inextricably associated with unusual power, for good or evil. And power of this degree can only be acquired by human beings through the help of other-than-human persons. Sorcerers can transform themselves only because they have acquired a high order of power from this source.

Powerful men, in the Ojibwa sense, are also those who can make inanimate objects behave as if they were animate. The *Midé* who made a stone roll over and over has been mentioned earlier. Other examples, such as the animation of a string of wooden beads, or animal skins, could be cited.[30] Such individuals also have been observed to transform one object into another, such as charcoal into bullets and ashes into gunpowder, or a handful of goose feathers into birds or insects.[31] In these manifestations, too, they are elevated to the same level of power as that displayed by other-than-human persons. We can, in fact, find comparable episodes in the myths.

The notion of animate being itself does not presume a capacity for manifesting the highest level of power any more than it implies person-attributes in every case. Power manifestations vary within the animate class of being as does the possession of person-attributes. A human being may possess little, if any, more power than a mole. No one would have been more surprised than Birchstick if the bear he faced had suddenly become human in form. On the other hand, the spiritual "masters" of the various species of animals are inherently powerful and, quite generally, they possess the power of metamorphosis. These entities, like the *ätíso'kanak,* are among the sources from which human beings may seek to enhance their own power. My Ojibwa friends often cautioned me against judging by appearances. A poor forlorn Indian dressed in rags might have great power; a smiling, amiable woman, or a pleasant old man, might be a sorcerer.[32] You never can tell until a situation arises in which their power for good or ill becomes manifest. I have since concluded that the advice given me in a common sense fashion provides one of the major clues to a generalized attitude towards the objects of their behavioral environment—particularly people. It makes them cautious and suspicious in interpersonal relations of all kinds. The possibility of metamorphosis must be one of the determining factors in this attitude; it is a concrete manifestation of the deceptiveness of appearances. What looks like an animal, without great power, may be a transformed person with evil intent. Even in dream experiences, where a human being comes into direct contact with other-than-human persons, it is possible to be deceived. Caution is necessary in "social" relations with all classes of persons.

Dreams, Metamorphosis, and the Self

The Ojibwa are a dream-conscious people. For an understanding of their cognitive orientation it is as necessary to appreciate their attitude towards dreams as it is to understand their attitude towards the characters in the myths. For them, there is an inner connection which is as integral to their outlook as it is foreign to ours.

The basic assumption which links the *ätiso'kanak* with dreams is this: Self-related experience of the most personal and vital kind includes what is seen, heard, and felt in dreams. Although there is no lack of discrimination between the experiences of the self when awake and when dreaming, both sets of experiences are equally self-related. Dream experiences function integrally with other recalled memory images in so far as these, too, enter the field of self-awareness. When we think autobiographically we only include events that happened to us when awake; the Ojibwa include remembered events that have occurred in dreams. And, far from being of subordinate importance, such experiences are for them often of more vital importance than the events of daily waking life. Why is this so? Because it is in dreams that the individual comes into direct communication with the *ätiso'kanak,* the powerful "persons" of the other-than-human class.

In the long winter evenings, as I have said, the *ätiso'kanak* are talked about; the past events in their lives are recalled again and again by *änícinábek*. When a conjuring performance occurs, the voices of some of the same beings are heard issuing from within the conjuring lodge. Here is actual perceptual experience of the "grandfathers" during a waking state. In dreams, the same other-than-human persons are both "seen" and "heard." They address human beings as "grandchild." These "dream visitors" (i.e., *pawáganak*) interact with the dreamer much as human persons do. But, on account of the nature of these beings there are differences, too. It is in the context of this face-to-face personal interaction of the self with the "grandfathers" (i.e., synonymously *átíso kanak, pawáganak*) that human beings receive important revelations that are the source of assistance to them in the daily round of life, and, besides this, of "blessings" that enable them to exercise exceptional powers of various kinds.

But dream experiences are not ordinarily recounted save under special circumstances. There is a taboo against this, just as there is a taboo against myth narration except in the proper seasonal context. The consequence is that we know relatively little about the manifest content of dreams. All our data come from acculturated Ojibwa. We do know enough to say, however, that the Ojibwa recognize quite as much as we do that dream experiences are often qualitatively different from our waking experiences. This fact, moreover, is turned to positive account. Since their dream visitors are other-than-human "persons" possessing great power, it is to be expected that the experiences of the self in interaction with them will differ from those with human beings in daily life. Besides this, another assumption must be taken into account: When a human being is asleep and dreaming his *òtcatcákwin* (vital part, soul), which is the core of the self, may become detached from the body (*mīyó*). Viewed by another human being, a person's body may be easily located and observed in space. But his vital part may be somewhere else. Thus, the self has greater mobility in space and even in time while sleeping. This is another illustration of the deceptiveness of appearances. The body of a sorcerer may be within sight in a wigwam, while "he" may be bearwalking. Yet the space in which the self is mobile is continuous with the earthly and cosmic space of waking life. A dream of one of my informants documents this specifically. After having a dream in which he met some (mythical) anthropomorphic beings (*mémengwécīwak*) who live in rocky escarpments and are famous for their medicine, he told me that he had later identified precisely the rocky place he had visited and entered in his dream. Thus the behavioral environment of the self is all of a piece. This is why experiences undergone when awake or asleep can be interpreted as experiences of self. Memory images, as recalled, become integrated with a sense of self-continuity in time and space.

Metamorphosis may be *experienced* by the self in dreams. One example will suffice to illustrate this. The dreamer in this case had been paddled out to an island by his father to undergo his puberty fast. For several nights he dreamed of an anthropomorphic figure. Finally, this being said, "Grandchild, I think you are strong enough now to go with me." Then the *pawágan* began dancing and as he danced he turned into what looked like a golden eagle. (This being must be understood as the "master" of this species.) Glancing down at his own body as he sat there on a rock, the boy noticed it was covered with feathers. The "eagle" spread its wings and flew off to the south. The boy then spread his wings and followed.

Here we find the instability of outward form in both human and other-than-human persons succinctly dramatized. Individuals of both categories undergo metamorphosis. In later life the boy will recall how he first saw the "master" of the golden eagles in his anthropomorphic guise, followed by his transformation into avian form; at the same time he will recall his own metamorphosis into a bird. But this experience, considered in context, does not imply that subsequently the boy can transform himself into a golden eagle at will. He might or might not be sufficiently "blessed." The dream itself does not inform us about this.

This example, besides showing how dream experiences may reinforce the belief in metamorphosis, illustrates an additional point: the *pawá-ganak*, whenever "seen," are always experienced as appearing in a specific form. They have a "bodily" aspect, whether human-like, animal-like, or ambiguous. But this is not their most persistent, enduring and vital attribute any more than in the case of human beings. We must conclude that all animate beings of the person class are unified conceptually in Ojibwa thinking because they have a similar structure—an inner vital part that is enduring and an outward form which can change. Vital personal attributes such as sentience, volition, memory, speech are not dependent upon outward appearance but upon the inner vital essence of being. If this be true, human beings and other-than-human persons are alike in another way. The human self does not die; it continues its existence in another place, after the body is buried in the grave. In this way *anícinábek* are as immortal as *átíso'kanak*. This may be why we find human beings associated with the latter in the myths where it is sometimes difficult for an outsider to distinguish between them.

Thus the world of personal relations in which the Ojibwa live is a world in which vital social relations transcend those which are maintained with human beings. Their culturally constituted cognitive orientation prepares the individual for life in this world and for a life after death. The self-image that he acquires makes intelligible the nature of other selves. Speaking as an Ojibwa, one might say: all other "persons"—human or other than human—are structured the same as I am. There is a vital part which is enduring and an outward appearance that may be transformed under certain conditions. All other "persons," too, have such attributes as self-awareness and understanding. I can talk with them. Like myself, they have personal identity, autonomy, and volition. I cannot always predict exactly how they will act, although most of the time their behavior meets my expectations. In relation to myself, other "persons" vary in power. Many of them have more power than I have, but some have less. They may be friendly and help me when I need them but, at the same time, I have to be prepared for hostile acts, too. I must be cautious in my relations with other "persons" because appearances may be deceptive.

The Psychological Unity of the Ojibwa World

Although not formally abstracted and articulated philosophically, the nature of "persons" is the focal point of Ojibwa ontology and the key to the psychological unity and dynamics of their world outlook. This aspect of their metaphysics of being permeates the content of their cognitive processes: perceiving, remembering, imagining, conceiving, judging, and reasoning. Nor can the motivation of much of their conduct be thoroughly understood without taking into account the relation of their central values and goals to the awareness they have of the existence of other-than-human, as well as human, persons in their world. "Persons," in fact, are so inextricably associated with notions of causality that, in order to understand their appraisal of events and the kind of behavior demanded in situations as they define them, we are confronted over and over again with the roles of "persons" as *loci* of causality in the dynamics of their universe. For the Ojibwa make no cardinal use of any concept of impersonal forces as major determinants of events. In the context of my exposition the meaning of the term *manitu*, which has become so generally known, may be considered as a synonym for a person of the other-than-human class ("grandfather," *ätíso'kan, pawágan*). Among the Ojibwa I worked with it is now quite generally confined to the God of Christianity, when combined with an augmentative prefix (*k'tci manĩtu*). There is no evidence to suggest, however, that the term ever did connote an impersonal, magical, or supernatural force.[33]

In an essay on the "Religion of the North American Indians" published over forty years ago, Radin asserted "that from an examination of the data customarily relied upon as proof and from individual data obtained, there is nothing to justify the postulation of a belief in a universal force in North America. Magical power as an 'essence' existing apart and separate from a definite spirit, is, we believe, an unjustified assumption, an abstraction created by investigators."[34] This opinion, at the time, was advanced in opposition to the one expressed by those who, stimulated by the writings of R. R. Marett in particular, interpreted the term *manitu* among the Algonkians (W. Jones), *orenda* among the Iroquois (Hewitt) and *wakanda* among the Siouan peoples (Fletcher) as having reference to a belief in a magical force of some kind. But Radin pointed out that in his own field work among both the Winnebago and the Ojibwa the terms in question "always referred to definite spirits, not necessarily definite in shape. If at a vapor-bath the steam is regarded as *wakanda* or *manitu,* it is because it is a spirit transformed into steam for the time being; if an arrow is possessed of specific virtues, it is because a spirit has either transformed himself into the arrow or because he is temporarily dwelling in it; and finally, if tobacco is offered to a peculiarly-shaped object it is because either this object belongs to a spirit, or a spirit is residing in it." *Manitu,* he said, in addition to its substantive usage may have such connotations as "sacred," "strange," "remarkable" or "powerful" without "having the slightest suggestion of 'inherent power', but having the ordinary sense of these adjectives."[35]

With respect to the Ojibwa conception of causality, all my own observations suggest that a culturally constituted psychological set operates which inevitably directs the reasoning of individuals towards an explanation of events in personalistic terms. *Who* did it, *who* is responsible, is always the crucial question to be answered. Personalistic explanation of past events is found in the myths. It was *Wísekedjak* who, through the exercise of his personal power, expanded the tiny bit of mud retrieved by Muskrat from the depths of the inundating waters of the great deluge into the inhabitable island-earth of Ojibwa cosmography. Personalistic explanation is central in theories of disease causation. Illness may be due to sorcery; the victim, in turn, may be "responsible" because he has offended the sorcerer—even unwittingly. Besides this, I may be responsible for my own illness, even without the intervention of a sorcerer. I may have committed some wrongful act in the past, which is the "cause" of my sickness. My child's illness, too, may be the consequence of my past transgressions or those of my wife.[36] The personalistic theory of causation even emerges today among acculturated Ojibwa. In 1940, when a severe forest fire broke out at the mouth of the Berens River, no Indian would believe that lightning or any impersonal or accidental determinants were involved. *Somebody* must have been responsible. The German spy theory soon became popular. "Evidence" began to accumulate; strangers had been seen in the bush, and so on. The personalistic type of explanation satisfies the Ojibwa because it is rooted in a basic metaphysical assumption; its terms are ultimate and incapable of further analysis within the framework of their cognitive orientation and experience.

Since the dynamics of events in the Ojibwa universe find their most ready explanation in a personalistic theory of causation, the qualitative aspects of interpersonal relations become affectively charged with a characteristic sensitivity.[37] The psychological importance of the range and depth of this sensitive area may be overlooked if the inclusiveness of the concept of "person" and "social relations" that is inherent in their outlook is not borne in mind. The reason for this becomes apparent when we consider the pragmatic relations between behavior, values, and the role of "persons" in their world view.

The central goal of life for the Ojibwa is expressed by the term *pīmädäzīwin*, life in the fullest sense, life in the sense of longevity, health and freedom from misfortune. This goal cannot be achieved without the effective help and cooperation of *both* human and other-than-human "persons," as well as by one's own personal efforts. The help of other-than-human "grandfathers" is particularly important for men. This is why all Ojibwa boys, in aboriginal days, were motivated to undergo the so-called "puberty fast" or "dreaming" experience. This was the means by which it was possible to enter into direct "social interaction" with "persons" of the other-than-human class for the first time. It was the opportunity of a lifetime. Every special aptitude, all a man's subsequent successes and the explanation of many of his failures, hinged upon the help of the "guardian spirits" he obtained at this time, rather than upon his own native endowments or the help of his fellow *änícinábek*. If a boy received "blessings" during his puberty fast and, as a man, could call upon the help of other-than-human persons when he needed them he was well prepared for meeting the vicissitudes of life. Among other things, he could defend himself against the hostile actions of human persons which might threaten him and thus interfere with the achievement of *pīmǎdäzīwin*. The grandfather of one of my informants said to him: "you will have a long and good life if you dream well." The help of human beings, however, was also vital, especially the services of those who had acquired the kind of power which permitted them to exercise effective curative functions in cases of illness. At the same time there were moral responsibilities which had to be assumed by an individual if he strove for *pīmǎdäzīwin*. It was as essential to maintain approved standards of personal and social conduct as it was to obtain power from the "grandfathers" because, in the nature of things, one's own conduct, as well as that of other "persons," was always a potential threat to the achievement of *pīmǎdäzīwin*. Thus we find that the same values are implied throughout the entire range of "social interaction" that characterizes the Ojibwa world; the same standards which apply to mutual obligations between human beings are likewise implied in the reciprocal relations between human and other-than-human "persons." In his relations with "the grandfathers" the individual does not expect to receive a "blessing" for nothing. It is not a free gift; on his part there are obligations to be met. There is a principle of reciprocity implied. There is a general taboo imposed upon the human being which forbids him to recount his dream experiences in full detail, except under certain circumstances. Specific taboos may likewise be imposed upon the suppliant. If these taboos are violated he will lose his power; he can no longer count on the help of his "grandfathers."

The same principle of mutual obligations applies in other spheres of life. The Ojibwa are hunters and food gatherers. Since the various species of animals on which they depend for a living are believed to be under the control of "masters" or "owners" who belong to the category of other-than-human persons, the hunter must always be careful to treat the animals he kills for food or fur in the proper manner. It may be necessary, for example, to throw their bones in the water or to perform a ritual in the case of bears. Otherwise, he will offend the "masters" and be threatened with starvation because no animals will be made available to him. Cruelty to animals is likewise an offense that will provoke the same kind of retaliation. And, according to one anecdote, a man suffered illness because he tortured a fabulous *windīgo* after killing him. A moral distinction is drawn between the kind of conduct demanded by the primary necessities of securing a livelihood, or defending oneself against aggression, and unnecessary acts of cruelty. The moral values implied document the consistency of the principle of mutual obligations which is inherent in all interactions with "persons" throughout the Ojibwa world.

One of the prime values of Ojibwa culture is exemplified by the great stress laid upon sharing what one has with others. A balance, a sense of proportion must be maintained in all interpersonal relations and activities. Hoarding, or any manifestation of greed, is discountenanced. The central importance of this moral value in their world outlook is illustrated by the fact that other-than-human persons share their power with human beings. This is only a particular instance of the obligations which human beings feel towards one another. A man's catch of fish or meat is distributed among his kin. Human grandfathers share the power acquired in their dreams from other-than-human persons with their classificatory grandchildren. An informant whose wife had borrowed his pipe for the morning asked to borrow one of mine while we worked together. When my friend Chief Berens once fell ill he could not explain it. Then he recalled that he had overlooked one man when he had passed around a bottle of whiskey. He believed this man was offended and had bewitched him. Since there was no objective evidence of this, it illustrates the extreme sensitivity of an individual to the principle of sharing, operating through feelings of guilt. I was once told about the puberty fast of a boy who was not satisfied with his initial "blessing." He demanded that he dream of all the leaves of all the trees in the world so that absolutely nothing would be hidden from him. This was considered greedy and, while the *pawágan* who appeared in his dream granted his desire, the boy was told that "as soon as the leaves start to fall you'll get sick and when all the leaves drop to the ground that is the end of your life." And this is what happened.[38] "Overfasting" is as greedy as hoarding. It violates a basic moral value and is subject to a punitive sanction. The unity of the Ojibwa outlook is likewise apparent here.

The entire psychological field in which they live and act is not only unified through their conception of the nature and role of "persons" in their universe, but by the sanctioned moral values which guide the relations of "persons." It is within this web of "social relations" that the individual strives for *pīmådäzīwin*.

NOTES

[1] Redfield 1952, p. 30; cf. *African Worlds*.

[2] Hallowell 1955, p. 91. For a more extended discussion of the culturally constituted behavioral environment of man see *ibid.*, pp. 86-89 and note 33. The term "self" is not used as a synonym for ego in the psychoanalytic sense. See *ibid.*, p. 80.

[3] See Basilius 1952, Carroll in Whorf, 1956, Hoijer, 1954, Feuer, 1953.

[4] Hallowell 1955, chap. 5.

[5] Bruno de Jésus-Marie 1952, p. xvii: "The studies which make up this book fall into two main groups, of which the first deals with the theological Satan. Here the analysis of exegesis, of philosophy, of theology, treat of the devil under his aspect of a personal being whose history—his fall, his desire for vengeance—can be written as such." One of the most startling characteristics of the devil ". . . is his agelessness" (p. 4). He is immune to "injury, to pain, to sickness, to death . . . . Like God, and unlike man, he has no body. There are in him, then, no parts to be dismembered, no possibilities of corruption and decay, no threat of a separation of parts that will result in death. He is incorruptible, immune to the vagaries, the pains the limitations of the flesh, immortal" (p.5). "Angels have no bodies, yet they have appeared to men in physical form, have talked with them, journeyed the roads with them fulfilling all the pleasant tasks of companionship" (p. 6).

[6] Hallowell 1934b, pp. 7-9; 1936, pp. 1308-9; 1951, pp. 182-83; 1955, pp. 256-58.

[7] Kelsen 1943, chapter 2, discusses the "social" or "personalistic interpretation of nature" which he considers the nucleus of what has been called animism.

[8] In a prefatory note to *Ojibwa Texts*, Part I, Jones says (p. xiii) that " 'Being' or 'creature' would be a general rendering of the animate while 'thing' would express the inanimate." Cf. Schoolcraft's pioneer analysis of the animate and inanimate categories in Ojibwa speech, pp. 171-72.

[9] Greenberg 1954, pp. 15-16.

[10] I believe that Jenness grossly overgeneralizes when he says (p. 21): "To the Ojibwa . . . all objects have life. . . ." If this were true, their *inanimate* grammatical category would indeed be puzzling.

Within the more sophisticated framework of modern biological thought, the Ojibwa attitude is not altogether naïve. N. W. Pirie points out (pp. 184-85) that the words "life" and "living" have been borrowed by science from lay usage and are no longer serviceable. "Life is not a thing, a philosophical entity: it is an attitude of mind towards what is being observed."

[11] Field notes. From this same Indian I obtained a smoothly rounded pebble, about two inches long and one and a half inches broad, which his father had given him. He told me that I had better keep it enclosed in a tin box or it might "go." Another man, Ketegas, gave me an account of the circumstances under which he obtained a stone with animate properties and of great medicinal value. This stone was egg shaped. It had some dark amorphous markings on it which he interpreted as representing his three children and himself. "You may not think this stone is alive," he said, "but it is. I can make it move." (He did not demonstrate this to me.) He went on to say that on two occasions he had loaned the stone to sick people to keep during the night. Both times he found it in his pocket in the morning. Ketegas kept it in a little leather case he had made for it.

[12] Yellow Legs had obtained information about this remarkable stone in a dream. Its precise location was revealed to him. He sent two other Indians to get it. These men, following directions, found the stone on Birch Island, located in the middle of Lake Winnipeg, some thirty miles south of the mouth of the Berens River.

[13] Cognate forms are found in Chamberlain's compilation of Cree and Ojibwa "literary" terms.

[14] Jones, *Texts,* Part II, p. 574*n.*

[15] The attitude manifested is by no means peculiar to the Ojibwa. Almost half a century ago Swanton remarked that "one of the most widespread errors, and one of those most unfortunate for folk-lore and comparative mythology, is the off-hand classification of myth with fiction. . . ." On the contrary, as he says, "It is safe to say that most of the myths found spread over considerable areas were regarded by the tribes among which they were collected as narratives of real occurrences."

[16] Bidney 1953, p. 166.

[17] Lovejoy and Boas 1935, p. 12; Lovejoy 1948, p. 69.

[18] See, e.g., Collingwood 1945, also the remarks in Randall 1944, pp. 355-56. With respect to the applicability of the natural-supernatural dichotomy to primitive cultures see Van Der Leeuw 1938, pp. 544-45; Kelsen 1943, p. 44; Bidney 1953, p. 166.

[19] Krech and Crutchfield 1948 write (p. 10): "clouds and storms and winds are excellent examples of objects in the psychological field that carry the perceived properties of mobility, capriciousness, causation, power of threat and reward."

[20] Cf. Hallowell 1934a.

[21] Actually, this was probably a rationalization of mother-son incest. But the woman never was punished by sickness, nor did she confess. Since the violation of the incest prohibition is reputed to be followed by dire consequences, the absence of both may have operated to support the possibility of her claim when considered in the context of the Ojibwa world view.

[22] Thompson 1946, p. 258.

[23] Hallowell 1926.

[24] Hallowell 1934a, p. 397.

[25] Sorcerers may assume the form of other animals as well. Peter Jones, a converted Ojibwa, who became famous as a preacher and author says that "they can turn themselves into bears, wolves, foxes, owls, bats, and snakes.... Several of our people have informed me that they have seen and heard witches in the shape of these animals, especially the bear and the fox. They say that when a witch in the shape of a bear is being chased all at once she will run around a tree or hill, so as to be lost sight of for a time by her pursuers, and then, instead of seeing a bear they behold an old woman walking quietly along or digging up roots, and looking as innocent as a lamb" (Jones 1861, pp. 145-46).

[26] Dorson 1952, p. 30.

[27] *Ibid.*, p. 29. This rationalization dates back over a century. John Tanner, an Indianized white man who was captured as a boy in the late eighteenth century and lived with the Ottawa and Ojibwa many years, refers to it. So does Peter Jones.

[28] Hallowell 1955, pp. 176-77.

[29] Dorson 1952, p. 31.

[30] Hoffman 1891, pp. 205-6.

[31] Unpublished field notes.

[32] See Hallowell 1955, Chapter 15.

[33] Cf. Skinner 1915, p. 261. Cooper 1933 (p. 75) writes: "The Manitu was clearly personal in the minds of my informants, and not identified with impersonal supernatural force. In fact, nowhere among the Albany River Otchipwe, among the Eastern Cree, or among the Montagnais have I been able thus far to find the word Manitu used to denote such force in connection with the Supreme Being belief, with conjuring, or with any other phase of magico-religious culture. *Manitu*, so far as I can discover, always denotes a supernatural personal being.... The word *Manitu* is, my informants say, not used to denote magical or conjuring power among the coastal Cree, nor so I was told in 1927, among the Fort Hope Otchipwe of the upper Albany River."

[34] Radin 1914a, p. 350.

[35] *Ibid.*, pp. 349-50.

[36] "Because a person does bad things, that is where sickness starts," is the way one of my informants phrased it. For a fuller discussion of the relations between unsanctioned sexual behavior and disease, see Hallowell 1955, pp. 294-95; 303-4. For case material, see Hallowell 1939.

[37] Cf. Hallowell 1955, p. 305.

[38] Radin 1927, p. 177, points out that "throughout the area inhabited by the woodland tribes of Canada and the United States, overfasting entails death." Jones, *Texts,* Part II, pp. 307-11, gives two cases of overfasting. In one of them the bones of the boy were later found by his father.

REFERENCES

African Worlds: Studies in the Cosmological Ideas and Social Values of African Peoples. 1954. Published for the International African Institute. London, Oxford University Press.

Baraga, R. R. Bishop. 1878. A Theoretical and Practical Grammar of the Otchipive Language. Montreal, Beauchemin and Valois.

Baraga, R. R. Bishop. 1880. A Dictionary of the Otchipive Language Explained in English. Montreal, Beauchemin and Valois.

Basilius, H. 1952. "Neo-Humboldtian Ethnolinguistics," *Word,* Vol. 8.

Bidney, David. 1953. Theoretical Anthropology. New York, Columbia University Press.

Bruno de Jésus-Marie, père, ed. 1952. Satan. New York, Sheed and Ward.

Chamberlain, A. F. 1906. "Cree and Ojibwa Literary Terms," *Journal of American Folklore,* 19:346-47.

Collingwood, R. G. 1945. The Idea of Nature. Oxford, Clarendon Press.

Cooper, John M. 1933. "The Northern Algonquian Supreme Being," *Primitive Man,* 6:41-112.

Dorson, Richard M. 1952. Bloodstoppers and Bearwalkers: Folk Traditions of the Upper Peninsula. Cambridge, Mass., Harvard University Press.

Feuer, Lewis S. 1953. "Sociological Aspects of the Relation between Language and Philosophy," *Philosophy of Science,* 20:85-100.

Fletcher, Alice C. 1910. "Wakonda," in *Handbook of American Indians.* Washington, D.C.: Bureau of American Ethnology, Bull. 30.

Greenberg, Joseph H. 1954. "Concerning Inferences from Linguistic to Non-linguistic Data," in *Language in Culture,* ed. by Harry Hoijer. (Chicago University "Comparative Studies in Cultures and Civilizations.") Chicago, University of Chicago Press.

Hallowell, A. Irving. 1926. "Bear Ceremonialism in the Northern Hemisphere," *American Anthropologist,* 28:1-175.

———— 1934a. "Some Empirical Aspects of Northern Saulteaux Religion," *American Anthropologist,* 36:389-404.

———— 1934b. "Culture and Mental Disorder," *Journal of Abnormal and Social Psychology,* 29:1-9.

———— 1936. "Psychic Stresses and Culture Patterns," *American Journal of Psychiatry,* 92:1291-1310.

———— 1939. "Sin, Sex and Sickness in Saulteaux Belief," *British Journal of Medical Psychology,* 18:191-97.

———— 1951. "Cultural Factors in the Structuralization of Perception," in John H. Rohver and Muzafer Sherif, *Social Psychology at the Crossroads.* New York, Harper.

———— 1955. Culture and Experience. Philadelphia, University of Penna. Press.

Hewitt, J. N. B. 1902. "Orenda and a Definition of Religion," *American Anthropologist,* 4:33-46.

Hoffman, W. J. 1891. The Mide'wiwin or "Grand Medicine Society" of the Ojibwa. Washington, D.C., Bureau of American Ethnology 7th Annual Report.

Hoijer, Harry, ed. 1954. Language in Culture. Memoir 79, American Anthropological Association.

Jenness, Diamond. 1935. The Ojibwa Indians of Parry Island, their social and religious life. Ottawa, Canada Department of Mines, National Museum of Canada Bull. 78, Anthropological Series 12.

Jones, Peter. 1861. History of the Ojibway Indians. London.

Jones, William. 1905. "The Algonkin Manitu," *Journal of American Folklore,* 18:183-90.

———— Ojibwa Texts. (Publications of the American Ethnological Society, Vol. 7, Parts I and II.) Leyden: 1917; New York: 1919.

Kelsen, Hans. 1943. Society and Nature: A Sociological Inquiry. Chicago, University of Chicago Press.

Krech, David, and Richard S. Crutchfield. 1948. Theory and Problems of Social Psychology. New York, McGraw-Hill.

Lovejoy, Arthur O. 1948. Essays in the History of Ideas. Baltimore, Johns Hopkins Press.

Lovejoy, Arthur O., and George Boas. 1935. Primitivism and Related Ideas in Antiquity. Baltimore, Johns Hopkins Press. Vol. I of A Documentary History of Primitivism and Related Ideas.

Pirie, N. W. 1937. "The Meaninglessness of the Terms 'Life' and 'Living,' " in Perspectives in Biochemistry, ed. by J. Needham and D. Green. New York, Macmillan.

Radin, Paul. 1914a. "Religion of the North American Indians," Journal of American Folklore, 27:335-73.

—— 1914b. Some Aspects of Puberty Fasting among the Ojibwa. Geological Survey of Canada, Department of Mines, Museum Bull. No. 2, Anthropological Series, No. 2, pp. 1-10.

—— 1927. Primitive Man as Philosopher. New York, D. Appleton & Co.

Randall, John Herman, Jr. 1944. "The Nature of Naturalism," in Naturalism and the Human Spirit, ed. by H. Krikorian. New York, Columbia University Press.

Redfield, Robert. 1952. "The Primitive World View," Proceedings of the American Philosophical Society, 96:30-36.

Schoolcraft, Henry R. 1834. Narrative of an Expedition through the Upper Mississippi to Itasca Lake, the Actual Source of the River .... New York, Harper.

Skinner, Alanson. 1915. "The Menomini Word 'Häwätûk,' " Journal of American Folklore, 28:258-61.

Swanton, John R. 1910. "Some practical aspects of the study of myths," Journal of American Folklore, 23:1-7.

Tanner, John. 1830. Narrative of the Captivity and Adventures of John Tanner, ed. by E. James.

Thompson, Stith. 1946. The Folktale. New York, Dryden Press.

Van Der Leeuw, G. 1938. Religion in Essence and Manifestation. London, Allen and Unwin.

Whorf, Benjamin Lee. 1956. Language Thought and Reality: Selected Writings of Benjamin L. Whorf, ed. with an introduction by J. B. Carroll; Foreword by Stuart Chase. New York, Wiley.

THE WORLD OF THE KERESAN
PUEBLO INDIANS

By Leslie A. White

WHEN CORONADO and his party entered the American Southwest in 1540 they found many Indian tribes living in towns, or pueblos, with rows of terraced houses two to four stories high. They were peaceful Indians who raised corn, beans and squash, cotton and tobacco. They had dogs and kept flocks of domesticated turkeys. They made a good grade of pottery and wove cotton fabrics on simple looms. They were the Pueblo Indians.

The land occupied by the Pueblo tribes was wild and beautiful. Great mesas of solid rock alternated with sandy plains. Deep canyons cut sharply into mesas and mountains. The lower elevations were a mile above sea level, but huge mountain ranges—the Jemez and the Sandias—raised their peaks ten and eleven thousand feet above the sea. Huge Ponderosa pines and Douglas firs grew high upon the mountain slopes; the mesas and lowlands were dotted with clumps of juniper, yucca, and cactus. Cottonwoods and willows followed the river valleys.

The pueblo country is an arid one. Streams are few and many of them are bone-dry most of the year. But during the summer months the rain may fall in torrents, quickly filling the dusty channels with swift and turbulent currents. The summers are hot, a brassy sun glares fiercely out of a deep blue sky, great white clouds are piled at random above a distant horizon. Lizards sun themselves on hot, flat rocks, or dart swiftly to cover at a sign of danger. But in winter bitter storms, bringing snow and ice, occasionally descend from the mountains, and all life is stilled for a time.

The actual holdings of the Pueblo Indians were meager indeed in comparison with the vast expanse in which they lived. They had little farms near their villages, either in valleys where irrigation was possible, or out on the barren plain or hillside. But most of the land was nature's domain, the home of deer and bear, of turkey, puma, and antelope. These great tracts were exploited for game and plant food, for minerals and dyestuffs, for boughs of fir for dance costumes, and willow twigs for prayersticks. Sacred springs were visited to fill the medicine bowls upon their altars. The hazards of the open country were faced when the pueblo peoples attended each other's ceremonies. And dangers there were, for wild nomadic tribes, the feared and hated Moshomi—the Navahos and Utes, the Comanches and Apaches—infiltrated their land, visiting them with murder and theft.

This was the world of the Pueblo Indians as the early Spaniards saw it, and indeed as the Americans saw it after the Treaty of Guadalupe-Hidalgo. The Indians themselves saw all of this, too. But they saw much more—and they still do today, even as in 1540 when Coronado broke in upon their world.

The world of the Pueblo Indians[1] was not created in the beginning; it was always there—or here. But it was somewhat different in the beginning than it is now. The Earth was square and flat; it had four corners and a middle. Below the surface of the earth there were four horizontal layers; each one was a world. The lowest world was a white one. Above that lay the red world and then the blue one. Above the blue world, and just beneath this world that we are living in today, was the yellow world.[2]

In the beginning the people were living deep down inside the earth, in the white world, with their mother, Iyatiku. Finally it was time for them to come out, to ascend to this world. Iyatiku caused a great evergreen tree, a spruce or a fir, to grow so that the people could climb up its trunk and boughs to the next world. But when the tree reached the next world above it found its way blocked by a hard layer of earth and rock. So Iyatiku had Woodpecker make a hole through the layer into the next world. The people climbed up into the red world and lived there for four years. Then it was time to climb up into the blue world. Again Iyatiku had a tree reach up to the world above, and again she had someone make a hole through the hard layer so the tree and the people could pass through.

At last the people were ready to ascend into this world. Iyatiku had Badger make a hole through the hard crust. He made so much dust in his work that there was danger that the people might be blinded, so Whirlwind Old Man went up and held the dust in his arms until Badger got through. Then Cicada was asked to line the opening so it would be smooth and safe to pass through. Iyatiku asked Badger to look out into this world and tell her what it looked like. Badger looked out. "It is very beautiful up there," he told Iyatiku, "there are rain clouds everywhere." So Iyatiku decided it was all right for the people to complete their ascent and to emerge into this world. Iyatiku had created societies of medicine men in the lower worlds and had given them their altars and ceremonies. These societies—the Flint, Fire, Giant, and Kapina medicine men—came out with the people. There were some evil spirits, too, who also came out. They were *kanadyaiya,* 'witches,' but no one knew this at that time.

They came out at a place in the north called Shipap. Everything was new and "raw." The earth was too soft for people to walk upon so Iyatiku had the mountain lion use his magic power to harden it. When it was sufficiently hard, the people came out. They stayed near the opening at Shipap for a time, but it was too sacred a place for permanent residence, so Iyatiku told them they were to migrate toward the south. She said: "I shall not go with you. I am going to return to my home in the white world, but I will be with you always in spirit. You can pray to me and I will always help you." Before she left she appointed a man to take her place. "You shall be Tiamunyi," she told him and the people. "You will be my representative among my people. You must look after them and work for their welfare." Then Iyatiku gave Tiamunyi an ear of corn. "Take this," she told him. "This corn is my heart. This is what you will live on; its milk shall be to you as milk from my breasts."

Iyatiku returned to the lower world and the people began their journey to the south. They stopped at a place and established a pueblo. They called it Kashikatchrutiya, or White House. They lived here a long time.

There were two sisters, Utctsityi and Naotsityi, living with the people. They were supernatural beings. Naotsityi felt superior to her sister and challenged her to a number of contests so that she could demonstrate her superiority. They had a number of contests, but Utctsityi always came out on top. Finally Naotsityi decided to go away, so she took her people and left. Naotsityi's people became the white people; the children of Utctsityi became the Indians.

In these early days lots of things happened. There was a girl who was out in the mountains one day picking pinyon nuts. She became impregnated by the Sun and in due course bore twin sons. She named the first born Masewi, the younger Oyoyewi. They grew rapidly and soon showed signs of great supernatural power. They were very venturesome and wanted to explore the world. Their mother, fearing for their safety, tried always to keep them at home. The boys were determined to go to the place of the sunrise to meet their father, and, ignoring their mother's protests, they set out. When they got to the Sun's house they announced that they were his sons and had come to meet him. But the Sun was unwilling to accept them as his sons and devised a number of tests to settle the question of paternity. In one of these tests he put the boys into a big oven full of glowing coals. But Masewi and Oyoyewi had some magic shells in their mouths which they spat out upon the fire and remained unharmed. Each time the boys passed the test so finally the Sun acknowledged them as his own sons. He gave them bows and arrows and throwing sticks of great potency and they returned home.

Masewi and Oyoyewi had many other adventures. They used to take trips far and wide to see what they could see. On one of these trips they met a huge woman-like creature. She was a Shkoyo. She was big and ugly and carried a basket on her back. She picked up Masewi and Oyoyewi and put them in her basket. When she got home she built a fire in her oven; she was going to roast the boys and eat them. But Masewi and Oyoyewi were too smart for her, and they killed her. On another adventure the two boys turned an entire pueblo and its houses into stone—all except one couple—for being inhospitable to strangers. Eventually it became clear to everyone that Masewi and Oyoyewi were supernatural; they were war-gods. They finally left the people and went to make their home in the Sandia mountains where they now live. But they are represented today in the Pueblos by two men, the war chiefs, who bear their names.

While the people were living at White House they came to know all about the world they were living in, and how to behave toward it. First of all there was the Earth, Naiya Ha'atse, 'Mother Earth.' It was the Earth that we live on. It was square and flat, although marked with mountains and valleys here and there. It was very large, also; one could not reach its edges in many days' journey, although one could easily see them on the distant horizons. Above the earth was Howaka, 'the Sky.' This was not merely empty space, but a real something, a structure that arched like a great dome above the earth upon which it rested.

At each corner of the Earth was a house and in that house lived a god. In the northwest corner was the House of Leaves, the home of Tsityostinako, or 'Thought Woman'; she could cause things to happen merely by thinking of them. Spider Grandmother lived in the House of Boards in the southwest corner. Turquoise House was in the southeast corner; Butterfly lived there. And in the northeast corner lived Mocking Bird Youth in Yatkana house.

The cardinal points were important. They were called "middle north," "middle east," and so on, meaning that the points were midway beween the corners of the earth. In addition to the four points on the horizons, zenith and nadir were distinguished and named. Each of the six directions had a color: the north was yellow, west blue, south red, east white, zenith brown, and nadir black. At each of the cardinal points lived a god. Shakak lived at Kawestima, the north mountain; he was the god of winter and of snow. Shruwitira, a man-like god, lived at Tspina, west mountain. A gopher-like god named Maiyochina lived at Daotyuma, or south mountain; he helped crops to grow. Shruwisigyama, a bird-like god, lived at east mountain, a fox-like god at the zenith, and a mole-like god at the nadir.

Each one of the six directions had its own animal: the puma lived in the north, the bear in the west, bobcat in the south, wolf in the east; eagle lived at the zenith, shrew at the nadir, and the badger in the middle—the middle of the whole world. Each cardinal point had also a woman, a tree, a snake, and a warrior. The women had colored faces, each one with the color appropriate to her cardinal point.

Thus, everything was well ordered in the world in which the Keresan Pueblo Indians found themselves, and neatly arranged according to the cardinal points.

There were still other gods, each with his, or their, home. In the middle east was Koaikutc, 'Sunrise Place,' located a short distance south of Yastya Kot, 'Dawn Mountain.' The Koshairi lived at Koaikutc, and just south of them the Kwiraina had their home at Shell Spring. In the northwest, but not at the corner of the earth, lived Gotsa, the patron of game animals. Whirlwind Old Man lived in the southwest near the house of Spider Grandmother. In the middle west, but not as far as the edge of the world, was Wenima, the home of the

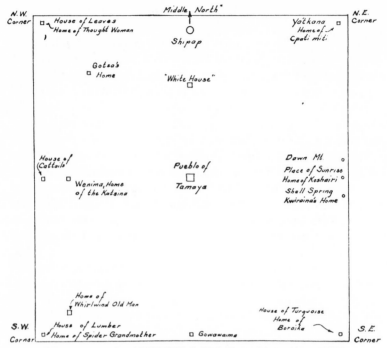

MAP OF THE MYTHOLOGICAL WORLD OF THE
PUEBLO OF SANTA ANA

From White, *The Pueblo of Santa Ana, New Mexico* (1942)

Katsina, the rain makers. Water Snake, with a horn on his head and
cloud designs on his sides, lived in the earth and the Rio Grande river.

It was while the people were living at White House that the way of
life which they have followed since that time was organized. They
raised corn, beans, squash, cotton, and tobacco, and they hunted deer
and turkey in the mountains. The medicine societies performed their
ceremonies in their houses. Two *kivas* were built for other ceremonies
and dances. The people learned how to make prayersticks and how to
pray to all the gods and spirits with them. They prayed with corn
meal, too.

When people died their bodies were buried, but their souls went
back to Shipap, the place of emergence, and returned to their mother
in the fourfold womb of the earth. Every year they would come back

to White House to visit their relatives. But when the time came for them to return, the living people wanted to accompany them. But Iyatiku told them that they could not do this, that they would have to wait until they died and became like little children again before they could reenter the place of their birth. So every year, now, the souls of the dead come back to the pueblos of the living and visit their relatives and eat the food that has been placed for them on their graves and on the road toward the north. The living entertain their dead relatives, but do not accompany them when they leave. Some people become *katsinas* after they die.

The *katsinas* used to come to White House during the summer to dance for rain and crops. It always rained after a visit from the *katsinas,* the crops grew abundantly, and the people prospered and were happy. But one time a quarrel arose between the people and the *katsinas*. Accounts differ somewhat as to just what happened, but, in any event, the *katsinas* felt that they had been insulted and they decided not to come to the Pueblo again to dance for rain. The people were staggered by the decision; without the *katsinas'* help they would have no rain and consequently no crops; they would starve. The *katsinas* finally relented to the extent of allowing the men of the Pueblo to impersonate them by wearing masks and costume, and to put on the dances just like the *katsinas* did. "We will be there with you in spirit," they told the people.

This was the way the Keres came to have the masked dances which they perform today. They had to learn to impersonate the Koshairi and the Kwiraina, too. These were the two groups of spirits whose homes were in the east, near the Place of Sunrise. They have great power to promote fertility of crops, animals, and people. They—or rather, their impersonators—have charge of dances today. The Koshairi act as buffoons in the plaza between dances and occasionally engage in scatological rites.

After the unfortunate quarrel with the *katsinas* at White House the people fell to quarreling among themselves. Iyatiku, their mother, deep down in her home within the earth, knew all about what had happened and she was deeply distressed. One night she changed the language of the people, causing each faction to speak a different tongue. The people decided to abandon White House. So they set out, one group going in this direction; another, in that. They settled at various places.

Sometimes they would live at a site for a time and then move on to some other place. Finally they came to establish their homes permanently where they are now found. This is why we find so many pueblo ruins today, and why the Pueblo Indians speak different languages.

Thus the great mythical era of the Pueblo Indians came to an end, and the modern era began. But by the time this change took place, the Indians had their culture—their institutions, their clans, medicine societies, officers, dances, and ceremonies—well established. The Cacique, or Tiamunyi, was the head of the Pueblo. He was the representative of the mother, Iyatiku. There were two war chiefs, Masewi and Oyoyewi, who represented the war-god twins. The *katsinas* and the Koshairi and Kwiraina were impersonated by appropriately initiated and costumed men. There were a number of medicine societies—the Flint, Fire, Shikame, Giant, and Kapina societies. Some of the pueblos had a Snake society which performed a ceremony with living snakes.

Life was not too difficult for the Pueblos, but they did have problems to face and solve. The most important one was to get enough to eat; in their arid land this problem sometimes became critical. And game was not always plentiful. There were enemies, the wild Moshomi, to be opposed. Sickness and disease were always to be reckoned with; sometimes a whole pueblo would be stricken. But the Pueblos had means and aids to cope with these problems. There were the vast powers of the supernatural world to be enlisted in their behalf. With good hearts, powerful songs, prayers, paraphernalia, and ritual they could accomplish anything.

Everyone worked and prayed for rain. The Cacique prayed and fasted. The medicine societies performed their ceremonies; men impersonated *katsinas* in dances; the Buffalo dances brought snow in wintertime; and even the scalps of slain Moshomi had power to moisten the earth. Cloud, rain, and lightning symbols were everywhere, on altars, medicine bowls, and masks; the horned water snake was painted on dance kilts. Carved and feathered prayersticks were offered to all kinds of spirits, in the mountains, in the springs, and in the heavens. The whole supernatural world was constrained by prayer and song to give up its fructifying fluid so that the people might raise abundant crops and have enough to eat.

There was a special society to bring success to hunters. This was the Shaiyak society. The mountain lion was the principal god of the hunt, but other predatory animals assisted also. The medicine men of the Shaiyak society had songs, paraphernalia, ritual, and prayers to insure success. Each hunter carried a *mokaich,* a little stone figure of the mountain lion, in his pouch. When a deer was killed the first thing the hunter did was to feed the *mokaich* by dipping his head and mouth in the fresh blood. The deer were taken back to the pueblo where they were received with ceremonial display and adopted into the village; their heads and horns were adorned with fluffy feathers and placed upon the housetops next to the chimneys.

The Moshomi, especially the Navahos, were not only ruthless men who killed and plundered the Pueblos; they were possessed of supernatural powers as well, and one had to have supernatural power to overcome them. Fortunately, the Keres had their twin war-gods, Masewi and Oyoyewi, who were ever ready to help them through their human representatives the war chiefs. There was also a society of warriors called Opi. This was composed of men who had scalped an enemy and "taken his clothes," i.e., his supernatural power embodied in a charm or medicine bag. To be sure, the enemy had to be killed in order to do this, but the mere killing was not as significant as overpowering him on the supernatural plane and taking his scalp. The Opi were the first line of defense against the nomadic marauders. The Flint society, too, had powers for war and helped the Opi and common men alike to overcome their foes.

Scalps were taken back to the pueblo where they were greeted with a war dance. They were adopted into the pueblo and kept in a special chamber in one of the ceremonial houses. They were fed, given cigarettes, and bathed periodically. Once they had become residents of the pueblo they had power to bring rain.

But a man who had come into direct contact with a slain enemy became contaminated in a supernaturalistic way. The power of the enemy was upon him, and his life would be in danger until he was put through a ceremony to cleanse him and restore him to his customary life within the pueblo.

As we noted earlier, there were some Evil Ones who came up out of the lower world with the people of the pueblos. They were *kanadyaiya,* or witches. They were human beings, like the others, but they had two hearts, one good, the other bad. When they grew up they expressed their evil nature by making people sick. They would shoot objects of various kinds—broken glass, cactus thorns, dirty rags, or sharp stones—into people causing them to become ill. Sometimes they stole a person's "breath-heart," his *tsats-winoshka*.

The *kanadyaiya,* or witches, had some affinity with owls and crows which sometimes enabled one to recognize them. But for the most part they could be detected only by medicine men. Along with rain making, the curing of sickness is an important function of the medicine men organized in the Flint, Giant, Fire, and other societies. The real doctors, however, were animal gods; the Indian medicine men must obtain their power to cure from them. The animal doctors include the bear, eagle, badger, wolf, and shrew. The bear is by far the most important of these. Medicine men wear necklaces of bear claws and put the foreleg skins of bears on their arms when performing curing rituals. The spirits of the animal doctors are induced to enter the curing chamber by means of songs. There they invest their respective stone figures and lend their powers to the medicine men. Wooden slat altars, meal paintings on the floor, medicine bowls, corn ear fetiches of Iyatiku, comprise the equipment of a medicine society. Some of the doctors have a quartz crystal which gives them second sight; this enables them to locate the evil spirits that have caused the sickness. Curing consists of withdrawing the objects which have been injected into the body. This may be done with eagle wing feathers, but it is usually accomplished by sucking. If diagnosis reveals that the sick one's heart has been stolen, it must be restored if the patient is to live. When the doctors retrieve a stolen heart it turns out to be a small ball of rags in the center of which are some kernels of corn. If these are in good condition the patient will live; if they are mouldy or scorched the sick one will probably die. In either case, he is given the corn to swallow.

When the Spaniards settled in New Mexico in the seventeenth century they brought new gods and spirits to the Pueblo Indians. At first the Indians were unwilling to accept these foreigners, but after the Great Revolt of 1680 failed they found themselves obliged to submit. The Catholic gods of the Spaniards came to live in the pueblos and were eventually adopted and assimilated to the Indian way of life and belief. A Catholic church was built in each pueblo, and each village acquired a patron saint. The birth of Jesus is celebrated every year, and Easter ceremonies are observed. Important among the

Catholic spirits are saints, particularly Santiago and his horse. Santiago, San Geronimo, and a comparable spirit with an Indian name, Boshaiyanyi, are impersonated by men who "ride" little hobby horses. They may take part in the celebration for the patron saint or they may come at other times. They ride through the corrals and sprinkle the horses with holy water. Santiago has great and beneficent power for horses.

Associated with the saints and the equestrian impersonations is the *gallo,* or "rooster pull," ceremony. A rooster is buried in the sand with only his head and neck protruding. Horsemen ride by until one of them succeeds in pulling the rooster out of the sand. When one has done this he dashes away as fast as his horse can gallop, pursued by the other horsemen. When the horseman with the rooster has been overtaken a fight over the possession of the fowl ensues. Bit by bit the poor bird is torn to pieces. "Rooster blood is good for rain." The foamy lather on the horses' flanks is like the foamy waters rushing down an arroyo after a heavy rain. At the end of the ceremony the riders go around to houses of persons named for the saint of that day where they are doused with water. This, too, helps to bring rain.

But, with rather few exceptions, the Keresan Pueblo Indians have not become Christians, or Catholics. They have merely adopted some alien spirits and have taken them into the pueblos to live. Santa Ana and Santiago have become *maiyanyi,* that is, spirits like Masewi and Oyoyewi, or Spider Grandmother. In an altar painting in one of the Pueblo missions John the Baptist has become Naotsityi, the mother of non-Indians; Jesus has become Utctsityi, the mother of Indians. Prayersticks may be offered to God as they are to Iyatiku and other Indian gods.

Despite more than three centuries of contact with Christian faiths, both Catholic and Protestant, the Keresan Pueblos remain Indian. Even some of the individuals who leave their pueblos to live among white men and adopt their ways cannot always succeed by any means. I once knew well an old man who had gone to a Presbyterian mission school as a young man. He became a Christian, or so he thought. He used to say grace before meals in Christian fashion, but, curiously enough, he addressed the Deity in the Keresan language even though his English was fluent. His transfiguration was never really accomplished, as the following incident makes clear. He told me one morning that he had dreamed that he had died and gone to heaven. "I went up to heaven," he told me, "and I stood there before God." "What was heaven like?" I asked, eager to know how an Indian would conceive of this place. "It was just like in a bank," he said, "God was sitting there at a big desk, just like in a bank." "What did God look like and how was he dressed?" I asked. "He was a white man and he was wearing a business suit." "I stood there before God," he said, "and finally God looked up at me. 'You've come,' he said. 'Yes,' I told him. 'Where is your license [credentials]?' God asked me. 'Right here,' I told him, and I handed him the Bible they gave me when I was in the Mission boarding school. God took the Bible and studied it for a while. Then he handed it back to me and said, 'No, this is not your license.' Then he pulled out a drawer in his desk and took out a prayerstick. '*This* is your license,' he said and he gave it to me."

We may be sure that when this old man left this world it was with a prayerstick in his hand—and in his heart.

Man's visions of his world are myriad and kaleidoscopic. The world that the Keres believed in and lived in is one of those visions. It was dramatic and picturesque; it was intimate and reassuring. Their vision has sustained them for centuries on end, and it will continue to do so as long as they remain Indians.

NOTES

[1] From here on, this essay is confined to the historic Keresan pueblos, namely, Acoma, Laguna, Santo Domingo, San Felipe, Santa Ana, Sia, and Cochiti.

[2] There are many versions of the origin myths. We shall try to present a fair consensus of them.

REFERENCES

Benedict, Ruth. Tales of the Cochiti Indians. Bulletin 98, Bureau of American Ethnology, Washington, 1931.

Boas, Franz. Keresan Texts. Publications of the American Ethnological Society, Vol. VIII, Parts 1 and 2, 1925, 1928.

Stevenson, Mathilda Coxe. The Sia. Eleventh Annual Report, Bureau of American Ethnology, Washington, 1894.

Stirling, Matthew W. Origin Myth of Acoma. Bulletin 135, Bureau of American Ethnology, Washington, 1942.

White, Leslie A. The Pueblo of Santa Ana, New Mexico. Memoir 60, American Anthropological Association, 1942.

NAVAHO CATEGORIES

By Clyde Kluckhohn

PAUL RADIN'S reputation has many bases. But I think that he is famed as much as anything for his analyses of primitive thought and for his intensive studies of the Winnebago. It seems appropriate, therefore, to offer a contribution upon some of the categories of another tribe that has been studied in depth. It is not yet possible to write a definitive account of Navaho categorization because some areas of thought remain to be investigated and because some available field materials still await analysis. Nevertheless, it may be useful at this point to bring together a provisional synthesis of some of the published and unpublished data.

An English-speaking informant once said to Wyman: "The Navahos are great categorists" (Wyman and Harris, 1941, p. 9). All field workers who have known even a little of the Navaho language have been struck by Navaho delight in sharply defined categories, by their pleasure in filing things away in neat little packages, their readiness to argue about small distinctions that would strike even a philosopher as hair-splitting. Indeed the formal structure of the language itself introduces elaborate classifications. For example, many verb stems "refer not to a characteristic type of event such as *stand* or *give* or *fall,* but to the class of object or objects conceived as participating in such an event, whether as actor or goal ... there is no simple verb *to give* but a number of parallel verb themes consisting of a certain sequence of prefixes plus a classificatory verb stem" (Hoijer, 1945, p. 13). Hoijer lists only the more frequently occurring classificatory stems that must be differentiated in a wide range of verbs: round object, long object, living being, set of objects, rigid container with contents, fabric-like object, bulky object, set of parallel objects, a mass, wool-like mass, rope-like object, mud-like mass.

It is evident that every Navaho must use a rather well developed sensitivity for categorization. Of course, the finer distinctions are the province of the various specialists, and it is they whom we shall have primarily in mind in the course of this paper. Nevertheless one should not underestimate the extent to which a representative Navaho adult man will both categorize firmly all sorts of objects and events outside his own occupational specialty *and* systematize all of these—crudely and yet with some coherence—in a master scheme. In my opinion, Reichard (1943, p. 360) goes too far when she writes: "Thus Navajo dogma connects all things, natural and experienced, from man's skeleton to universal destiny, which encompasses even inconceivable space, in a closely interlocked unity which omits nothing, no matter how small or how stupendous. . . ." Yet I know from experience and from reading the literature on the Navaho what she means. The more articulate and thoughtful Navahos, especially some of the ceremonialists, do exhibit a tendency in this direction.

It therefore appears inviting to examine in some detail standard Navaho categories in various spheres, trying to discover the criteria, explicit and implicit, applied in each area and seeing the extent to which some criteria tend to pervade all or many areas. It will be more convenient to use Western categories for the broad divisions, but I shall indicate the major places where this does violence to Navaho thinking. I shall begin with the supernatural world because it is here, on the whole, that Navaho thought exhibits its most distinctive elaborations and shadings. In fact, Goodwin (1945, p. 506) sees the main distinction between the ceremonialism of the Navaho and the closely related (biologically and culturally) Western Apache in the fact that "the latter people have not bothered to go in for minute classification; the Navaho have."

The Supernatural World

Detailed documentation will be found in Haile (1947a, 1947b), Kluckhohn and Wyman (1940, esp. pp. 184-90), Reichard (1950), Wyman and Kluckhohn (1938), Wyman (1957).[1] These sources do not agree completely on every point, but there is a highly satisfactory consensus on most issues. Much of such disagreement as exists is to be attributed to the same phenomenon among the Navaho themselves. There are a host of matters on which all unacculturated Navaho are unanimous. There are others where regional and generational variations are prominent. There is also contention traceable to the competitive rivalry of various "schools" of ceremonialists. In other instances it is a question of sheer ignorance. I have, for example, shown (Kluckhohn, 1938) that a sample of 60 women (out of about 210 in this particular Navaho group) were—age group for age group—much less familiar with ceremonial categories than the men of the same band. However, the women aged fifty years and over were quite positive on the main outlines of Navaho theology.

The most fundamental category is that represented by a Navaho word which is commonly translated "holy" but which is more precisely rendered as "supernatural." For this term is applied to all individuals, things, and events that are beyond ordinary experience, charged with a special kind of power and danger. "Holy" has the wrong connotation because the word is applied also to evil people and events (e.g. witchcraft). "Supernatural" does not have its paired opposite to designate the phenomena of the mundane world. "Earth-surface People" are regularly contrasted with "Supernatural People," but there is no general category embracing everything in ordinary experience.

Within the supernatural sphere there are distinguished "behavior" (literally: "here and there [in a place] one person goes"),[2] "myth," and "beings."

Behavior. Colloquially one can render the Navaho word as "something is going on" or "something is being done." Contextually, it becomes perfectly clear that the meaning is something like this: "An organized attempt is being made to influence the course of events by supernatural techniques."[3] The word is applied freely to a major ritual, a small ceremony; to witchcraft, to ritual practices employed in trading and gambling; to events directed in the supernatural world by supernaturals. It designates any *act* in the supernatural sphere, as opposed to words or "personalities."

There is a major dichotomy of behavior relating to the supernatural. English-speaking informants will frequently speak of "the good side" and "the bad side." Navaho terminology on this point is not altogether consistent. Navahos use a variety of words which can be roughly translated as "evil," "ugly," "bad" (cf. Kluckhohn, 1956) to refer to all ritual activities that are culturally disapproved, that involve an improper and malicious use of supernatural techniques. The distinction is approximately that between all forms of evil magic and ceremonialism (which is defined as "good"). Actually, the use of magic in trading and gambling with aliens and, to some extent, personal enemies is condoned, but these behaviors are close enough to witchcraft in the narrow sense that informants uniformly group them "on the bad side."

Navahos who pride themselves on their rigor will deny that there is any generic term in Navaho for "witchcraft." They grant that in loose, popular usage two words that properly designate two of the special techniques of witches are in fact used to cover the whole range of culturally prohibited behaviors which strict Navaho thinking classes only vaguely together. The categorization of these is primarily by techniques:

1. Poison Witchcraft. The Navaho term means literally "by means of it something is being done terminatively," but the technique is exclusively that of administering noxious substances.

2. Spells. The Navaho term is "evil-wishing"—i.e. witchcraft by a technique primarily verbal.

3. Pellet Witchcraft. The technique is that of magically shooting dangerous foreign objects into the victim's body. The word is literally "they cause something, emaciation" (by these injections).

4. Frenzy Witchcraft. The technique involves administration of narcotic plants, especially Datura, and is used primarily to obtain women. The stem refers to recklessness in any form.

Actually, to represent Navaho thinking fully a dotted line should be run between 3 and 4. While all four of the above will be mentioned and associated by every unacculturated Navaho, careful analysis of the data shows a less explicit subclassification. The first three are grouped together on the ground that these three kinds of "witches" (and only these three) move about at night as were-animals and participate in the Witches' Sabbath. There are also two named subvarieties of "Spells." While small differences in technique are specified for each, the basis of the subclassification seems clearly to be that one is connected with Game Way[4] (a hunting rite) and the other with Eagle Way, a Navaho chant.

The "good side" includes a very large number of ceremonies. The most sweeping and clear-cut distinction is that between "chants" and all else.[5] The Navaho word which means "chant" or "sing" refers to those ceremonials differentiated by a simple and consistent operation: those which include singing accompanied by some kind of rattle. Chants are subdivided fundamentally in two ways. The first refers merely to the duration, and one hears therefore of one-night, two-night, five-night, and nine-night chants. Or a patient may have only an "excerpt" from a chant or other ceremonial. This may be a blackening or a making of a sacrificial figurine (cf. Haile, 1947a).

The other subdivision is according to the "ritual" by which they are carried out: Holy[6] Way or Ugly[7] Way or Life Way.[8] Several chants provide for performance according to all three rituals; a much larger number for performance by Holy Way and Ugly Way only. The ritual is selected in accord with the assumed etiology of the disease of the patient being treated. If the illness is thought to be caused by angry supernaturals, Holy Way is appropriate. If the "cause" be the ghosts of fellow tribesmen or (sometimes) witches, Ugly Way is selected. The Life Way ceremonials are primarily for those suffering from injuries attributed to accidents, either recent or past. Special circumstances may call for some combination of rituals within a performance of a single chant (Haile, 1947b, p. 9). Each ritual implies certain choices of procedures, equipment, songs, and symbolism. Thus in Angry Way subritual reds are turned in, blues out; in Peaceful Way blues are toward the figure, reds out (Haile, 1947b, p. 12). Holy Way ritual makes provision (at least in the case of certain chants) for three subrituals: Weapon Way,[9] Angry Way, and Peaceful Way. Here likewise the decisive factor is the "diagnosis" of the origin of the illness.

The specific chants which may be conducted according to one or more of the rituals and subrituals are loosely associated by the Navaho into subgroups which are derived in the first instance from the particular corpus of mythology on which the chants are based and, in the second instance, from well-known techniques or features prominent in or distinctive of these connected chants. Thus, for example, in Holy Way we get:

I. Shooting-Chant subgroup

   Hail Way
   Water Way

   Shooting Way, Male Branch
   Shooting Way, Female Branch

   Red Ant Way
   Big Star Way

   Flint Way, Male Branch
   Flint Way, Female Branch[10]

II. Mountain Chant subgroup

Mountain Top Way, Male Branch
Mountain Top Way, Female Branch (Old Woman's Branch)
Mountain Top Way, Cub Branch (Her Son's [woman
  speaking] Branch)[11]
Mountain Top Way, Male Shooting Branch
Mountain Top Way, Female Shooting Branch[12]

Excess Way, Male Branch
Excess Way, Female Branch

Way to Remove Someone's Paralysis[13]

Moth Way

Beauty Way, Male Branch
Beauty Way, Female Branch

III. Those Which Have Impersonators of the Supernaturals

Night Way, Rock Center Branch (Darkness Beneath
  the Rock Branch)
Night Way, Big Tree Branch
Night Way, Water Bottom Branch[14]
Night Way, Pollen Branch
Night Way, Across the River Branch

Big God Way
Plume Way
Dog Way
Coyote Way
Raven Way

IV. Wind-Chant subgroup

Navaho Wind Way, Male Branch
Navaho Wind Way, Female Branch

Chiricahua Apache Wind Way

These four groups all represent Navaho classification with fair consistency. However, only Group III is consistently given the same Navaho designation,[15] perhaps because these chants may be given only "while the thunder sleeps." There are other small subgroups: Eagle Way and Bead Way; one subgroup containing only one chant (Hand Trembling Way); and three (probably more[16]) extinct Holy Way chants of uncertain affiliation: Earth Way, Awl Way, and Reared in Earth Way.

Some principles of Navaho classification, including a few that we shall meet more than once again, emerge from study of the above table. There is the tendency exhibited in a number of cases to specify a male and a female part. The chant names refer either (a) to a central episode in the accompanying myth (e.g., Red Ant Way) or to a particular episode taken as basic for the elaboration of a particular branch (e.g., Night Way, Across the River Branch); or (b) statement of symptom or etiology (e.g., Excess Way and Hail Way). There is also a manifestation of the tendency to syncretism which appears elsewhere in Navaho chant classification: the Mountain Top and Shooting Chants are mingled. There may also be syncretism between Navaho Wind Way and Hail Way and the Game Way complex (Wyman and Bailey, 1946, pp. 214-15).

The foregoing does not begin to exhaust the ways in which Navahos classify their ceremonials. For example, chants of Group III may be given without the masked impersonators in which case they are called "just visiting" chants (Haile, 1947c, p. 36). There are the *features* (with sandpaintings, prayersticks, jewels, and various other paraphernalia which may or may not be added). There are the public exhibitions[17] and "vaudeville acts" which can be included as "extras" with certain chants. There are the "etiological factors" specified with some chants and influencing the precise details of their conduct: Upper Regions Side or Thunderstruck Side; From Under Plants (the reference is really to snakes as the cause of illness); Striped Side.[18] If one asks a chanter what ceremonial he is conducting, his answer will vary[19] with a number of circumstances, but if he trusts you and feels that you understand the language and the ceremonial system and really want him to be precise, he is perfectly capable of coming out with something like the following: "Holy Way, Male Shooting Branch; nine nights; Angry Way and Peace Way subrituals; Thunderstruck Side: with Sun's House and Dark Circle of Branches."

Actually, there are still further specifications possible which it would take too long to explain here. To give just two instances: (1) careful ceremonialists distinguish two forms of Shooting Way, Female Branch, with one held to be of Jicarilla and the other of Navaho origin (Kluckhohn and Wyman, 1940, p. 155); (2) the order of the component ceremonies of a chant may be reversed to cure a singer who has given a chant too often—this is designated a "reverse chant" (*ibid.*, p. 107).

To turn to the "non-chants" there are (leaving aside small, essentially personal songs and rites for crops, livestock, good luck in traveling, girl's adolescence, and the like) the following groups:

> Blessing Way (in five varieties)
> Prayer Ceremonials (three main varieties)
> War Ceremonials (at least two varieties)
> Hunting Ceremonials (many varieties)
> Rites of Divination (four varieties)

Blessing Way is sung but not to the accompaniment of a rattle. Although it is short and of fixed duration (two nights), it is stated by almost all Navahos to be the very keystone of their whole ceremonial system. In addition to its existence as an independent ceremonial, each chant has "its Blessing Way part,"[20] and many minor rites such as the Girl's Adolescence Ceremony are essentially built up out of Blessing Way. Blessing Way is differentiated in function as well as in form and content; its purpose is not to cure illness but rather "for good hope" (e.g. for a pregnant woman or a person about to start on a journey). The named varieties of Blessing Way are:

> Talking God Blessing Way (Two Go for Water Blessing
>   Way; also, Night Way Blessing Way)
> Enemy Monster Blessing Way
> Chief Blessing Way
> Mountain Peak Blessing Way (Eagle Way Blessing Way)
> Game Way Blessing Way

All except one of these names and synonyms refer to mythic episodes and/or related ceremonials (syncretism again). Chief Blessing Way is designated by a main though not exclusive function of this rite—the induction of a "chief" or "headman." Most informants when they say simply "Blessing Way" in Navaho have in mind Talking God Blessing Way, though a few vigorously maintained the primacy of Chief Blessing Way.

The prayer ceremonials are mainly associated with Blessing Way, even though they have forms given in connection with chants conducted according to Ugly Way ritual. They are not sung but often include drypaintings of pollen on buckskin (rather than the "sandpaintings" made of sand, charcoal, and minerals on the floor of the hut). Alone among Navaho ceremonials they have a duration of four nights. Prayer ceremonials are intended primarily for cure of witchcraft and for protection against witches. The names of each of those still well known today have a definite witchcraft implication: Self-Protection, Bringing Up, and Bringing Out.

Just as the prayer ceremonials "fall on Blessing Way side," so most[21] of the war ceremonials are felt to have a marked affiliation with Ugly Way ritual. The myths of Ugly Way chants and war ceremonials frequently interlock (cf. Haile, 1947b, p. 6) and are, indeed, at some points almost indistinguishable. With one exception, war ceremonials have been extinct or obsolescent for some time save as preserved in fragments of rites ("excerpts," especially some of the "blackenings") and some myths. Enemy Way, the public part of which is widely known to the English-speaking population of the Southwest as "the Squaw Dance," is still very frequently performed, though only during the summer months. This is the treatment for "ghost infection" from aliens, whereas the Ugly Way chants are for illness caused or threatened by native ghosts. But Enemy Way falls out of the chant pattern in three respects: (a) not a rattle but a rattle-stick is used, and the singing is accompanied by a potdrum; (b) the ceremonial lasts *three* nights; (c) Enemy Way is not unequivocally in charge of a single individual; two, if not four, persons share the responsibility. Navaho differentiation of Enemy Way as non-chant is reflected in the fact that the patient of Enemy Way is called by a different term from that applied to the patients in all chants.

Navaho informants are agreed that the other war ceremonials (Enemy Monster Way, Monster Men Way, Two Went Back for Scalp Way, Ghosts of Every Description Way, and Where the Two Came to their Father Way) are not chants, but it is not so clear how, in other particulars, they fit into the Navaho scheme of ceremonial categories. Some excerpts were revived and rather popular during and immediately after the Second World War, but only the myth and drypaintings of the last-named have been recorded in detail (Oakes, 1943). The first two may represent rather minor versions of a basic ceremonial. Oakes's principal informant says (Oakes, 1943, p. 57) that Enemy Monster Way was another "side" of Where the Two Came to their Father that was used in enemy country on the battlefield. Two Went for Scalp Way may be merely an old synonym for the basic native-ghosts chant, Upward-Reaching Way. Ghosts of Every Description Way may be a special designation for the end of Enemy Way or for a slightly unorthodox combination of Upward-Reaching Way and Enemy Way (cf. Kluckhohn and Wyman, 1940, p. 190). From the Oakes monograph and from scattered fragments of other information, some resemblances to Blessing Way and to the prayer ceremonials are evident: drypaintings and prayers are prominent; prevention and protection are intended as much as (or more than) cure. On the other hand, while Oakes's informant admitted the similarity of his rite to Blessing Way, he likewise insisted that it was separate, "has nothing to do with it" (Oakes, 1943, p. 56). One painting is from Blessing Way, but "this is used because it gives a personal blessing which has nothing to do with war" (*ibid.*). In sum, the evidence indicates that these war ceremonials were regarded as being in a special category but with felt linkage to chants conducted according to Ugly Way ritual.

The game ceremonials[22] are also substantially extinct. There were two main divisions corresponding to the hunting of deer and the hunting of antelope. The known varieties of ritual deer hunting are named again partly on the basis of technique (e.g. Encircling by Fire or Tiptoe) or myth (e.g. Big Snake Way and Talking God Way).

Types of divination are distinguished by technique: hand-trembling, stargazing, listening, and *Datura* divination. In each case the practitioner goes into a kind of trance to "diagnose" the cause and history of an event (illness, loss, theft, adultery) and to make a prognostication of a favorable course of action (what ceremonial to have for an illness, where to hunt, when and how to raid or retaliate in war). It is also relevant to remark that "diagnosticians" seldom carry out other ceremonials. Divination is a specialty, and Navahos rather generally assume implicitly it is an exclusive one. In fact, some evidence (cf. Kluckhohn, 1939) indicates that strong temperamental and selective factors operate to distinguish between "diagnosticians" and other ceremonialists. All other ceremonials are learned; one becomes a diagnostician by a sudden "gift." To a lesser extent, singers of Blessing Way are likely to stick to this specialty, not becoming either chanters or "diagnosticians." They do often carry out prayer ceremonials. Presumably because of close affiliation between one technique of divination (hand trembling) and the chant of the same name, these chanters also strongly tend to restrict themselves to this single chant (cf. Kluckhohn and Wyman, 1940, p. 169).

Beings. Almost everything known to the Navaho is personalized in the supernatural context: animals, plants, mountains, winds, and rain. "They are conceived as existing 'in man form'" (Haile, 1943, p. 67). "A number of natural phenomena are taken possession of by . . . 'one who lies within it' . . . this inner form is a being independent of the object which it happens to occupy. To instance, the sun disc . . . is quite distinct from its carrier . . . 'who carries a round object here and there in daytime'" (*ibid.*, p. 68). The personalized "inner forms" of animals, plants, and inanimate natural phenomena are addressed in prayers and mentioned in myths and ceremonials. They are legion, and there does not seem to be an evident Navaho classification of them except insofar as they are often grouped in pairs, frequently as either male and female or older and younger.

As to the Navaho "gods" (as this word would usually be understood in the tradition of the West), there are many. The sun appears really in three guises: as object, as "inner form" of this object, and as a completely individualized being who is one of the major Navaho supernaturals. (The moon,[23] on the other hand, appears only under the first two aspects, and although the earth is invoked as "the earth, our mother," the earth likewise does not seem to be completely individuated[24]). The wife of the sun, Changing Woman[25] is regarded by many Navahos as the principal Navaho divinity. Another "school" assigns this place to an hermaphroditic deity (whose name means literally 'breast-grabber') who is portrayed as the creator. There are grounds for suspecting that Breast-Grabber represents a foreign, not fully assimilated element in Navaho theology, and one which has in recent times been sharply remodeled under Christian influence. In the main stream of Navaho thought, the principal divinities appear to be the Sun and Changing Woman; their children, the Hero Twins; First Man and First Woman. Note that just as the dual form is prominent in the Navaho language, the main deities appear in pairs. Changing Woman herself is often equated with a remarkably similar personage, Turquoise Woman. The Hero Twins are differentiated in accord with Navaho kinship terminology into "older brother" and "younger brother." Each of the Twins has an "alias." Monster Slayer appears as Reared in the Earth, Child of the Water as Changing Grandchild. These terms are used when Navaho lore wishes to emphasize special manifestations of their "personalities" (Reichard, 1950, p. 482). There is also another "form" of the Twins: The Stricken Twins (*ibid.*, p. 481).

Reichard (1950, chap. 5) has grouped Navaho divinities:

Persuadable deities
Undependable deities
Helpers of deity and man
Intermediaries between man and deity
Unpersuadable deities
Dangers conceived as deities
Beings between good and evil
Order of monsters, dangers, and beings-in-between

This is not a Navaho categorization, though a correct ordering of certain regularities in Navaho statements. Reichard herself (p. 53) says her classification is "intended to be suggestive rather than definitive." Navaho categories remain to be satisfactorily worked out. There are three terms in common use. The first, "Supernatural People,"[26] seems to be the generic one which can be applied to all individual divinities and personalized powers, to all "people" of the preemergence world as contrasted with Earth-surface People, even to chanters when they are saturated with supernatural power at the height of a ceremonial. Neither the Navaho nor Father Berard Haile have been able to translate the second Navaho word, so the latter proposes (1947c, p. 37) using Anglicized ye-i. The ye-i occupy a prominent place in Navaho legend, but sometimes the word or its correlate, 'Maternal Grandfather of the Supernatural Monsters,' is used to designate divinities who are not represented as monstrous animals. The third term which is literally 'Failed-to-Speak People' would appear to be a colloquial usage, deriving from the fact that the impersonators of the divinities at the public exhibitions attending some chants never talk but only hoot, holler, and sing.

Navaho deities are strikingly less fully categorized than the ceremonials, though each ceremonial tends to be associated with a particular figure. Changing Woman is, so to speak, patron of Blessing Way and the prayer ceremonials. The Sun is prominent in the Shooting Way complex. First Man and First Woman are connected with all evil magic. Breast-Grabber is first and foremost the tutelary deity of hunters. The Hero Twins, great warriors, bulk large in most ceremonials telling of war. Black Supernatural, however, conducts Enemy Way. Reviewing the evidence thus far available, one must conclude that for some reason the Navaho were not interested in an elaborate grouping here. They found it sufficient to speak of the Supernatural People and then to name each individual divinity and personalized "inner form." The other two terms do not appear to be more than colloquial variants, handy in specific contexts. Haile (1947b, pp. 6-7) regards the *ye-i* and the Failed-to-Speak ones as an identical subclass of the Supernatural People. They were created by First Man. The myth Haile quotes lists seven: Talking God, Calling God, Male God, Female God, Shooting God, Whipping God, and Red God. In Night Way, however, there are six each of "Male God" and "Female God" (i.e. ordinary male and female *ye-i*) and the following possible additional impersonators: Black God, Monster Slayer, Born for Water, Water Carrier (Gray God), Hump Back, Fringed Mouth, Red Failed-to-Speak, Destroyer, Whistling Failed-to-Speak, Shooting Failed-to-Speak (Haile, 1947b, p. 37).

Myth. Roughly speaking, alike from the point of view of the observer and of the Navaho, one distinguishes the more secular from the more sacred stories, although the same Navaho word is applied to both. "More" is a necessary qualification, because in Navaho feeling the supernatural world is involved in all. Definitely in the "sacred" category belong the legend—or rather the various legends—dealing with the emergences of the Navaho from the eleven lower worlds (a very widely distributed plot among Indians of Western North America but with variations and elaborations more or less special to each tribe or group of tribes). Likewise "sacred" are the myths that are the rationale for the various ceremonials. As a matter of fact, the emergence myth or part of it is incorporated into the justificatory legend of many ceremonials. In a somewhat intermediate class are the legends of the different clans. These often begin with part of the emergence story and then recount the wanderings and subsequent development of that clan. Most on the "secular" side are what would usually be designated as "folktales." These are the Navaho equivalent of Aesop's Fables or of Brer Rabbit. The best known to most Navahos are the Trotting Coyote Stories. There are also other quasi-obscene cycles like those of Tooth-Gum Woman. Some tales, like some chants, are reserved for the winter months (Haile, 1954, p. 39).

While themes and passages of the emergence and ceremonial myths and clan legends (and even the folktales) weave in and out of each other in a manner most bewildering to a non-Navaho, they still constitute in some sense a fairly unified corpus. A knowledgeable Navaho who is recounting or talking about mythic materials will say most definitely but at a point that strikes an outsider as altogether arbitrary, "here Blessing Way begins." The origin legends of numerous ceremonials may be almost identical up to a certain point and then they "branch off." Beauty Way (cf. Wyman, 1957) and Mountain Top Way are independent continuations of the story of the war against the Pueblo Indians of Taos, a story which the Navaho seem to regard as having been begun in the myth of Monster Way and that in turn in the emergence story. The origin legend of the divinatory rites of star-gazing and listening appears to take off from the buzzard episode of Enemy Way. As Wyman (1945, p. 382) says:

As more Navaho myths are recorded the more apparent it becomes that the total mythology possesses a somewhat limited number of episodes and incidents of types thereof which recur over and again in the origin legends of different chants. It is almost as in the construction of the chants themselves, where a limited number of types of ceremony are combined in different ways and with various individual minutiae ... With a store of legendary events to pick from, and evidence in the existing myths that "picking" must have occurred in the past, the temptation to create new combinations and thus new myths would seem to be present.

Discussion. Navaho beliefs and practices relating to the supernatural certainly constitute a ramified system. From the Navaho viewpoint everything is related to everything else. It has not been possible to specify in detail here all actual relationships. Most chants are connected with particular animals. Many are related to specific mountains (especially the sacred mountains of the four directions) and to other localities. Every ceremonial has a color, directional, sex, number, and sound symbolism. The intricacies remind one of the contrived systematic symbolism of Joyce's *Ulysses*.

In part, these interrelationships are made quite explicitly and consistently. "Causation" is a keynote. You begin by finding out what "caused" your illness or who stole your property or indulged in adultery with your wife; where the enemy or the game animals are at the moment. A course of action is then indicated in "logical" terms. The system with its categorizations tells you. If the diagnostician maintains that you have "Thunderstruck" sickness, then obviously you must have recourse to a practitioner of one of the Shooting Ways. The chanter, on the basis of his information on what details divination has revealed and his knowledge of the full mechanics of etiology as set forth in the myth, will know what ritual, subritual, branch, and features of Shooting Way are indicated; what divinity or divinities must be given special attention in the symbolism of the chant.

And at points almost inseparable the keynote is "origin." Is "ghost sickness" attributable to native or foreign ghosts? Was there a failure in treatment because superficial "diagnosis" prescribed Enemy Way but, as the legends show, the story of Enemy Way begins "farther back" in Monster Way and therefore it was this latter that was required? Technique likewise receives some accentuation, often following the familiar principles of sympathetic and holophrastic magic. Mountain Lion Way is one branch of Game Way because mountain lions are notably successful as hunters of deer. Since some forms of witchcraft utilize the clothes or offal of the victim, an appropriate prayer ceremonial for someone suffering from such a technique is one which incorporates "in a good way" some part or product of the person. Technique is also a basis of naming in a descriptive sense. Thus Flint Way is popularly called Hoof Way (from the hoof rattles used); Chiricahua Wind Way is popularly designated by one of its refrains or is called Toothgum Way; Blessing Way is referred to as No Sleep from the all-night performance of the second night.

Other general principles of Navaho classification appear at a number of points. For the Navaho everything comes in twos (or in fours, the multiple of two and the number of the directions recognized by the Navaho). The pair may be male and female, older and younger, "outer" and "inner," siblings or counterparts, without reference to relative age. Many divinities appear in duplex or multiplex forms. Holy Young Man and Holy Boy appear to be the same "person," as do Changing Woman and Salt Woman. Indeed, Changing Woman also appears as White Shell Woman and as Turquoise Woman. Reichard (1950, p. 76) suggests that First Man and First Woman are the respective manifestations of Sun and Changing Woman in the worlds below and that (p. 77) First Woman is "a rudimentary archetype of Changing Woman." She likewise implies that various aspects of the Sun's personality are represented by:

Breast-Grabber (the darkness of the sun)
Black Supernatural (the darkness of the sun)

Talking God
Speechless God

She specifically proposes (p. 79) that Coyote, the "exponent of irresponsibility and lack of direction," "seems to be an uncontrolled aspect of either the Sun himself or his child." Similarly, Changing-Bear Maiden "is the female apotheosis of evil as Changing Woman is of good" (*ibid.*, p. 414).

How the Navaho name (i.e. classify) a supernatural depends upon quite standardized features of context. The elder of the Hero Twins is called Monster Slayer when arrayed in armor, Holy Man otherwise (*ibid.*, p. 55). Place and situation are also determinative of the various appellations of the twins: Reared-in-the-Earth, Child-of-the-Water, Holy Boy, Changing Grandchild. There is also a marked tendency to project into the supernatural world the main categories of persons found in the actual world. The supernatural beings include parental categories (Sun and Changing Woman; First Man and First Woman; Male Supernatural and Female Supernatural); children (First Boy and First Girl; the Hero Twins and some of the "inner forms" of natural phenomena—e.g. Thunder Boy and Thunder Girl); Changing Grandchild; the "maternal grandfather of the *Ye-i*," and so on. It may be significant that the relationship between maternal uncle and maternal nephew, so important in Navaho social organization in recent centuries, has only a minor place in Navaho myth and ceremonialism. Breast-Grabber, the hermaphrodite, is the supernatural representation of the culturally recognized category of the transvestite. The most pronounced tendency is pairing by sex: Rock Crystal Boy, Rock Crystal Girl; Whiteshell Boy, Whiteshell Girl; Dawn Boy, Dawn Girl; White Corn Boy, Yellow Corn Girl; Evening Light Boy, Abalone Girl; Mirage Stone Boy, Carnelian Girl; Soft Goods Boy, Soft Goods Girl.

While categorizations of ceremonials, myths, and beings are interrelated and cross-cut in a number of explicit and consistent ways, there remains the fact that the relative elaboration of categories in various spheres is markedly diverse. Many supernatural beings are named but if there is any Navaho classification it remains almost completely implicit except to the degree that it merely echoes the ceremonial system. Categories within the myths are also reflections of the ceremonials save for the very loose segregation of emergence myth, ceremonial myths, clan legends, and folktales. A plausible guess is that this divergence rests upon a quite pervasive theme of Navaho culture: action. The cases where the Navaho are least equivocal on their classifications involve operations of the observation of action. A ceremonial either does or does not employ rattles (chant or non-chant). Prayer ceremonials are extremely reminiscent of Blessing Way, but there is a simple operational test: no singing. The presence of certain features immediately places certain ceremonials by ritual or subritual, chant subgroup, or chant (e.g. passing through hoops signifies a ceremonial according to Ugly Way ritual). Navahos categorize ceremonialists (there are Navaho terms for each category below) as well as ceremonials, and here again they resort to observation of behavior. A *chanter* is one who sings with a rattle[27] *and* knows a ceremonial of at least five nights' duration. A *curer* may sing wth a rattle but is never observed to carry on more than an excerpt of a ceremonial. Curers who specialize in certain excerpts are named according to a primary activity (e.g. "blackeners"). *Apprentices* and *helpers* are designated on the basis of the functions they are noticed to perform. A diagnostician is known and referred to on the basis of the technique he is seen to carry out.

The Navaho are interested in words insofar as they categorize events with some precision. They are not interested in words just as expression of belief. The words of a chant myth must be just right because they prescribe a course of behavior that must be followed with minute exactness. But the test of correct behavior for a Navaho invariably stresses what is to be done and exactly how it is to be done. No unacculturated Navaho could possibly comprehend the Christian controversies over, say, the Arian and Monophysite heresies unless he were shown that accepting one or the other position inevitably involved different ritual practices. Hence, I suspect, the intricate classification of all ceremonial behaviors. A Navaho wants to know minutely where he stands here. Myths and beings are important only insofar as they affect ceremonial action, and there is little probability of error here so long as rites are correctly classified.

The Inanimate World

As already indicated, this title is really a misnomer from the Navaho point of view, though artifacts (in general) and some other inanimate phenomena are not held to have "inner forms." It will not be possible to review this sphere at such great length. I shall content myself with some general remarks, with one example in some detail, and with the introduction of material illustrating somewhat different principles of classification.

Within the natural world there is a strong tendency to classify into "male" and "female" (rains, winds, mountains, mesas, etc.). Actually, as Reichard points out (1950, p. 176), the distinction is in no simple sense the literal one of sex but rather that between "coarser, rougher, and more violent" versus "finer, weaker, and more gentle." So far as some types of artifacts and some mineral and (dead) biological forms, there are broad classes deriving from the classificatory categories of Navaho verb stems. Particularly common are "hard goods," "soft goods," and "woven goods."

The Navaho speak of "the upper regions" which include sun, moon, constellations, individual stars, rains, clouds, and thunders. (There are a number of publications on Navaho starlore, the most comprehensive being Haile, 1947d.[28] Representations of constellations and of stars of the first magnitude may be found in Navaho drypaintings, on gourd rattles, on prayersticks, and on masks. The Big Dipper, Cassiopeia, Cervus, Pleiades, Hyades, Scorpio, Orion, and the morning and evening stars are generally known, but more detailed knowledge is esoteric. Translations of the Navaho names in Haile's list follow:

> Man with his feet ajar (Cervus)
> Big first one (Scorpio)
> Rabbit tracks
> Butterfly
> Big white stars in the east and west (morning
>   and evening stars)
> Big red star
> Pronged star
> Fire Supernatural
> Monster Slayer and Born for Water
> Black Big Star
> Blue Big Star
> Yellow Big Star
> Igniter of Flash Lightning
> Igniter of Thunder
> Monthless (Coyote's) Star (Canopus?)
> Dawn's Star
> Porcupine
> Horned Rattler

Slim First One (Orion)
Pinching Stars (Hyades)
Cornbeetle
Bear
Thunder
Flash Lightning
Male Revolving One (Ursa Major)
Female Revolving One (Cassiopeia)
Red Heavens
Dawn
Skyblue
Evening Twilight
Darkness
Trails of the Sun
Milky Way
Big White Star
Big Yellow Star

As is evident, the nomenclature is primarily descriptive, secondarily mythological. "Male" and "Female" appear once again. Many constellations are conceived as having human or animal form, and individual stars or groups of stars in them are designated as their body parts: legs, knees, hips, body, liver, kidney, arms, head; or appurtenances such as head feather or cane; each has an "igniter" which illuminates the entire group. A very few of the constellations are held to be interrelated in some way. The Pleiades, Hyades, and Orion form a central group.

Winds and directions.[29] Winds are differentiated by color: dark, white, yellow, blue-spotted; or by their manner of travel: left-handed, running sunwise, running sunward, and so on. We also get "small wind," "inaudible wind" ("which in summer at times blows inaudibly with a cool breeze, even in hot weather"), and "smooth wind" ("when it is cold and there is a warm breeze even in cold weather"). Then there are "whirlwind" and "big-jumping wind" (cyclone). Each of these has, of course, its supernatural linkages. The last two named are associated with witchcraft. Supernaturals "without meanness" have two souls of "inaudible and smooth wind." Dawn Woman and Talking God "breathe by means of white wind." Dark Wind became the "soul" of First Man, Blue Wind the soul of First Woman. Earth-surface People and Supernatural People alike get their being from one or more winds.

The cardinal directions are ultimately referable to the points where sky horizon edge and earth horizon edge meet. One can also refer to "upper regions" and "dark upper." Popular conception assigns color to the cardinal points and in this sequence: white to sunrise or east; blue to south; yellow to sunset or west; dark to north. The phenomena assigned to these cardinal points are: dawn in the east; horizontal blue in the south; horizontal yellow (evening twilight) in the west; darkness in the north. The corresponding "inner forms" are Dawn Man; Evening Twilight Woman; Horizontal Blue Man; Darkness Woman.

In interpersonal communication, in addition to distinguishing left and right, sunward and sunwise, the Navaho use many variations upon the theme of "this side of" (a specified point) or "the other side of." The language possesses many suffixes which divide space into zones and circles or into lines and directions with some precision. "Near me" and "nearer me than you" are refined by adding "at a point away from me and from you," "at a point distant from both you and me"; "way over there where he is," "away from where we are," etc.

Artifacts. There is considerable terminology—mainly descriptive—attached to weaving, silversmithing, pottery, basketry, ceremonial objects, and to the equipment used in the respective technologies. Only the first two reveal much typology. The Navaho, for example, distinguish only three types of pots (Tschopik, 1941, p. 7), two on the basis of function. Navaho treatment of artifacts does bring out particularly clearly one frequent feature of Navaho categorization: that of inclusiveness rather than exclusiveness, designating a whole or any of its parts by the same term. For example, the same word is used to refer to "medicine bundle with all its contents," "contents of medicine bundle," or "any separate item of these contents" (Reichard, 1950, p. 8).

Property. Haile (1954) has discussed such Navaho concepts as goods which could be bartered at will (pp. 8, 48-49); this concept included slaves; "hard goods" and "soft goods" (pp. 20-21); "labor by arm" (p. 44—to work out the value of a gambling wager); wife-asking and gifts to the bride's mother (pp. 13-14, 46-47); exchange gifts (p. 50). They illustrate the familiar Navaho combination of inclusiveness and fine distinctions.

Biological Phenomena

Here again Navaho categorization intergrades with that in the supernatural sphere. But, as Haile (1943, p. 67) says:

anthropomorphism may be said to be applied with a slight difference to plants and animals, than it is to natural phenomena proper. Thus, a study of ceremonial usage and popular practice reveals that plants and animals are conceived as existing... "in man form," and that they can remove their plant and animal form at will.... This man form is indestructible, and there is some evidence, though not conclusive, that plant and animal forms likewise are indestructible.

The basic contrast is between "one who speaks" (human beings) and "nonspeaker" (plants and animals). The latter category is broken down into vegetation, trotting beings (i.e. quadrupeds), flying beings, and crawling beings. The last three are subdivided into "night travelers" and "day travelers." There are also "Travelers on the Earth Surface" and "Travelers in Water."

The only thorough study of Navaho biological classification thus far published is that by Wyman and Harris (1941).[30] On Wyman's major study of Navaho entomology one preliminary communication (Wyman and Bailey, 1952) has appeared. Wyman, however, permits me to quote the following from his forthcoming monograph:

A few striking species from well outside the Navaho country... were shown to informants to test their reactions. They did not hesitate to equate them with species which somewhat resembled them, and they named them appropriately. Therefore, it is evident that although Navahos may be confused by certain types of insects found within their own domain, they react with assurance when confronted with species which bear a clear resemblance to their own valid Navaho genera.

Wyman and Harris say (p. 9):

The Navajo classify plants in at least three separate ways... first, plants are male and female. Another relation is that various groups are used for curing the same disease or for the same purpose, or are used in the same way. Still another is that they have similar characteristics, such as being prickly or sticky, and within these groups there are large, medium, and small or slender kinds. These three types of category are independent, except that when plants are named according to size the larger one is likely to be "male," while the smaller one is "female." They form, however, classifications within classifications, physical characteristics or "sex" being used to distinguish plants within a usage group.... There is an extraordinary similarity between the names for supposedly allied plants in the works of the pre-Linnean herbalists, such as Gerarde's herbal of the sixteenth century, and many of the Navajo names for plants.

Of the 456 uncultivated plant species collected in the area, there were only three for which no Navaho name was given when shown to two or more informants, and for one of these a use was known. This does not mean that every plant is well known, but it does mean that the people are observant of their plant surrounding and can readily distinguish between plants of major, secondary, or minor importance, in their lives. . . . There is great variation in the names which may be applied to a particular plant unless it is a commonly used species, and even then the name given may vary with the informant and how he uses that plant. One informant explained this variation as follows: "most plants have at least three names, the real name, the way-in-which-it-is-used name, and a descriptive name." . . . Certain informants were inclined to give long descriptive names, while others have only the briefest names.

Wyman and Harris remark in a later study (1951, p. 55) that the complete or partial correspondence between materials from the eastern and far western portions of the Navaho territory, gathered about a generation apart,

is eloquent testimony for a rather remarkable uniformity in fundamental native botanical nomenclature over a wide expanse of territory, which exists along with enormous individual variation in the use and application of the nomenclature, and ingenious inventiveness in manufacturing new descriptive names when occasion demands.

Navaho propensity for being a little fussy about categories is reflected in the fact that there is not just a single term for "white man." They distinguish: "Anglo white man," Mexican, Mormon, and Texan. As a result of the Second World War, the English are "islanders"; the French "those of 'crazy' speech"; the Germans "metal hats"; the Russians "lawless ones." Asiatics are termed simply "slant-eyed ones." Negroes are "black Mexicans."

Ceremonial lore (as usual) supplies much information on the identification and classification of animals, both real and mythological. We find, for example (Haile, 1947a, pp. 5-7), the following "travelers on the earth surface": pig, chicken, cat; blue, gray, rock, white, gliding, and digging lizards; the horned toad; snakes; rattler, bull, garter, water, malpais; bear, porcupine, badger, black squirrel, white squirrel, long-tailed rock squirrel, chipmunk, weasel; and the following "travelers in water": toad, frog, armadillo (!), duck, "water lizards" (salamander), box turtle, otter, beaver. The land turtle is also assigned to this group. Many more animals are identified by the Navaho than those listed above. Reichard (1950, pp. 396-8) lists about a hundred. She notes that birds of different genera are sometimes classified as "male" and "female" of the "Navaho species" (e.g. cowbird is given as the female of Brewer's blackbird).

The famous Navaho "Big Fly," although apparently mythological, has recently been identified biologically by Wyman (Reichard, 1950, p. 390). The most interesting of the mythological animals are the "enemy monsters" or "enemy terrors," who include: Bony Bear; Throwing Monster, Kicking Monster, Horned Monster (Burrowing Monster), Crushing Rocks, Cutting Reeds, Eye Killers, Tearing Cactus, Water Monster, Traveling Rock. Psychoanalysts will please note that all of these are the fruits of the self-abuse of the wives of the chiefs in the lower worlds and of various kinds of sexual misbehavior on the part of certain Supernatural People.

Reichard (1948) has published a little on Navaho ornithological taxonomy. She notes (pp. 11-12):

the tribal scheme of classification—analogous, religious—should be kept in mind. It includes male and female divisions, some of which may separate genera, although too they may be rationalized so as to bring subspecies, species, or genera together. The categories will certainly be set up to include birds believed to contribute similar powers to ritual; to differentiate large and small, perhaps intermediate sizes; other classes may be determined by calls, colors, marking, odor, and habits.

In the same paper she has made (pp. 7, 9) some useful observations on Navaho categorization in general:

Navajo categories are inclusive, complementary, analogous, rather than distinctive, exclusive and homologous—they are more religious than scientific. . . . For instance, myth relates that the first world was inhabited by insects specifically mentioned, and the group includes bat. The Navajo know perfectly well that bat is not an insect, but they have established a connection between insects and a so-called 'helper'—bat is believed to have been a supernatural power of deliverance. Wolf, mountain lion, bobcat, and lynx are associated as predatory animals but their group also includes badger "because," as the Navajo explain, "he is their friend."

. . . . .

All natural objects are divided by the Navajo into male and female, meaning, in addition to sex, that there are contrasting types: aggressive and compliant, active and passive, kinetic and potential; coarse, rough, severe compared with fine, gentle, mild. Plants are so classified, the smaller varieties often being female. Plants are grouped also because they purport to cure the same diseases, that is, they fulfill a similar purpose; and because they have the same character—prickly, spiny, hairy, sticky . . . such or similar categories dominate in all Navajo classifications.

Social Organization [31]

In principle, this subject ought to be treated at as great length as the supernatural world, but there is not enough space nor has this topic yet been worked out as fully as ceremonialism. I must limit myself to some definitely established categories, showing how the familiar categorizing principles of duality, sex, overlapping circles, syncretism, and description repeat themselves in this area.

In the old days—and to a considerable extent still—Navahos meeting each other for the first time would very quickly communicate their respective positions in the social world by stating their clan affiliations. But this would always be done for both sides of the family. A Navaho is a member of his mother's clan but is "born for" his father's clan. As a matter of fact, the exchange of information takes place in stereotyped phrases which result in the establishment of one of the following positions:

"The two of us are of one clan."

"He [she] is the one for whom I am born" (i.e. he belongs to my father's clan).

"He is born for my clan, [as] I belong to his father's clan."

"We two are born for each other" (i.e. our fathers and mothers are clan brothers and sisters).

"We started out together in birth" (i.e. our fathers are of the same clan).

"He [she] is not my relative."

From the position reached, there emerge immediately many specifications of interactive behavior: kinship terms, the kind of joking that can properly be carried on, mutual obligations. Marriage or sexual intercourse is permissible only for men and women finding themselves in the last category.

There are somewhere between fifty and seventy Navaho clans, varyingly distributed in Navaho country, but most local groups will include representatives of about twenty clans, though membership is likely to be concentrated primarily in four to six clans. Clan names refer to places, origin (e.g. Ute or Chiricahua Apache), mythology (e.g.

Two Visited Water). In certain instances individuals who agree that they belong to the same clan will use different names, invoking the clan story. In other cases it is reasonably certain that as the Navaho tribe grew larger and spread out over wider territory a clan differentiated into two or more parts which gradually adopted different names while continuing to regard themselves as closely related.

This, in part, was presumably the origin of the "linked clans" or "clan groups." These cannot be designated as "phratries," for the Navaho do not name the various groups of associated clans. They refer to them merely as "partner clans." In theory, the prohibitions and mutual reciprocities prevailing among clan members are extended —with some diminution of intensity—to all associated clans. In recent practice the linked clans have played a minor role, particularly as far as those on one's father's side are concerned. Most adult, relatively unacculturated, Navahos will mention with some positiveness at least two or three "partner clans" into which they are forbidden to marry and toward the members of which they owe certain obligations. But the specification becomes vague and uncertain so far as the clan "for which I am born" (i.e. father's clan) is concerned.

Some alleged clan groupings would also appear to exhibit the syncretistic tendency. In general, Navahos welcome affiliation and secure placement in the world of social organization. The legends give a number of examples of this sort (Reichard, 1950, p. 12). The People-of-the-large-yucca-place affiliated with the Moving Mountain clan because their red arrow holders looked alike. Similarly, Base of the Mountain and Poles Strung Out clans recognized "partnership" because of similarities in headdress and equipment.

Into the intricacies of Navaho kinship terminology, some details of which remain to be worked out satisfactorily, I can enter only briefly. Relatives ("my kin") are distinguished from affinal relatives ("Those for whom I carry burdens"[32]). There are few affinal terms and relatively little discrimination by sex of speaker and relative designated: daughter-in-law; brother-in-law and sister-in-law (one term); "one married into [my, your, his] clan"; "he is married with him" (men who are married to women of the same clan but otherwise unrelated). Another term means both son-in-law and father-in-law, but ordinarily mother-in-law and son-in-law refer to each other by a word meaning "one whom he [she] does not see or look at."

Either parent may designate all children, regardless of sex, "my children." In general, however, the sex of the person speaking or referred to is taken into account. Mothers and fathers use distinct terms for their sons and daughters. An individual of either sex distinguishes "my brothers" from "my sisters." A male cross-cousin is "with me he goes around"; a female cross-cousin is called by another word which has not been etymologized. Relatives of the same order (e.g. "uncles") on the two sides of the family are differently designated because they belong to different clans. In some cases, reciprocal terms are utilized, sometimes with slight variations in the pair.

Ordinal as well as classificatory principles are employed: older brother, younger brother; older sister, younger sister. Parents differentiate (not in address but in reference) the ages of their children: "with whom birth started" or "the starting born one" or "who was born in the lead"; "the one in next position"; "the one between"; "one in position three" (four, etc.); "the concluding born." Generational lines are in some cases indicated by prefixes. Thus we get "twice daughter's children again" (i.e. a niece's children's children, both on the brother's and sister's side).

Language[33]

Here the categories exist in quite clear-cut form and are followed with great consistency by unacculturated Navahos, but are not, with two exceptions, named by the Navaho themselves. The Navaho do refer to a "respect language" which involves the use of a certain form of the third personal pronoun prescribed for speech to specific classes of relatives and persons of superior status. There also is, or was, a "war language," used by warriors. This was largely a matter of special vocabulary, though certain special inflectional forms were apparently involved also. In fact there is also an esoteric ceremonial terminology, but the Navaho do not call this a special "speech."

There are three major form classes in Navaho: particles, nouns, and verbs. "These differ mainly in the amount and kind of grammatical inflection they undergo." Particles (pronouns, numerals, modifiers, conjunctions, and other "relaters") are not inflected, though they often take one or more proclitics and enclitics. There are a number of nice discriminations that are typically Navaho with respect to pronouns. Thus "it" as the object of a verb has several different forms, depending upon whether "it" is thought of as definite or indefinite or as a place. The third person subject pronoun indicates whether the subject is ordinary or a place or what Sapir called "person of preferred interest." The latter designates the hero of a story as opposed to others, a Navaho as opposed to a member of another tribe, and so on. Possessive pronouns distinguish "my milk" in the sense of "milk owned by me" from "my milk" in the sense of "milk that came from my breasts."

There are few Navaho "nouns" in the sense of the "free forms" called nouns in Indo-European tongues. These Navaho nouns are not inflected save for an occasional plural. Other "nouns" or complex phrase-like constructions that function as nouns are really verbal forms which are inflected. No Navaho nouns have gender.

Each verb "consists of a theme—composed of a stem or set of stems with or without a thematic prefix—which may occur alone or with one or more non-thematic prefixes." The stem, though this must be selected in accord with categories discussed below, conveys an image which remains constant. Otherwise, meanings in Navaho (for communication is overwhelmingly by the verb) are derived from the assembling of elements that are generalized and colorless in themselves. Navaho might be called a chemical language: the basic process is that of utilizing the varying effects of small elements in different combinations.

Verb themes never occur as free forms and are usually provided with from three to seven or more distinctive stems, with or without a thematic prefix. Non-thematic verb prefixes are of two kinds, derivational and paradigmatic. The former are mainly adverbial in function, while the latter denote concepts of aspect, mode, tense, number and the pronouns for the subject, object, and indirect object. . . . Most verb themes . . . require one or another set of derivational prefixes in addition to the appropriate paradigmatic elements. Such derivations (i.e. verb themes plus derivational prefixes) are called verb bases. Many themes appear in several bases and some, like the theme "one round object moves," in more than a hundred bases. . . . Verb bases fall into two major categories, neuter and active. Neuter bases are conjugated for person and number in only one paradigm (the stem is invariant throughout the paradigm), but active bases have seven required paradigms: imperfective, perfective, progressive, future, iterative, customary, and optative.

In addition, both neuter and active verbs may have transitive and intransitive forms. Many verbs have separate stems for singular, dual, and plural. The dual is an important category in the Navaho verb, as are paired forms in the various spheres previously surveyed. Then there are the classificatory forms of transitive verbs referred to at the beginning of this chapter. Most of these bear a fairly obvious relationship to the perceptual world, but others are conventional. Who, for example, would guess that "sorrow" is in the round object category?

Next to "neuter and active," the primary emphasis would seem to fall upon "aspect." This category defines the geometrical character of an event, stating its status with regard to line and point rather than its position in an absolute time scale or in time as broken up by the moving present of the speaker. Thus the interest is in completion or incompletion of action (perfective vs. imperfective) rather than in tense (past or present). Certain Navaho locutions supply, roughly, the functional equivalent of the tenses of Western languages, but Hoijer doubts that even a true future exists in Navaho (". . . the future, so-called, is better interpreted as an inceptive progressive—that is, as an aspect rather than a tense category").

Navaho verb categories center very largely about the reporting of events, or better, "eventings." These eventings are divided into neuters, eventings solidified, as it were, into states of being by virtue of the withdrawal of motion, and actives, eventings in motion. The latter are further subdivided into imperfectives, eventings in process of completion; perfectives, eventings completed; progressives, eventings moving along; and iteratives, eventings repeated over and over again. The customary reports eventings repeated by force of habit or custom; the optative, a desire that an eventing take place; and the future, the expectation that an eventing will occur.

But this is not all. A careful analysis of the meanings of Navaho verb bases, neuter and active, reveals that eventings themselves are conceived, not abstractly for the most part, but very concretely in terms of the movements of corporeal bodies, or of entities metaphorically linked with corporeal bodies. Movement itself is reported in painstaking detail, even to the extent of classifying as semantically different the movements of one, two, or several bodies, and sometimes distinguishing as well between movements of bodies differentiated by their shape and distribution in space.

. . . in three broad speech patterns, illustrated by the conjugation of active verbs, the reporting of actions and events, and the framing of substantive concepts Navaho emphasizes movement and specifies the nature, direction, and status of such movement in considerable detail. Even the neuter category is relatable to the dominant conception of a universe in motion; for, just as someone is reported to have described architecture as frozen music, so the Navaho define position as a resultant of the withdrawal of motion.

Summary

I have reviewed some of the evidence on what Navahos group together, how they do so, and in accord with what principles. The Navaho attain to many genuine concepts: i.e. not arbitrarily labeled classes to which a common response is made on the basis of rote memory but rather identifications of new instances on the basis of defining properties. In some instances only one or two attributes are sufficient for the Navaho to identify a category. For example: a ceremonial where singing takes place to the accompaniment of a rattle is immediately identified as "chant"; ceremonials without singing and featuring drypaintings made of pollen rather than sand and minerals are classified at once as prayer ceremonials; stories about "trotting coyote" and told only in winter are assigned to one and only one class of "myths"; a ceremonial context where color and other symbolism occurs in an "improper" way will unhesitatingly be classified as "witchcraft."

In more instances there are overlapping classifications based upon the three criteria specified by Wyman and Harris (1941):

Duality by sex. This criterion appears (though not consistently) in the classification of ceremonials), supernatural beings, stars and other natural phenomena, plants and other biota, kinship terminology, and language. Sometimes it is associated with another attribute that is also utilized independently in other connections: size.

Use or purpose: ceremonials, plants, artifacts, witchcraft.

Descriptions according to perceptible or symbolic similar characteristics. This principle of classification appeared to greater or lesser extent in every sphere examined.

In some cases these concepts are definitely disjunctive: i.e. one or another of the attributes is used in identifying or categorizing. Such overlapping classifications are not in conflict in the Navaho mind. They are merely different and correspond usually either to varying contexts of discourse and/or to varying knowledge of the speakers.

Some other recurring tendencies in Navaho categorization need mention in review. There is a marked tendency for all systems (with the exception of language?) to be referable at one or more points in the final analysis to Navaho theology and to the associated terminology thereof. The supernatural system appears in many ways to be the ultimate paradigm for all systems.

There is also a strong tendency for entities to be segregable into aspects. Natural phenomena have their "inner forms." Human and divine nature is never portrayed as either completely good or completely evil: both elements are always present, though in varying proportions. Every ceremonial must have "its Blessing Way part." The most respected chanter must know something about witchcraft—"else he would go dry." Lightning comes as zigzag, forked, and flash. The segregations of Supernatural People appear to be largely by "aspects of personality": either in the form of complementary facets (as in the case of Changing Woman and Changing Bear Maiden) or of manifestations varying by context (cf. various names for the Hero Twins and for Changing Woman).

As a matter of fact, the personal dimension is prominent throughout much Navaho categorization. The language seems to organize both the natural world and the mechanical world in terms of direct bodily reference. Navaho avoidance of completion and overdoing relates back to the body and emotional experience. Most perceptual decisions have a personal reference. Reichard remarks (1950, p. 3): "Navaho dogma is based upon a cosmogony that tries to account for everything in the universe by relating it to man and his activities." And (*ibid.*, p. 148), "the universe is conceived as a place for man, and all natural phenomena are interpreted as his allies or enemies."

Finally, there is a pervasive difference between Navaho categorization and ours about which I have not yet succeeded in being articulate. Reichard characterizes this as "inclusive rather than exclusive." She writes (*ibid.*, p. 5):

for one purpose or another Navaho culture is divided into categories most elements of which have some features in common, but in order to make a category "complete" in the Navaho sense, it should contain at least one feature of an opposed or related category. In other words, categories are inclusive rather than exclusive.

Some of the phenomena do fall along these lines. Yet I am not quite comfortable with the phrasing because of syncretistic and other tendencies that have been noted in the evidence.

NOTES

[1] Specific citations will be made only on central and controversial issues or where there are additional details quite relevant to this chapter but too involved to recapitulate here. Recordings of the terms in Navaho will be found only in this technical literature.

[2] Two frequently heard forms refer, respectively, to a whole ceremonial and to a single one of the component ceremonies.

[3] Haile (1951, p. 46) renders the basic term as "to restore by ceremonial."

[4] Two Navaho enclitics are translated "way." One means more precisely "in the direction of" or "on the side of." The other may be literally rendered as "by means of" or "with." Another enclitic (used with slightly different intent) means "if ritual [or Way] is directive" (Haile, 1947b, pp. 6-7).

[5] It is convenient, following Haile, to use "ceremonial" for all organized religious activities "on the good side"; "chant" for the corresponding Navaho term; and "rites" for "ceremonial which is not a chant." However, Navaho gives us here only one clear-cut term—that for chant.

[6] Could perhaps more correctly be rendered as "Supernatural" (see section below on *Beings*). But "Holy Way" is enshrined in the literature.

[7] Has also been rendered as "evil" and "ghost."

[8] Haile (1947b, p. 9) thinks we may regard Life Way ritual as merely a sub-division or phrase of Holy Way. This definitely does not appear to have been the native point of view—at least during the last twenty years. There are, however, some slight indications making it conceivable that Life Way ritual is an offshoot of Holy Way. Earlier (1938, pp. 650, 652) Father Berard tended to regard Life Way as a separate ritual.

[9] Also rendered as Fighting Way and Injury Way (cf. Wyman and Bailey, 1946, p. 214).

[10] Perhaps these two chants should be considered a separate group, governed by Life Way ritual. The evidence is conflicting. See Wyman (1944, p. 365), Wyman and Bailey (1945, p. 358), and Haile (1947b, p. 7).

[11] Some data indicate that this is simply a variant of the Female Branch, named in terms of an etiological factor.

[12] Navaho opinion is not clear-cut as to whether these belong in II or in I.

[13] May be only a special prayer rather than a distinct chantway. No information is available on actual performance.

[14] These first three may all be the same branch with the different names designating the *ye-i* of different localities as etiological factors.

[15] The Navaho do, however, regularly use a term "partner chants" for these groupings. The same Navaho word meaning "partner" is used in designating linked clans.

[16] See Wyman (1951).

[17] The forms without public exhibition are referred to as "just-visiting-here-and-there chants" or as "inside" or "interior-way chants" (Haile, 1938, p. 647).

[18] Striped Side may refer to a subritual rather than an etiological factor—specifically, the term may designate Navaho Wind Way, Male Branch, Injury Way (Kluckhohn and Wyman, 1940, p. 111). However, there are many other etiological factors. Wyman and Bailey (1946, p. 214) think that Deer's Wind Way, Scolder Wind Way, and Hail Wind Way refer to etiological factors rather than branches. Father Berard (1938, p. 644) lists: Bear-does-it-Way: Thunder-

does-it Way; Big Snake-does-it Way; Horned Toad-does-it Way; Changing Bear Maiden-does-it Way.

[19] He may, for instance, simply name the ritual or an etiological factor or specify the chant without mentioning the branch.

[20] In the main, this is to correct omissions (Haile, 1947b, p. 5). Father Berard to the contrary notwithstanding, there are grounds for regarding Blessing Way both as an independent rite and as a ritual analogous to Holy Way, Life Way, and Ugly Way.

[21] Little is known about the Gesture Dance, and what has been recorded is conflicting.

[22] Bead Way and Eagle Way which are concerned with the ritual trapping of eagles are today considered chants. Ritual bear hunting had strong connections with the various Mountain Top Way ceremonials.

[23] Some accounts (see Reichard, 1950, p. 390) associate Breast-Grabber similarly with the moon, but I suspect syncretism here—a tidying up of the system by Navaho intellectuals.

[24] There are some indications (Reichard, 1950, pp. 407, 431) that Earth and Changing Woman are equivalent, but this is not nearly as explicit as the three forms of Sun.

[25] Also known as White Shell Woman, although occasionally White Shell Woman is considered the sister of Changing Woman (Reichard, 1950, p. 482).

[26] Usually rendered into English as "Holy People."

[27] In a few cases present practice is not completely consistent (Kluckhohn and Wyman, 1940, p. 40).

[28] My summary is taken from Wyman's (1948) review, much of it word for word.

[29] The section (except for the final paragraph) is taken exclusively from Haile (1943) and often in the same words. This publication is little known in the United States.

[30] Cf. G. Dieterlen, "Classification des végétaux chez les Dogon," *Journal de la Société des Africanistes,* 22:115-58 (1952).

[31] This section is based primarily on materials in Haile, 1941.

[32] The reference is to the obligation of the husband to work for the wife's family.

[33] This section is based largely on Hoijer, 1951. Unless otherwise indicated, passages in quotation marks are from this article.

REFERENCES

Goodwin, Grenville. 1945. "A Comparison of Navajo and White Mountain Apache Ceremonial Forms and Categories," *Southwestern Journal of Anthropology,* 1:498-506.

Haile, Berard. 1938. "Navaho Chantways and Ceremonials," *American Anthropologist,* 40:639-52.

———— 1941. Learning Navaho. Vol. I. Saint Michaels, Arizona, Saint Michaels Press.

———— 1943. "Soul Concepts of the Navaho," *Annali Lateranansi,* 7:59-94.

———— 1947a. Navaho Sacrificial Figures. Chicago, University of Chicago Press.

Haile, Berard. 1947b. Prayer Stick Cutting in a Five Night Ceremonial of the Male Branch of Shooting Way. Chicago, University of Chicago Press.

———— 1947c. Head and Face Masks in Navaho Ceremonialism. Saint Michaels, Arizona, Saint Michaels Press.

———— 1947d. Starlore among the Navaho. Santa Fe, Museum of Navajo Ceremonial Art.

———— 1951. A Stem Vocabulary of the Navaho Language: English-Navaho. Saint Michaels, Arizona, Saint Michaels Press.

———— 1954. Property Concepts of the Navaho Indians. The Catholic University of America, Anthropological Series No. 17.

Hoijer, Harry. 1945. "Classificatory Verb Systems in the Apachean Languages," International Journal of American Linguistics, 11:15-23.

———— 1951. "Cultural implications of some Navaho linguistic categories," Language, 27:111-20.

Kluckhohn, Clyde. 1938. "Navaho Women's Knowledge of Their Song Ceremonials," El Palacio, 45:87-92.

———— 1939. "Some Personal and Social Aspects of Navaho Ceremonial Practice," Harvard Theological Review, 32:57-82.

———— 1956. "Some Navaho Value Terms in Behavioral Context," Language, 32:140-45.

Kluckhohn, Clyde, and Leland C. Wyman. 1940. An Introduction to Navaho Chant Practice. Memoirs of the American Anthropological Association 53.

Oakes, Maud. 1943. Where the Two Came to Their Father. New York, Pantheon Books.

Reichard, Gladys A. 1943. "Human Nature as Conceived by the Navajo Indians," Review of Religion, 353-60.

———— 1948. "Navaho Classification of Natural Objects," Plateau, 21:7-12.

———— 1950. Navaho Religion. 2 vols. New York, Pantheon Books.

Tschopik, Harry, Jr. 1941. Navaho Pottery Making. (Papers of the Peabody Museum of Harvard University 17.) Cambridge, Mass.

Vestal, Paul A. 1952. Ethnobotany of the Ramah Navaho. (Papers of the Peabody Museum of Harvard University 40.) Cambridge, Mass.

Wyman, Leland C. 1944. Review of Origin Legend of the Navaho Flintway by Berard Haile, American Antiquity, 9:363-65.

———— 1945. Review of The Story of the Navajo Hail Chant by G. A. Reichard, Review of Religion, 380-83.

———— 1948. Review of Starlore among the Navajo by Berard Haile, The American Indian, 4:45-7.

———— 1951. "Notes on Obsolete Navaho Ceremonies," Plateau, 23:44-48.

———— 1957. Ed. Beautyway, A Navaho Ceremonial. New York, Bollingen Series 53, Pantheon Books.

Wyman, Leland C., and Clyde Kluckhohn. 1938. Navaho Classification of Their Song Ceremonials. Memoirs of the American Anthropological Association 50.

Wyman, Leland C., and Stuart K. Harris. 1941. Navajo Indian Medical Ethnobotany. University of New Mexico Bulletin 3.

———— 1951. The Ethnobotany of the Kayenta Navaho. University of New Mexico Publications in Biology 5.

Wyman, Leland C., and Flora L. Bailey. 1945. "Idea and Action Patterns in Navajo Flintway," Southwestern Journal of Anthropology, 1:356-77.

Wyman, Leland C., and Flora L. Bailey. 1946. "Navajo Striped Windway, an Injury-Way Chant," *Southwestern Journal of Anthropology*, 2:213-38.
————— 1952. "Native Navaho Methods for the Control of Insect Pests," *Plateau*, 24:97-103.

ACKNOWLEDGMENT

I am grateful to Dr. Leland C. Wyman for careful criticism of an earlier version of this paper.

THE GOTR CEREMONY
OF THE BORO GADABA

By Karl Gustav Izikowitz

DURING MY VISIT to India in 1952 I was fortunate enough to observe the so-called Gotr ceremony among the Gadaba on the Koraput plateau in Orissa. These ceremonies had supposedly disappeared and until now there existed only a description of them written down according to the narration of various informants.[1] As this ceremony is considered the most important among the Gadaba and only seldom takes place, it was indeed an unusual opportunity for me to have been able to witness it with my own eyes.

The Gadaba are often spoken of as a single tribe, but actually the name covers several tribes on the Koraput plateau and its eastern slopes in Orissa. These tribes resemble each other and dress alike, but they do not speak the same language and it is possible that they do not have the same form of society. In a recently published work Bhattacharya[2] shows that the language of one of the Gadaba tribes, Ollari, belongs to the Dravida group. There are several other Gadaba, but these have not been investigated. The tribe with the most members speaks the Munda language; they are the so-called Boro or Moro Gadaba, i.e. the big Gadaba or, as they call themselves, the *Gutob*. For the sake of simplicity I shall use the term Gadaba to cover also Boro Gadaba.

In addition to the Munda-speaking tribe there are others in the vicinity, the Pareng, who are neighbors of the Gadaba to the south. As an example of how the names of the tribes can vary we can mention that the Poya Gadaba who live at Salur sometimes call themselves Gadaba, sometimes Pareng, though they do not speak the Munda language. These two names very likely include groups which live in a similar way in spite of differences in language. To the southwest the Gadaba have as their neighbors the Bondo, also Munda-speaking, who in their turn are neighbors of the Didayis in the Machkund valley. While the Bondo have been described by Elwin, there has as yet been no research done on the Didayis.[3] These two tribes are the southern-most representatives of the Munda-speaking peoples.

In addition to these tribes there a great number of different kinds of peoples on the Koraput plateau. The Joria and other Gond tribes have many members, as is also the case with the Oriya-speaking Doms and Hindus of different castes. The Gadaba inhabit a larger part of the plateau but are concentrated round Nandapur Taluk.

The Koraput plateau itself is practically without forest. Only on the hills and the steep slopes is there any woods left. But the Gadaba say that this is a recent phenomenon. The old men assure us that as recently as in their youth there was still plenty of forest. The last of it is supposed to have been cut down around the time of the First World War, when there was still valuable timber here. Therefore the peoples of the Koraput plateau nowadays have a great deal of trouble in collecting fuel. Very likely there has also been a considerable migration of people to the plateau, and this would naturally make the fuel shortage still more acute.

The Gadaba are mainly farmers, but they also have herds of buffaloes, cows, and goats. On dry land they raise mainly *ragi* (Eleusine coracana) as well as a number of other cereals. Because of the lay of the land they can only irrigate the canyon-like, deepened river beds, which they widen as far as possible. Here they raise only rice. As this river-bed section is limited, they can obtain only a relatively small quantity of rice. This is eaten only at more important feasts. The rest of the rice, as is the case with the valuable oil-plant seeds, *niger* (Guizotia abyssinica), is a money crop. Thus the Gadaba live mainly on a gruel made of *ragi* flour and water.

Since the rice is already sown and set before the monsoon comes, the irrigated fields with their fresh green color down along the river bottoms form a sharp contrast with the dried red-brown landscape in general, giving the appearance of a land of green rivers.

The villages are arranged rather irregularly. In the center there is usually an open place and in the middle of this a big *bo* tree (Ficus religiosa) under which there is a *sodor*. It consists of stones, both standing upright and lying flat, and it is here that the village council meets with the members seated on the stones. These have been placed here in memory of the descendants of the village founder. Each pair of stones (one upright and one flat) has been placed here on the occasion of the great Gotr ceremony in memory of the parents of the dead chieftain, because the leadership here is inherited and comes in a direct line from the village founder. Sometimes the *bo* tree has become so old and big that it has actually grown over a part of the stones. One could probably determine the age of a village by the number of such stones.[4]

The larger villages are often divided into sections, each of which contains one sib. Only one biological family lives in a house, but the married sons prefer to have their houses near their fathers'.

In a Gadaba village there are seldom only Gadabas. Often there are also Doms, who constitute a section of their own, and some Hindu families as well. On the other hand one can find Hindu villages where there are a minority of Gadabas who apparently have joined the village at a later period.

In addition to the chieftain there can be assistant chieftains, and every village has also a *barrik* (herald) who is always a Dom and who stands ready to serve the chieftain. In larger villages there are also the *dissari* (shaman) and several other functionaries.

The Gadaba are divided up into a number of patrilinear, totemistic, and exogamous clans which for the most part are spread over the whole territory. Only in a few villages does the majority belong to one clan, this being the case especially in the southwestern section.

The clans are divided into sub-clans, often many in number, all of which consider themselves not only related but also originating from the same village. The name of such a sub-clan sometimes indicates its local origin; in other cases it can also indicate special occupations they have had in ancient times, but often the names cannot be explained. One such sub-clan is called *kuttum,* and it is a part of this group from the same village who join in the Gotr ceremony.

The sub-clans are furthermore divided into sibs; these in turn are divided into groups of relatives from the same village, which frequently form their own sections. It is therefore a segmented community.

Apart from this there are friendship relationships of several different degrees. These contribute to the formation of groups of families which constantly exchange services and things with each other. We shall here mention two of these: The relationship with the *panjabhai* and the *moitur,* which may be considered sacred bonds of friendship. Families which have made such sacred compacts may not intermarry. Consequently they form together an exogamous group. *Panjabhai* is actually an Oriya term and means originally one of the five brothers who make up the *panchyat*, the group which governs the village. The Gadaba have no such group. The proper term among the Gadaba is really *dissel*, but this word is rarely used. A *panjabhai* is the one who is to take over the buffaloes containing the spirits of the deceased at the Gotr ceremony. But he has other functions as well. *Moitur* (originally a Sanskrit term) is a kind of a general sacred friend who even in other situations plays an important role. During his lifetime a Gadaba goes through a succession of different kinds of friendship relationships, from more playful ones in childhood to the sacred ones of adult life beginning at the time of his marriage.

The year is divided into two main seasons. When the rainy season comes, it is time to begin the sowing on the dry lands, that is, about the middle or end of July.

During the rains the people are wholly occupied with their farming; not before January, when the crops have been harvested, does a new season begin. First of all they make preparations for weddings, and it is not unusual for a large number of couples to marry at the same time. During the dry period there is plenty of food and leisure and it is then that all the big feasts take place. But the same ceremonies are not repeated every year.

One can divide their life into a production cycle and a life cycle. In the former there is a complicated system of ploughing, rotation of crops and fallowing. This cycle covers several years before the rotation of its components begins again. Connected with production are a series of ceremonies, in part related to farming and in part to other things which are repeated every year. Many of these ceremonies are identical with the more important Hindu feasts.

The life cycle, which extends from birth to the final death feast, Gotr, follows its own rhythm and its own continuity. It begins with birth, the shaving feast, marriage, and certain lesser ceremonies, but by no means ends with one's death and cremation. To the physical phenomena are added the social factors. Ten days after the cremation there is an important ceremony, and several years after that, perhaps after a generation or more, the cycle ends with Gotr. This final feast of life is, according to the Gadaba, the greatest and the most significant of them all, and to arrange such a feast is "the highest" Gadaba activity.

One can throw light on the motivation of the Gotr by examining more of the beliefs of the Gadaba about the spirits of the dead. They believe that these spirits wander about restlessly and can, sooner or later, cause trouble. "If one is rich and does not hold a Gotr, the cattle will die and the harvest will be poor," is a usual explanation. "One can also become sick. Many kinds of illness are caused by *goigigi*" (spirits of the deceased), they say. This is a sure sign that the deceased relatives are angry. If anyone becomes seriously ill one can be sure that the spirits of the dead have caused this because no Gotr was held.

It is then advisable to make a serious promise on one's oath. To do this they take two reeds from the plant *Sátreng*. They cut off one ear of a calf, whereupon they let the calf pass between the two reeds as they drink the blood of the calf's ear. They say: "I let the calf pass between the *Sátreng* reeds. Do not be angry from this day on for I shall hold a Gotr and you shall be honored." "When one has held a Gotr the harvest is generally good," they say.

But these rhythms or cycles are interwoven, and therefore the ceremonies of the life cycle are placed at that time of the year when food, leisure, and place are most available. On the other hand the production cycle surplus is "pumped into" the different feasts of the life cycle. The two cycles together form a life stream in time, and all actions float along through the canals which are made by the relationships, that is, by the structure.

One may well ask the question: how can we say what is important and what is less important when it is a matter of ceremony? But one can measure the amount of work that is done, the economic efforts that are made, and the relationships which are involved, all based on statements from the people themselves. Since a number of social factors are implied in the different ceremonies and rites, it is important to determine their significance. This varies a great deal in the different communities, and a determination of a ceremony's rank is a very important method.

Everyone emphazises the fact that it is only the great men, the so-called Morolok, that is, those who are rich, who can arrange a Gotr. It is not sufficient that one person be rich; preferably the whole sib (*kuttum*) should be wealthy. As a matter of fact, it can be said, that the largest part of a Gadaba's savings go into the Gotr feast and that one must save all his life in order to be able to arrange such a feast. It is probably for this reason that they wait so many years before giving the feast for all the relatives who have died. The Gadabas can even leave their entire fortune to be used for a Gotr. I have run into several such cases, where it was said that the man had made a will according to which his property after death was to be used for a Gotr. This is called *Saraigú,* which means "how to spend money." It is no doubt also the Gotr which motivates the Gadaba to do extra work, for example on the Assam tea plantations, to make extra money.

I have obtained some information on what a Gadaba thinks a Gotr should cost, but the figures can not possibly be correct. Probably there is a good deal of exaggeration in these figures because of the social importance of the feast. One must buy or raise a certain number of buffaloes since, as we shall see later, a buffalo is given away for every deceased member of the family. In addition, one must have a certain supply of buffaloes to be used as gifts at similar feasts as well as at weddings and the like. Since these animals are not used in ploughing or other work among the Gadaba but are an investment, it is obvious that they also eat up a considerable part of the poor pasturage which the people have for all their animals. This is capital which does not draw interest until after a very long time and which in the long run becomes rather expensive to keep.

Only a few people actually have these resources, and it is usual that now and then one must borrow animals from relatives and friends. What this can imply I shall show later when I describe the feast. Along with buffaloes one should also have a certain number of cattle and goats ready for slaughter for the meals which are to be served. But often one receives these animals as gifts at the different feasts, a debt which one must later pay back.

At most of the important feasts it is necessary to cook the food in new pots which are bought especially for the feast in the Hindu pottery-making villages. Also used are quantities of rice, salt, eggs, and vegetables, especially chilis and turmeric. Unfortunately I cannot give the cost for a family with a given number of members, but I would imagine that the foodstuffs involved would surely run to as much as a whole year's income for a very well-to-do family. But this is certainly only a minimum. In addition there are certain services which must be paid for, such as chopping and carrying wood, husking rice, making leaf bowls, and all the other work, most of which however is done by the members of the *kuttum*. When it comes to gathering wood the *kuttum* membership is generally not sufficient, so other people in the village must be called upon to help.

The first Gotr which I had the opportunity of witnessing took place in a little village or hamlet, Kammarguda, and it began immediately after the *pus porob* feast, on the 10th of January, 1952. Long before —the villagers said three years before—they had begun to buy up the buffaloes that would be needed. The final preparations followed. This meant, first of all, husking the rice and making bowls of leaves, which are often used in this area. Husking rice takes considerable time and from morning till night the women of the Gotr-celebrating families are busy husking the rice with their heavy pestles. The mortar itself is simply a little hole in the earth which has been hardened with cow manure. In Kammarguda the high point of the feast is reached a month later, that is, the first Friday after the full moon of the month of *magh*. This day was supposed to bring good luck, and in this particular case it was a *dissari* from a neighboring village who had decided on the day.

Searching for all the fuel which is needed for the cooking of the food means a great deal of trouble for the Gadaba, since nowadays it is quite a distance to the forest. Formerly the custom was to suspend this matter until the last moment but they then had a better supply of fuel than at present.

Around two o'clock A.M. after the first day, they took two stones and placed them where the *dissari* had decided, not far from the house belonging to the Kirsani family. One of the stones was laid flat on the ground and the other was placed upright behind it. The *dissari* then placed an egg on the flat stone and mumbled something. Simultaneously with this act he decided when the actual final ceremonies would be held. At the same time two big poles or branches of a *simili* or red silk cotton tree (Salmalia malabarica) were taken into the village and driven into the ground on each side and just behind the upright stone. This was followed by the beating of drums all throught the night.

The next morning a buffalo was taken into the village and tied to the two *simili* poles. The people explained to me that this buffalo (one of the finest I have seen in this region and with enormous horns) was the *raja bongtel,* the king of buffaloes, and that it contained the deceased spirit of Kulia Kirsani. Kulia had died five years before and had been chief of the Kirsani families.

Women belonging to the families celebrating the Gotr then fed this buffalo with rice and other food while they wept loudly. Eventually all the older inhabitants of the village joined in the chorus of wailing. Then nothing happened for a while except that the husking of rice and other preparations for the feast continued. The buffalo however was taken in every day for ceremonial feeding.

A week or so before the high point of the feast the *panjabhai,* who in this case was Duaro Kirsani from Alungpada, the nearest neighboring village, arranged a feast for the Gotr families.

On the eighth day before the final day of the feast the actual Gotr ceremonies begin. The first day all the Gotr families and all the relatives from other villages who were invited gather together. They now make a larger fence of *simili* branches and all the buffaloes which are meant to be given away at the Gotr are now taken in and fed ceremonially every day. Besides rice and curry, which are served in fine leaf cups, they are given beer to drink. The people pat the buffaloes and wail their lamentations, and I even saw a number of women claw their cheeks with their nails so that the blood ran, while they beat themselves on the head and wept uncontrollably. The buffaloes, which contain the deceased spirits of the families, that is to say, the spirits of all those who have died since the last Gotr feast, are now washed with lukewarm water just as one does when there are important guests in the village, and then they are rubbed with oil. One now hears the drums night and day, and the wailing songs fill the whole night. The men dance in front of the row of buffaloes, dances which may be described as a kind of war dance, for the men have weapons in their hands. They yell and whistle wildly, and some of them wear rows of brass bells. When this twenty-four-hour period is over, the relatives go home, and during the following day only the inhabitants of the village feed all the buffaloes, in this case nine, twice a day.

In addition to the special place, *gotr munda,* where the buffaloes are tied, there are two other places of importance. One of these is the family's own stone place (*nggom munda*) which on this occasion was in the immediate vicinity of the huts of the Kirsani family. The other one is a bit outside the village, not far from the area where the deceased are cremated. Characteristically a number of big stones stand there in memory of earlier Gotr ceremonies. This place is called *gotr langbo,* that is to say, gotr "out in the fields," and each *kuttum* has its own stones there. In a Gadaba village one can usually point out the different stone places for each family.

At this point a decision is made concerning which members of the family on both sides, *bongso* and *somdi,* are to contribute animals. *Bongso* is the patrilineage and *somdi* the female relatives who have married into the family. They then ask who will give buffaloes and who will give oxen, goats, and the like. They must keep their promises and not substitute any other animals. The *bongso* give buffaloes and the *somdi* oxen. But these animals must later be paid back at weddings or other important feasts.

The following day, the seventh day before the final ceremony, they carry, with the help of the inhabitants of the village, a large stone to *gotr langbo,* and place there also a branch of the *simili* tree for each deceased person. The seventh night the buffaloes remain in the village, while the Gotr families and the other inhabitants sing and dance the whole night through. In the morning and evening the buffaloes are fed. If they refuse to eat, force is used. The important people among the guests are invited to have a bath in warm water and those who bathe give from two to five rupees to each of the people who help them. They spend this money at the next market where they buy dried fish and share it in the village. This happens one day before the final day. Of the two families in Kammarguda who were arranging a Gotr ceremony only the Kirsani family had a *nggom munda,* because only rich people can acquire one. Both of these stone places later become permanent.

The feast had been set by the *dissari* for the first Friday after the full moon, but at the last minute he changed this so that the final stage began on Sunday, the 3d of February, at eight o'clock in the morning. At that time they tied all the buffaloes, numbering twelve, to the poles of *gotr munda.* They fed them with both cooked and uncooked rice and gave them beer to drink.

The relatives came about ten o'clock. They too fed the buffaloes. They then bathed themselves in hot water and consumed a dinner prepared by both of the Gotr families for all the guests. They then danced in front of *gotr munda,* before the buffaloes, at which time all the men were anointed with rice beer and turmeric. After this the relatives went home.

On Monday the only ceremony was the feeding of the buffaloes. There was wailing and dancing and, of course, an endless beating of drums, which during the last days continued both night and day.

The buffaloes stood in their places until Tuesday morning, and after being fed again they were driven off. At about two o'clock they were brought back and were once more tied at *gotr munda*. Later in the afternoon a cow was slaughtered in order to make a feast for the chief of Alungpada, who is the *panjabhai* of the Kirsani family. The Alungpada people arrived late in the afternoon with a cow as a gift, a couple of stones for *gotr munda,* and bunches of banana leaves. After this came a *moitur* with his followers from Devulpada, also bringing stones. These people placed the stones on the *nggom munda* of the Kirsani family. Then the groups from both villages gathered and ate together.

On Tuesday evening additional groups from Tikkirapada joined the celebration, bringing with them two bulls, a basket of rice, and a pot of beer. The people from the village of Sankai came also, and they brought along two small cows as well as rice and beer. The eating and dancing continued all night.

Wednesday was the last day and the climax of the feast. After a ceremonial feeding early in the morning the buffaloes were decorated with mirrors and combs which were placed on their horns. A piece of cloth of *kereng* or other material was draped over their backs.[5] The buffaloes were then rubbed with turmeric. Later, about eleven o'clock, to the music of drums and shawms (oboes) and the noise of loud wailing they were led, at the front of a procession of all the relatives, out to *gotr langbo*. At the same time they also carried food to the family's cremation place, where it was offered as a sacrifice. At *gotr langbo* they had made a fence similar to the one within the village at *gotr munda*. They also set up another stone, as at *gotr munda*. Even in this case it was placed there by the Alungpada people. But of the original twelve buffaloes there were now only nine left, for three had been taken away. Of these nine, five were to be taken by the Alungpada, the *panjabhai* of the Kirsani family, and one was to go to the Kirsani's *moitur* in the village of Lugum. The three remaining came from the Pujari families and were to go to Kangarapada, the Pujari's *panjabhai*. Of the three buffaloes which were taken away from the village before the nine were led out, the Alungpada chief took one, which was at once taken to his village and slaughtered the night before the big feast. The third was allowed to remain in the village for the time being, since it limped and had difficulty in walking. It was to be taken by the Kirsani's *moitur* in Lugum.

This division of the animals was made known officially on Wednesday morning. The buffaloes containing the spirits of the deceased had thus been carried away from the village, and the first phase of the rites was completed; that is, the spirits of the deceased had been removed from the actual village region.

Within the village and just outside it tremendous crowds of people had now gathered. It seemed as if the people of the whole territory had come to witness the spectacle, and one could now feel an intense excitement in the air. The men were naked except for a breech cloth which had been drawn tight around the hips and between the legs. The breech cloth was as short as possible, so as not to hinder movement. The men stood in groups and waited for what was going to happen, looking like fighters or athletes ready for a contest. It was clear that they now waited impatiently for the climax of the drama. But they could concentrate and control their feelings.

Suddenly there could be heard music and whistling, screams and yells from the hills round about. From different directions came processions of men, armed with axes, knives and spears, and every kind of weapon they could get. They came towards the village like troops to an accompaniment of music. Those who first arrived at the village were the people from Sankai, who turned out in great numbers. They all carried weapons which they waved in the air as they danced. As soon as they came within the boundaries of the village they had to surrender all the dangerous weapons to an especially appointed policeman, a man who was considered sober and responsible. But this was, as fas as I could understand, an exception. There was some fear of bloodshed and fighting on such occasions; thus as a substitute for their weapons the men were given long sticks or clubs with which they later danced.

When the Sankai people came in leading a buffalo, they brought it to the Kirsani's house for display. As soon as that was done, they led the buffalo out of the village. The custom is that the buffaloes contributed by relatives and friends are to be taken outside the village on the last day and torn to pieces. But, instead of turning it over to the waiting crowd, the Sankai people ran off with the buffalo toward their own village. The situation was that the Kirsani had once borrowed a buffalo from the Sankai, so the Sankai gave this buffalo as a present but then took it back at once as payment for the debt.

But the Alungpada people would not stand for this, and soon there was a terrible quarrel which turned into a real fight. The Alungpada and Sankai men beat each other with clubs, and the women screamed and tried to separate them. Some of the women hung on to the clubs to prevent the men from using them. The fight got hotter. Several men were struck on the head and the blood ran in streams. This episode lasted a long time, but it was not the end of the drama.

One troop after another marched in to the accompaniment of drums and shawms. People came from several villages leading one or more buffaloes, first to the Kirsani's house, then to the Pujari's. Those who brought several buffaloes sometimes took one back, in this way taking care of an old debt. One person gave the Gotr families several buffaloes, but took back the number which was owed. At once, certain Gotr men ran off beyond the village with the remaining buffaloes, usually stopping in the shade of a tree. All the men followed and it did not take long for them to knock a buffalo to the ground and throw themselves over it. Soon there was a tangled mass of fighting men all over the buffalo, and each one tried to tear out the animal's entrails with his bare hands. Some crawled over the pile of men and others tried to wedge themselves underneath. Those who got hold of a piece stuck it inside their belts.

There was a stench of entrails, excrement, and blood, and everyone was more or less covered with the same. It was impossible to say whether the men were drunk or simply intoxicated with emotion. There was battle in the air. People quarreled, and the fighters had constantly to be separated. Outside the village an enormous crowd had gathered. Men, women, and children from the whole region had come to see the brutal spectacle, and some women had set up stands with food and drink for the hungry and thirsty. It was like a big market, and everyone was festively dressed. But the atmosphere was charged in the extreme, and the excitement increased every time a new buffalo was thrown down and torn to pieces by the wild mob. Each one wanted to assure himself of a bit of the entrails for it is in the entrails that the buffalo's enormous strength resides, according to the Gadaba. The men explained that the piece they succeeded in grabbing they would later bury in their fields, thus insuring a good harvest. No less than twelve buffaloes were torn to bits within a few hours; not until this was accomplished and the heat began to be intense was the spectacle over. Then, each village group gathered in the shade of a tree to rest and eat the food they had brought with them.

During this time Kammarguda's own men cleaned up the field of battle and one saw heads, forelegs, and hind parts of the buffaloes dragged into the village where they would again be divided up.

About two o'clock the intermission was over and the whole crowd went to the *gotr langbo,* where the original buffaloes containing the spirits of the deceased were standing. The bereaved families came, wailing their lamentations; they stroked the buffaloes, and finally removed from them the mirrors, combs, and pieces of cloth with which they were decorated. When this was done the *panjabhai* of both the Kirsani and Pujari families rushed to the buffaloes, then took them and disappeared with them in the direction of their villages as fast as the buffaloes could go. This was the end of the ceremonies in Kammarguda and the spirits of the deceased had now been carried away by the families' helpers, the *panjabhai,* who later slaughtered them in their own villages, one after another at great feasts, and finally devoured them all. With this, the deceased relatives of the Kirsani and the Pujari were considered "finally dead," to use the Gadaba's expression. The dangerous spirits, *goigigi,* had at last been killed.

But the actual feast was not yet over. The market was in full swing and the men demonstrated their cleverest sword dances. A team of fencers composed of young boys from Tikkirapada was especially outstanding. They had their teacher and their own music with them. To the delight of the crowd they did a certain kind of sword dance which simulated fencing between two opponents. The whole thing was very formal and acrobatic. They made brilliant stabs at each other and parried them with a kind of wooden shield made for the occasion, rectangular in shape and with a spike sticking out from the upper edge. They fenced from a sitting position and wrestled and threw each other over their shoulders. All the fighters were painted with turmeric and rice flour and had a black cross on their faces. It was apparently a very skillful team, as the audience was most enthusiastic.

Later on in the afternoon the crowds separated and went to their homes, but a great number of guests remained in the village. The idea was that the evening should be concluded with a dinner for the invited guests who had brought gifts of animals and other things, but unfortunately the fuel had given out. This, however, did not matter so much, because the Alungpada people had already slaughtered a couple of buffaloes and some of the participants in the Gotr ceremony were therefore invited to their village. The celebrants came back to Kammarguda late at night, quite intoxicated and very noisy.

The next morning the people were out early gathering fuel so that a dinner could be given. Thus far in the feast only one cow had been slaughtered, but now so many cows had come as gifts that ten could be slaughtered at once. The pink haunches were set up in a row on the fence as if they were on exhibition; they were later to be given away.

The guests then gathered for the festive dinner, which lasted far into the night. When they left next morning their departure was accompanied by many formalities. The people were especially ceremonious towards the *panjahbai* and *moitur,* whom they embraced and whose feet they touched. Several of the guests took with them a haunch of beef or at least a leg.

The following day there was another dinner, but it was only for the officials of the village. The guests were the chief of Devulpada, the village of which Kammarguda is a part, and the *barrik,* the herald of Kammarguda, the *dissari,* and a number of the closest relatives in the village. At the end of the dinner there was the presentation of the so-called *moali,* or obligatory gifts. Sukra Kirsani's mother's brother (*māmung*), Budda of the village Tukum, had contributed a buffalo for the Gotr. He received a brass bowl and a brass pot. Kulia Kirsani was one of those for whom the Gotr was given. His sister received a *moali* from Sukra Kirsani's wife. Kulia is Sukra's father; his mother is dead. Sukra's wife thus gave a *moali* to her father-in-law's sister, that is to say, to her husband's aunt. Sano Pujari held the Gotr in memory of his father Somo. His mother's brother, Angra Bordenaik of Tikkirapada, who gave a buffalo, also received a *moali* in the form of a brass pot. Thus, in the family who gives a Gotr, the husband gives a *moali* to his mother's brother, from whom he has received a buffalo, and his wife gives a *moali* to his father's sister, in case her husband's mother is dead.

As is usual among the Gadaba, there was a quarrel that lasted for hours involving the gifts. The phrase "It is not sufficient" and the insistence upon additional gifts with the bargaining and haggling that follows recurred again and again. It seems to be taken for granted that one is never to be contented but should try to get as much as possible. The Gotr was now finally finished, and the guests left with the remains of the slaughter as presents. Only the old *dissari* who had been constantly occupied and had been given too much to drink, did not get farther than a few meters beyond the village, where he fell down, dead drunk, and at once went to sleep.

This is a description of what I observed in Kammarguda. One might ask what happened in the villages before the people left for Kammarguda and what happened in the friendship villages. This, of course, I can not say, since Kammarguda was my point of vantage. However, during the same spring I was able to witness several other Gotr ceremonies, and I shall try to describe what happened as seen from the other side, that is, how the preparations were made among the *moitur*. I observed such a case at a Gotr between two different villages. In one case there was a family involved whose chief was Sida Muddili, of the village Kinchop, which strangely enough is not a Gadaba village but one inhabited by the Pareng. This man's *moitur* was, however, a Gadaba, the second chief in the village Godi Honjaro, Kanja Muddili. These villages are only three or four kilometers apart. As a *moitur,* Kanja brought with him no buffaloes but two large stones, one of them for a seat and the other to be stood upright. These had been fetched long before I came to the village, and in order to carry them, the people had made a structure of bamboo poles. The day of the final phase, the procession was started by a majority of Honjaro's male inhabitants. They also carried a number of *simili* poles with them. The women were to come the next day. Among the inhabitants of Honjaro village was another *moitur,* Sukro Bordenaik, who had no animals with him. He received two buffaloes on the Gotr day from his friend in Kinchop, and later he received two more. These were not counted in with the Gotr but were taken care of informally. At the actual Gotr, fourteen buffaloes were led away and torn to pieces. But later on, when Sukro arranges his Gotr, he will pay back the four buffaloes to Sida or his relatives. Sukro gave a special *moitur* feast for his friend in Kinchop immediately after the Gotr ceremony.

It was the *barrik* of Honjaro who called the people together and organized the march. Before they started the women came forth and pressed rice and turmeric on the stones and on the foreheads of the people who carried them. Then they marched off in single file, with music being played at the head of the line. When they had come a bit beyond the village they stopped and there groups of men began a sword dance. One pair of skillful dancers after the other swung their sabres above and at each other. One got the impression that this was a way of showing their skill. But why they do this and what its meaning is I was not able to discover. The march continued with several pauses to allow the bearers of the heavy stones to rest. In the discussion between the men I heard that they were wondering how Sida of Kinchop was going to divide up his animals. Discussions about such division of property is very usual among the Gadaba. It must be difficult for them to remember and keep straight all the debts from the past. Upon their arrival in the village the music started up and there was a general mêlée, the men dancing with drawn swords and swinging axes. The guests were greeted more formally in the Pareng village than in other places where I had been. The stones were placed according to ritual and the celebration of the Gotr followed the same general lines as in the feast described above.

In this short study I shall not dare to try to explain each and every phase of the Gotr feast. That would require a more general and thorough analysis of the Gadaba community than I am prepared to make here and also considerably more material than I have been able to collect during five short months. The Gotr ceremony is a kind of *rite de passage,* and, according to Van Gennep's scheme, these rites are a transition from one to another of life's phases.[6]

All these ritual actions are a kind of "social transformer," which mark the transition not only in life but from one kind of action to another kind: for instance, the transition from a magic or religious action to one of productive-technical character, or the reverse. Such a social transformation, at least when it concerns the life-rhythm, is composed of a number of different elements of which the physical change is one. An emptying phase, or an eliminating of dangerous or wicked elements, is the second; and the preservation of the good is the third. This takes place through the collecting of economic means, and through solemnization, in which religious, magic, and dramatic means come into use.

In the Gotr the physical factor is someone's death. And with this in mind a person can also make preparations, in this case a will. Later there is a succession of other actions, but this order of events, which applies especially to Gotr and perhaps also to other death feasts, does not necessarily apply to all kinds of *rites de passage* among all peoples. The order can vary. One needs only to contrast the child marriage of India, which long afterwards is followed by consummation, with what is usual in Europe. In the former case the solemnization comes much earlier than the living together. Among many peoples on the earth the reverse is true.

In the Gotr, the final ceremony after death comes after a very long time, perhaps ten years, perhaps a generation or more. As has been indicated, a Gotr implies tremendous economic effort for a family and their relatives and a really impressive accumulation of wealth. In earlier times when money did not exist it was still more difficult. The herds of buffaloes must be increased, as well as everything else, and the longer one delayed the more buffaloes and other goods were consumed. The life span was relatively short for these peoples, and it was not always certain that they could collect all that was necessary during a lifetime. If one knew all the factors it would probably be possible to make an equation for economic growth or accumulation in relation to mortality and thus figure out the time for a Gotr, or the interval between two Gotr ceremonies.

Among many peoples where the burial rites are of greatest importance they often wait a very long time before carrying out the final ceremony. This is so, for example, among the Muong tribe in Tonkin, where I myself have seen coffins containing the bodies of prominent people now dead which have lain on the beams inside the house for years, awaiting a respectable funeral. This was surely related to the economic surplus and the accumulated means which were available. A Gotr is actually a sort of social measure of one's success in life. It is without any doubt the Gadaba's most expensive feast, absorbing the greater part of their surplus. Thus it is rather obvious that the Gotr is connected with social prestige or at least with the respectability of the donor of the feast. On the other hand, one might say that the Gotr is only a means for prestige between relatives and individuals.

It would be interesting to know what the connection is between certain dominants within the life cycle and the production cycle, that is, the time organization on the one side and the structure on the other. One does not need to go further than the Hindus to find an example, for among them marriage is without a doubt the dominating life feast. In order to clear up this problem a series of similar investigations would have to be made in different communities.

The stones and the two poles made from the *simili* tree, which are erected at the beginning of the ceremony, are very important. Apparently, this is a kind of isolation of what is holy, just as one sets up an entrance or gateway to an altar. The promise, under oath, to arrange a Gotr when one makes use of two reeds may be considered a parallel phenomenon.[7] The essential thing in the Gotr ceremony seems to be the people's wish that the dangerous spirits of the dead (*goigigi*) should definitely disappear for good, which is accomplished by driving them out from the village to the "final place"—even here there are *simili* poles—where they are taken over by the *panjabhai,* the helper-in-time-of-need. He and his people eat up the buffaloes; a kind of analogy to this funeral custom exists in South America and is there called *endocannibalism.*[8]

This idea that the spirits of the dead reside in an animal and are later carried away is nothing other than the old motive of the scapegoat. Frazer[9] mentions several examples among the Todas and another tribe in southern India, but the whole concept resembles to an even greater degree the Juggernaut cult, which nowadays is centered in the Puri temple in Orissa. Even here the dangerous gods are carried off on a cart to be kept outside the region during the perilous rain period in a special temple building. I have seen a similar phenomenon in the Koraput section, where the people make a small model of a cart drawn by oxen, containing some kind of illness demons, which, following a ceremony, are thrown out of the village.

It is this ceremony which represents the elimination of the dangerous elements. But how is the good element preserved? The spirits of the dead are one thing and life power[10] is another and it is the latter that is to be preserved. I think I may assume here that the bringing of stones by relatives and friends is involved. The Gadaba say that by seating themselves on the *sodor,* the stones which are erected at the Gotr ceremony to the memory of the descendants of the founder of the village, the council members are in some way influenced by these ancestors so that their deliberation will benefit the people. The life power of their forefathers would thus supposedly be bound by these stones and influence those who came after. It seems therefore that they bless the descendants who stand on the newly placed stones, and it is indeed considered more important to bring a couple of stones than anything else to a Gotr. This is certainly no unusual phenomenon; the Koya, the neighboring tribe erect a stone for a certain person before he leaves for the tea plantations in Assam.[11] I think we may assume that this is done so that the traveler's life power will be bound to the village and can return home if he should die.

Perhaps the most difficult thing to explain is why certain people bring buffaloes which are later torn to pieces by the crowd. One thing has already been mentioned, that is, that the buffaloes' entrails are credited with great power and that they increase the fertility of the fields. I would imagine that this has something to do with a sort of general strengthening of the life power or power in general. The buffalo is known to be one of the strongest animals in the area and this is true particularly of the wild buffaloes, which still exist rather near the Gadaba territory. It is therefore possible that the buffaloes are a symbol of power and strength. But that is something which requires a thorough study. It may also be possible that there is some connection between this and the Khond tribes' so-called *meriah* sacrifice. When they were forbidden to tear a human being to pieces, they began using buffaloes.

In a ceremony there is often an intensifying element, and this finds expression in certain aesthetic actions, such as the Gotr songs, drumbeating, dances, and the like. It would also be of interest to try to analyze the dramatic elements in the Gotr feast. That they are not significant here is perhaps because the Gotr in its entirety is enormously dramatic and it is unnecessary to add extra elements. The actual fights and the tearing of the buffaloes are dramatic enough.

We thus see in the Gotr ceremony an example of a "social transformer" and its different elements among the Boro Gadaba. It is not until one begins to understand the Gotr and all that it implies for these people that one can gain any understanding of their life and activity. They produce, carry out magical acts, pray, make sacrifices and work hard in order to get a surplus which they can put aside for the future. Years and years go by while they struggle over bits of earth. At the same time they want to show that they are respectable. There are even faint trends towards *potlatch*, which is, however, hindered because of lack of means. Instead one tries to get at one's neighbor by making him ashamed, by calling out in front of the crowd that his gifts are not sufficient. But a Gadaba is forced to save and to be stingy for the final goal, Gotr. Into this ceremony is pumped whatever is left of his savings after the expense of other ceremonies and gift-giving. The result is the availability of the good life power along with increased prestige. The life power of the ancestors can not be seen, but it influences the harvest and health and it appears again in the production rhythm and closes the circle exactly as in the grounding of an electric circuit. In this way, security is obtained in everyday life. It is through the Gotr that the valuable things are carried on, "Gotr is the highest," say the Gadaba.

In this paper I have preferred to use the term "social transformer," which is a somewhat broader concept than Van Gennep's "scheme." A "social transformer" is an institution which contains elements in a certain standardized order. This institution is a part of the life cycle, thus a *rite de passage*. It has a physical basis, whether it be birth, puberty, marriage, death, or some other of life's elements. The main principles and the meaning of it are to protect against or annihilate the evil and to preserve the good in life.

In order to accomplish this there must be a separation, or seclusion, from everyday life. At the climax of the feast intensifying elements come in, in the form of aesthetic or dramatic means. It may also be necessary to strengthen the good with various magic rites.

In such a "transformer" three different systems are interwoven. As a part of the life cycle the feast carries the individual over from one status to another. An element of prestige is also implied in this process. The life cycle absorbs the accumulation from the production cycle. The production cycle brings in a material result and gives out a religious result. This influences in its turn the good will of the powers, and this again has its effect on the production cycle, there to be again strengthened with more rites for a maximal result.

We have also to determine the relationships between individuals and groups. Here we have the exchange of gifts, friendship, and the like, and the structure forms channels for such transformations which often occur at feasts. But such exchanges form their own cycle, which is bound to the other two. Through this interaction the structure also creates feed-back systems.

Through the dominants in the life and production cycles we obtain the "main leads" for the currents between these cycles, to use the analogy of the electric circuit, and the less dominant elements (as, for instance, hunting in the production cycle, where agriculture is the dominant) can be looked upon as auxiliary "leads."

Of great importance for the individual are the actual principles that the evil shall be "emptied out" and that the good shall be preserved or increased.

It may seem bold after an analysis of a single feast to draw such general conclusions. But they must be taken as they are meant: as ideas suggested for further research in the rites of the life cycle. For my part, I tend to believe that in a community everything does connect, but that it does this in a very definite way, in a sort of system of closed interlocking loops, the different items of which—institutions, rites, actions—are complementary to each other.

NOTES

[1] C. von Fürer-Haimendorf, "Megalithic Ritual among the Gadabas and Bondos of Orissa," *Journal of the Royal Asiatic Society of Bengal,* Vol. 9, 1943.

[2] Sudhibhushan Bhattacharya, *Ollari, A Dravidian Speech* (Department of Anthropology, Government of India. Memoir No. 3, 1956).

[3] Verrier Elwin, *Bondo Highlander* (Bombay, 1950).

[4] In the village of Alungpada there are 15 *sil birrel* (upright stones) and 31 flat stones. If we assume that they erected a stone for the headman of the family every generation, about 25 years to the generation, this *sodor,* and thus the village also, must be at least 300 years old. There are, however, other villages which have definitely larger *sodor,* and by counting the stones in these one could obtain a chronology of Gadaba villages. In some of the villages the *bo* tree is so old that the stones have been enclosed in the trunks.

[5] *Kereng,* or *kisalop,* is a fiber which comes from the bark of a bush, Calotropis gigantea. It is allowed to decay, and is then pounded and spun into thread.

[6] A. van Gennep, *Les rites de passage* (Paris, 1909).

[7] *Ibid.,* p. 25.

[8] S. Linné, "Darien in the Past," *Göteborgs Kungl. Vetenskaps- och Vitterhets-samhälles handlingar,* Femte följden, Ser. A, Band 1, No. 3 (Göteborg, 1929), pp. 227 ff.

[9] J. G. Frazer, *The Scapegoat,* Part VI of *The Golden Bough* (London, 1913).

[10] I have not found evidence of any definite concept of an individual soul among the Gadaba, but rather a belief that each person has within him a certain

"life power" (*birrel*). Apparently the stone binds the life power. I have developed this point in "Fastening the Soul," *Göteborgs Högskolas årsskrift*, 47:14 (1941).

[11] C. von Fürer-Haimendorf, "Megalithic Ritual," p. 173. It is probable that the stone "fastens" the life power of the person in question so that it comes back to the village in case the person should die.

REFLECTIONS ON
THE ONTOLOGY OF RICE

By Jane Richardson Hanks

IN A SMALL, rice-growing community of central Thailand,[1] when a supply of the new rice for the family's meals is first withdrawn from the bin, the mother selects an auspicious moment, then lights the candles and incense of her offering. Every step in the growth of the grain—plowing, planting, transplanting, and harvesting—has been accompanied by rituals shared or monopolized by women. Ordinarily a woman boils the milk-white grains over a wood fire in the kitchen and brings them in the big pot to the eating-space of the house for the elders, the men, and the children. The individual plates are buried under great mounds of rice. Each person dips with his fingers or a spoon into the heap before him, after mixing a portion of it with a few bits of spiced fish or vegetables from one of the little dishes in the center. The cook tends to the needs of others before she serves herself. At the end of the meal, each person may make a little gesture of thanks before leaving.[2]

Rice itself is considered drearily tasteless, and the hot and spicy fish and vegetables are only to add flavor to help one consume as large a quantity of rice as possible. In privation rice may have to be eaten alone, but "famine" in this abundant land consists in going without rice, even when fish and vegetables abound. What makes these people gorge themselves on this admittedly vapid food? We also ask about the woman's role. Women all over the world cook and serve others before themselves. But, when ordinarily field work and rites in agricultural societies are delegated to men, why do women in Thailand assume such an important role?

Let us consider what a person is. A human body is but the perishable harbor of a *khwan*,[3] that indestructible soul-stuff which is born, eon after eon, as man, animal, insect, or other, until at last, by reaching *Nibbhan* ('Nirvana'), it is freed from the cycle of rebirth. Just as a man must be fed and cared for by a woman throughout life, so must this separable entity that is the (or his) *khwan*. *Khwan* are delicate and flighty; many are the ceremonies to restore them. At rites of passage, or on return from a long, debilitating ordeal like military service, a candidate is given a large ceremony (*tham khwan*) to strengthen his *khwan*. Delicious food is offered, on which the *khwan* is known to linger and feed. The candidate also eats bits of this food for the benefit of his *khwan* as well as his body.

Between earthly existences, the tiny *khwan* lives in a tree under the care of a female spirit, *Maeae* ('Mother') *Syy*. Like a "fairy godmother" she continues her protection for a short time after the *khwan's* birth, until it is well incorporated in its human frame. Food is meager in the tree, for the only sources are the occasional offerings by people "to the ancestors," as at a water libation ritual (*truad nam*), at a wedding, or a funeral. Since there is more food during a human existence, the *khwan* is eager to be reborn. A woman alone can implement its reincarnation. She has no obligation to do this, for every *khwan* is an independent entity, unrelated to all others, responsible for its own fate. Yet in mercy alone a human mother begins a role of lifelong care by receiving the *khwan* into her womb at conception. To raise it she subjects herself to tedious food taboos and endures the pain of childbirth. After birth, she nurses with her milk "which is her own blood, purified to a pure white color." Thus, though the *khwan* of her child is not related to her, its body is part of her body. Some women have this female capacity to nourish to an unusually large degree. Their character (*nitsaj*) and ample milk supply enable them easily to bear and raise child after child. They are known for and as *liang dii* ('feed [another] well').

Thus the *khwan* is sustained by, and its incarnation grows from, the physical nourishment of a woman's body. What is to sustain it after a woman's milk gives out? Rice, because rice, too, is nourishment from a maternal figure. "Every grain is part of the body of Mother Rice (*Maeae Posop*) and contains a bit of her *khwan*." When weaning is to rice, there is no break in female nurture for body and *khwan*. Actually there is a cluster of female deities "concerned with our bodies," including *Maeae Thorani* ('earth'), *Maeae Nam* ('water'), and the Mother of the Fish. Mother Rice is the most important of these to the rice farmer, yet he is indebted to all of them to produce the sustaining grain.

A cardinal tenet of Thai life is that for every gift there must be a return, and so the nurture of a mother must also be reciprocated. A human mother is accorded lifelong obedience and respect, and, in her old age, food and care. Similarly one must reciprocate the care of the Rice Mother with gifts of food and feminine luxuries, and a place in the farmer's house during the hot, dry season. Women alone conduct these rituals because the men are said to be too easily captivated by the Mother's beauty, and might elope with her.

The idea that to nourish is to give life has been socially translated to a general feeling that a gift of food is especially acceptable, important, and appropriate. On a multitude of occasions foods are prepared, arranged with care, and offered to others. Most of the activity on any occasion of ceremony revolves around food preparation and serving. There is tremendous satisfaction not only in giving a feast, but in serving one's family the daily meals. A reputation for generosity with well-cooked foods is an integral part of leadership. Buddhist precepts have reinforced the importance of food giving. A major source of merit[4] is to give the priests their daily meals as well as to feed others, especially the poor. Offered food may not be refused lest one sinfully deny to the donor the opportunity of acquiring merit.

What are the interrelations of merit and rice? If a person has a store of merit he is successful in all his undertakings. For a woman, there is no merit in merely having a child, but she knows she has merit if she has an easy time in childbirth. A fine crop of rice is viewed by the farmer as indirect evidence of his merit. Merit allows a *khwan* to enter a rich instead of a poor family and a person to be skillful, wise, and lucky in life. If he is wisely attentive to the Rice Mother, she is pleased and gives him a large crop which is a means to acquire more merit. The less wise, less courteous get a smaller crop. But frequently Mother Rice manifests her mercy by giving a good crop to persons of apparently less merit, such as the poor and the wicked. In this sense, the mercy of the Rice Mother may mitigate the inexorability of the moral law that governs an individual's approach towards *Nibbhan*.

What, then, is the ontology of rice in Thailand? As each person partakes of rice, he demonstrates that he (or at least someone) has reciprocated his obligations in the past, and by eating it contracts new obligations to reciprocate. Rice nourishes his soul, which is eternally dependent on feminine mercy.

NOTES

[1] This data comes from Bang Chan, a community in central Thailand now under study by the Thailand Research Project of Cornell University, to which I am indebted for the opportunity of field research.

[2] The gesture, a *waj*, was not observed at meal-time in Bang Chan. It is reported by Pràja Anuman Rachadhon in southern Thailand.

[3] To be sure, the complete person is recognized to have other aspects than body and *khwan*, e.g. *winjaan, cetaphud, phii*, but these aspects need not concern us here.

[4] Merit, acquired by good works and beliefs, raises an individual successively nearer to his goal of *Nibbhan*. A *khwan* also desires rebirth so as to increase its store of merit.

THE PRIMITIVE PRESENCE IN
PRE-CLASSICAL GREECE

By Thalia Phillies Howe

SINCE the pioneer work of Durkheim, Freud, and Jung, it has been recognized that the myths of a given people reflect its social history, its experiences both actual and imaginary. It is as though all the elements which are part of the original substance of a myth hover in suspension within the cultural atmosphere of a society; out of this atmosphere, from time to time, bits are extracted, isolated, and given verbal or bodily (ritual) expression or both. Eminent ethnologists such as Paul Radin and Bronislaw Malinowski have observed such processes among myth-makers of modern times.[1]

Now it is entirely possible that some Greek myths also had similar origins, as the work of superior poetic intellects who extracted a core of ideas, a mythic theme that was introduced initially as a simple spontaneous narrative before a single narrow audience. The further development of such a myth would then have become the work not only of the originator but also of a succession of poets reworking and enlarging the original theme to a more complex scheme and proportions. In an age of incipient art, where there do not as yet exist literary forms of specific structure, such as the drama or novel, and where individual authors' rights are transferable, a given theme may be left intact by the purists among the bards and thus transmitted unretouched; but, more likely it is taken up by restless, gifted spirits who transform it as their genius compels.[2]

As the materials for myth are selected and detached from the social atmosphere and are crystallized about a theme, protagonists are chosen to carry the theme who are usually not derived from historical figures but are, instead, generalized social prototypes. Normally these protagonists are given names which are integral to the core of the myth and which, by their descriptiveness, frequently indicate something of its subsequent development. For example, the name of Perseus is derived from the root which means "to cut," and Perseus can thus be designated as the "Cutter," an apt designation for the Gorgon's decapitator.[3]

But the analyst of myth, in addition to a thorough knowledge of linguistic techniques,[4] must also have a thorough and sympathetic grounding in the workings of literature, say that of a writer as extraordinarily sensitive to words as James Joyce, who writes inside out, deliberately, to show how the creative genius links and ties, loops and weaves his words and ideas together. It is precisely this Joycean interlacing and manipulation of the names that cluster about the Jason and Medeia myth that makes one realize, contrary to frequent assumptions, how important is the role of the individual creative mind in the formation of such a myth. While its form may be looser than that of epic for instance, in myth, too, one may find evidence of the proper selection, organization, and integration of imaginative and social materials, the work of genius.

As first observed in Hesiod's *Theogony* the Jason and Medeia myth reveals the mythopoeic process in embryo. On first analysis it is observable that the name of Iason, as the Greeks called that hero, suggests the simple reversal of the first syllable of his father's name, *Ai*son. Then, starting from line 956 in the *Theogony,* we hear how *Ai*etes (note again the phonetic reversal of *Ia*son) was born and how *Ai*etes begat *Mēd*eia. Then, after a few lines, the goddess, *Dem*eter (note here the phonetic reversal of *Med*eia) is coupled with a certain *Ia*sion, after which the poem reverts to the myth again and tells us how the son of *Ai*son led away from *Ai*etes the daughter of *Ai*etes, and how the son of *Ai*son, Iason by name, had as his son *Mēd*eios who was also trained by Cheiron like his father.[5]

Now if *Ai*etes, *Ai*son, and *Ia*son as father-in-law, father, and son had been actual people this similarity of names could only have been a coincidence.[6] But they were not actual people. In each case the myth-maker had free choice of names, and plainly he chose not to range very far. He stayed within the simplest kind of phonetic scheme, the sound *Ia* and its reversal *Ai*.

In a scholion under fragments from Hesiod's *Catalogue of Women,* this phonetic pattern recurs. It begins: "and of *Ai*son and Poly*mēd*e, according to Hesiod, *Ia*son was born," and it continues, "whom Cheiron brought up in woody Pelion." This scholion, reporting what is the oldest tradition, gave a name that contains *mēd,* for its root, as the name of Jason's mother.[7]

The consistency of this scheme becomes more than phonetic, however, when we realize that the two sounds also separate according to the male and female genders—all the *Ia* and *Ai* sounds pertain to the males, and, with the apparent exception of *Mēd*eios, the son, the females revolve about the sound *med*. Now in addition to consistent phonetic patterns and separation of these according to gender, let us see whether these roots form consistent patterns of meaning as well. What do the names of these figures mean and how do their actions relate to these meanings?

When, at the end of the *Iliad* ancient Priam is fumbling his way into the Greek camp, to his great relief he meets Hermes disguised as a messenger. In blessing the messenger, Priam calls him *aisios,* 'auspicious,' 'sent by the gods as a good omen.'[8] Plainly it is this same root that forms part of such Homeric terminology as *aisymneter,* 'ruler, prince,' and *aisymnatas,* 'judge.' *Ai*son, then, suggests a personage who obtains his authority by his extraordinary skill in omens, by which he brings about judicious and fortunate decisions.[9] He is beyond the ordinary, he is "in the know."

Aietes himself, the father-in-law of Iason, is no less fortunately placed in the social terminology than Aison, for as Odysseus says: "we came to the island *Ai*a, where dwelt fair-tressed Kirke, a dread, divine enchantress, own sister to *Ai*etes of baneful mind."[10] Aietes, then, was brother to the greatest sorceress of antiquity, who dwelt in the "auspicious," "*omened* places," "*Ai*a," and was called by Homer "Aiaian Kirke." Aietes himself was *olophronos,* 'baleful,' a worker of "deadly evils," a concept we associate with sorcerers and the supernatural powers of the shaman. And, indeed, did not Aietes possess the brazen-hoofed, fire-breathing bulls by which he hoped to get rid of Iason and deprive him of the Fleece? Who could obtain and control such magical beasts except a wizard, or the wizard's daughter?

Aison > Aietes > Aia > Kirke—we begin to move in a world early- or even pre-Greek as these names grade backward in time from respectable and judicious augury to deadly sorcery. How deep into this territory, foreign or simply primeval, does Iason penetrate? At the least he was intended to set foot in it or else he would not have been chosen as the son and son-in-law of two such cultural figures of specific connotation.

His own name, Iason, probably derives from the verb *iasomai* which, both in its roots and its earliest Homeric usage, means 'to heal.' His name also appears under the word *iatrike*, 'medicine,' in ancient lexicons. And then there is the reference to his teacher, Cheiron, who taught the art of healing to Asklepios, the father of medicine himself.[11] Now Cheiron's methods of healing represented, as Jaeger describes them, "the forces of magic and spells which still passed for medicine in the old-fashioned Greek world of Pindar," where the old centaur cured "with soothing potions" and "kindly incantations."[12]

Thus there was always a suggestion of healing clinging to Iason's name. Observe also that the *iatroi*, the 'healers,' who bound up the wounds of Odysseus, like Cheiron "checked the black blood with a spell."[13] These *iatroi* are further described as "peerless" and "wise above many men," "the worth of many men," that is, as superior to others in the community by reason of their knowledge.[14]

Homer, however, also implies that his heroes, even while lending their ears to the Olympian gods who will help them institute a "well-ordered and meaningful world,"[15] at the same time continue to employ their lips and hands in the old ways:

Who, pray, of himself ever seeks out and bids a stranger from abroad, unless it be one of those that are masters of some public craft, a prophet, or a healer of ills, or a builder, aye, or a divine minstrel, who gives delight with his song. For these men are hidden all over the boundless earth.[16]

Now these men, professionals, bards, and builders alike, all combine their special technical knowledge with oral techniques. But one normally may not stop to realize that oral ritual probably also played an important part in preclassical times in the construction of large and complex public works, the building of a penteconter for instance. Homer, the poet, does not describe the building of the ships that assembled at Aulis. Malinowski, the technical observer, records the complex ritual with which the Trobrianders surround the constructing of their large and handsome canoes. These are great open boats that, like the Greek, held crews of up to sixty and more persons and crossed the open seas.[17] In the making of such craft, ritual is indispensable because the charm and incantation employed in it "builds in" the assurance that even the most mechanical skill cannot. Roes, in her work on Dipylon ships, points to certain wheel-shaped decorations on their prows which she interprets—how else?— as magical symbols to insure good fortune.[18] Though he began to pay more and more attention to Olympian powers, Geometric Greek man, for a while at least, no more neglected his former dependence on magic than he did any other kind of technical knowledge. For in the early period magic was still conceived of as an extension of practical knowledge, actually closer to science than to religion. How closely these old animistic and magical beliefs were kept functioning along with the advancing Olympian faith is best shown in the building of the Argo, Iason's ship. Because this magnificent ship was intended, like the Trobrianders' ships, for a venture both unusual and precarious, special care was taken to include in its construction a "divine" beam from the speaking oaks of Dodona. More than once on its voyage for the Fleece, the beam spoke up and saved the floundering crew of heroes and demi-gods. And who fitted this animistic beam of Dodona to the Argo?—the Olympian Athena herself.[19]

Iason, we shall find, is far more deeply enmeshed in this world of sorcery than his actions or his name would lead us to believe. There is an arresting statement in the Fourth Pythian Ode of Pindar in which the hero introduces himself to Pelias by stating that it was Cheiron, who, in addressing him, was *accustomed* to calling him by the name of Iason. An ancient footnote explains this odd circumlocution by stating that Iason was also known by the name of "Diomēdes," a fact corroborated by inscriptions on two vase paintings that were done within the same decade as the *Fourth* Pythian Ode (ca. 460 B.C.), and on which Iason appears and is labelled "Diomedes."[20] Thus we have for this myth the striking unification of names for the protagonists—Iason-Dio*medes-Med*eia.

Who then is Medeia really? If Iason be the hero as male, Medeia is his female aspect, with Diomedes as their intermediary link, while their son *Med*eios similarly shares their name.[21] But *Med*eia later bore yet another son, and his name was *Mēdos*. Him she bore after she broke with *Ia*son and had found a suitable substitute for *Ia*son in the king of Athens, named *Ai*geus.

We still have to consider the meaning of the name Medeia, to observe whether it has any bearing on the name Iason and whether she is truly his feminine counterpart. Her name it seems, stems from *mēdomai*, the meaning of which comes closest to the Old English word 'bethink,' which has not only cognitive connotations, but also sensory and emotional ones.[22] Then we note that this root *mēd* combines with descriptive prefixes to form the names of certain females who are all distinguished for their knowledge of drugs. In addition to *Mēde*ia there are Aga*mēde*, Heka*mēde*, and Peri*mēde*. In the Homeric epic these women mix magic potions by which men's spirits and lives are revived.[23]

Thus, it seems that early Greek culture recognized two kinds of dispensers of healing: females whose names were distinguished by the use of the stem *mēd* and who brewed drugs for internal use; men, *iatroi,* whose title stems from the same name as Iason's and who healed with external applications and sometimes with incantations. Among the *iatroi* named by Homer is Achilles, who was trained in medical skills by Cheiron, that same teacher of Iason, Medeios, and Asklepios.[24] Also, let us not forget the important Homeric fact that this hero was closely associated with other extraordinary supernatural powers, namely his horse which, like the oaks of Dodona, was gifted with human speech. To describe this animistic beast, Homer uses the same epithet that he does for Kirke, *audēëssa,* literally 'en-*chant*-ress.'[25] Moreover, it should be noted that there is a scholion to the effect that both the early lyric poets Ibycus and Simonides regarded Achilles as a "divinity of healing whom Medeia finally wedded in the underworld."[26]

This is a strange union, and, especially when viewed in isolation, might easily be dismissed as a later fanciful invention. But it is not so strange, really, when placed in its proper cultural context, for most of these figures are closely related by blood or intermarriage, and certainly by their magical capacities; where they are not conjoined by family they are united as a peer group by reason of their knowledge and their superiority to others, as Homer describes them.

Among the various other *iatroi* with supernatural powers of healing were Autolykos and his two sons, while his daughter Polymede was the wife of Aison.[27] There were also the sons of Asklepios, Podaleiros and Machaon.[28] Cheiron has given special training not only to Asklepios, but also to Medeios and to Iason and Achilles, both of whom eventually married Medeia.[29] Kirke, sister to Aietes, then became aunt to Medeia, and they in turn are related to Agamede through their common ancestor Helios.[30] In fact all these figures, male and female, form a closed in-group corresponding to the kind of relationship that Malinowski studied in the living situation:

Magic had to be handed over in direct *filiation,* from generation to generation. Hence it remains from earliest times in the hands of specialists, and the first profession of mankind is that of wizard or witch.[31]

Perhaps it was for this reason that even in the Classical Period there remained in Greece a class of physicians known as Asklepiads, described by Cohn-Haft as "some sort of guild oganization of the profession along family lines." In fact, "normally, medical knowledge descended from father to son as son followed father in the profession."[32] But this condition would hardly distinguish this profession from any other craft in general, except for two other factors which were part of the profession from the beginning: first, the continued high social status of the physician. Although he practiced a *technē*, a craft, the physician was not disdained as other craftsmen were.[33] Secondly, the secrecy normally surrounding this professional knowledge made it a craft apart. One of the solemn provisions of the Hippocratic Oath was that from the moment of admittance the pupil must keep secret this knowledge; from the beginning he was initiated into its mysteries as into a religious rite.[34] Thus, the original social traditions were retained intact even after the original primitive methods of practice had, for the most part, been superseded.

But the shaman was not only altered in time into the honorable physician, but eventually found new professional opportunities, as tribal chieftain or king.[35] This, in fact, was the ultimate fate of Aison, Aietes, and certainly of Aigeus, king of Athens. Also, among the second dynasty kings of Athens was *Mĕd*os, the mythical ancestor of the *Mĕd*ontidae, "whose name," says Hignett in his *History of the Athenian Constitution*, "seems derived from their kingly power." The Medontidae were, as they claimed, of the *genos basilikos,* and as late as the fifth century B.C. they owned land close to the Akropolis, the ancient residence of the Attic kings.[36]

Let us examine Medeia herself, as an individual figure. There is something so excessive and strange about her behavior that many have regarded her as of alien origin. Certainly her love for Iason was most unclassical and incontinent and involved her in all kinds of opportunistic maneuvering on his behalf. For him she murdered her own brother and charmed fire-breathing bulls and the dragon of the Fleece; she repeatedly saved the princely crew of the Argo; and, finally, she butchered old Pelias to regain Iason's lost heritage. Her costume, too, was certainly exotic with its elaborate eastern dress and tiara or Phrygian cap. And she frequently carried her box of magical herbs in her hands. But this extraordinary dress is to be expected, for the sorcerer or shaman in any society is usually distinguished by a bizarre costume.[37] Now in Medeia's case, since the social role of the shaman, which once marked her origins, had long since declined, there remained only the memory that she had once been unusual and different in the community. Such a figure, once familiar and different, gradually became unfamiliar and foreign.

When a people do not as yet have a strong historical, or even a well-developed chronological scale, memories and concepts which involve time not only telescope or expand, but may also suffer other, strange changes. The memory of the sorceress type remained vital and integral to this myth and its culture, while the actual figures and their dominant social role had virtually disappeared from the community. But in the case where there still remains hearsay knowledge of such figures, the primitive mind may argue that such things continue to exist, but not locally—only further off, among foreign peoples. Hence we may say that where chronological accuracy does not yet appear, then not only may events be made to telescope in time, but there may arise a *substitution* of space for time. This must happen throughout the development of myth, legend, and fairytales, and probably in part explains why it is that so many of the protagonists are exotic and the liveliest events seem to be taking place in the present yet in distant realms.[38]

In Medeia's case, however, more than historical or cultural misconception is at work to cause this transposition of time for space; what is at work is a mistrust of her extraordinary powers. There were those of her creators who expressed a perfectly human inclination to put a good physical distance, the edge of the world in fact, between themselves and the very idea of the Medeias of this world. So it is also that Aia, the island of the great sorceress Kirke, is set by Homer at the "risings of the Sun and the dwelling place of Dawn."[39] Hence there came to be a dual tradition in regard to Medeia's origins: for Pindar, for example, she was of Greek birth, a queen of Corinth even; for Euripides, a royal barbarian, a witch of Colchis, whose powers were of a kind that left men uneasy since they were very potent and arbitrarily used.[40] This was particularly true of her powers of rejuvenation, for according to early legend, she was regarded as having rejuvenated Aison and Iason at different times, and she was also entrusted with the rejuvenation of Pelias, though here she deliberately defaulted.[41]

What does rejuvenation mean in these cases? The answer is found in the kind of help Medeia rendered Aigeus as he passed through Corinth on his way to Delphi, a childless man, desperate at his own impotence. By her promise to cure this difficulty she was assured of sanctuary in Athens.[42] Hence the implications of rejuvenation are clear. But how does she come by this power? Medeia, as has been noted, was derived from *mēdomai,* but there is another noun with the same pronunciation as her name, though deriving from a quite different root, namely *medea,* which means 'genital organs.'[43] This verbal pun on her name was an inevitable connection for any myth-maker to make, so characteristically open is myth to verbal and phonetic possibilities. Thus Medeia, by reason of the sound of her name, was endowed with a gift of great, but arbitrary, power.

The ancient shamaness was relegated to the more comfortable distance of Colchis, partly to put at rest the psychological fears of Greek man, and partly because she had become outmoded. Yet she could be thus relegated because her social role had declined in importance, and not only in regard to healing and magic.

To understand this social decline, we need only recall that Medeia and the other women of supernatural powers plied their craft with the use of herbs and drugs taken from field, garden, and grove. Thus Medeia is rendered in paintings with her coffer of herbs, or holding a sprig. Sometimes she extends to Iason a wreath, the symbol of her magical powers which made his victories possible.[44] Thus, too, the women of Greek lands since Cretan times are depicted holding wreaths or dancing amid groves and plants, for the green growing things were their special area of knowledge, and by binding them the women exhibited their control over them.[45] What such females indicate is a familiar level of economy, in which the tending of gardens and a modest planting of a narrow field is commonly the work of women and children, while the men hunt or go off to war. At that point of domestic economy society depends on women, for they particularly possess the knowledge to make gardens grow. Thus their role as food-getters is important, and, by the same token, so is their social role. But as the population increases and agriculture rather than horticulture is predominantly practiced, a shift involving heavier labor in fields at a greater distance from home, the women retire to the care of the house. As their role as food-getter markedly declines, so in due proportion does their social role.[46]

This cultural concept of Medeia as a mistress, though not a divinity, of horticulture suggests that her beginnings extend back through Cretan times to the simple economy of a neolithic people. But it was a concept which still survived in popular memory, not as part of religious belief, but as myth with social-economic content. Medeia represents, not a goddess, but a particular aspect of fertile and gifted womankind. As Bouché-Leclerq has said, and considerably before Jung developed the concept of archetypes, it is not so much the question of whether an individual by the name of *Medeia* ever existed "as the fact that a certain set of attributes belong together, and cohere in a recurrent type."[47] While Iason stems from the archetypal concept of the *iatros,* Medeia *is* the archetype, and as such she antedates the Cretans; she is as old as the first green shoot planted by woman with a coaxing chant, half spell and half lullaby.

Lastly, it is this same fertile confluence of current and recurrent ideas that may well have made the *Theogony* draw Demeter and Iasion into contiguity with the Medeia and Iason myth. For the poet, immediately after the reference to the "neat-ankled Medeia," describes thus the goddess whose name *Dem*-eter suggests the reversal of *Med*-eia:[48] "Demeter, bright goddess, was joined in love with the hero *Ia*sion in a thrice-ploughed fallow in the rich land of Crete, and bare Plutus. . . ." Demeter, of course, is female fertility personified; while Iasion's name means the "Enlivener," the "Freshener," here, of the Earth. It was, then, not merely a fondness for alliteration or verbal play that caused the similarity of sounds in this quartet of names Iasion-Demeter, Iason-Medeia, to appear within these same few lines of the *Theogony.* It was primarily the connotations of fertility inherent in each name. We have, therefore, a group of names, tightly interwoven nuclei of sound and thought, that determine not only the immediate terminology of the myth, but can even temporarily attract other units similarly related in sound and thought but which have no direct connection with the myth.

It is my opinion that this core of names, with their interlocking sound patterns, their divisions into male and female genders, and their correspondence of meanings, all of which were originally culturally determined—that this core may well have been recognized and brought together by a single primitive Greek myth-maker, one with the verbal gifts of a James Joyce. It is certainly possible that such consistency arose within the psychological disposition and reaction of a single mind.

If so, no matter what else eventually accrued to the core of the myth—and a very great deal did—as the work of other minds, there would always have remained this individually and consciously conceived nucleus resting upon a shamanistic core and having male and female counterparts, in which the female prevailed and proceeded either to reinforce or deplete the male as the need might be. This was the center of the myth: Jason and Medeia as representations of two basic archetypal conceptions of a primitive stage. They are earlier materials that have been converted into myth at a turning point of an evolving society.

And that society? I would hazard it was Crete, as it shifted from a late neolithic to a more developed stage of culture, a culture which was in turn to form a basic part of the Greek. This later cultural fusion happened as Pausanias quite simply tells us: when Herakles came from Crete to found the Olympic games, that is, to mark the establishment of the classical Greek world, he brought with him four men: Paionios, Epimedes, Idas and Iasion.[49] Of these, Idas stands for Cretan Ida itself, while Paionios, like Paieon in Homer, was one of the *iatroi*; there was also near Athens the temple of Apollo Paionios and Athena Paionia, divine Healers.[50] Epimedes, too, is merely an eponym of primitive wisdom and medicine. And as for Iasion, it is hoped there is no need to identify him further.

NOTES

[1] P. Radin, *The Trickster* (1956) and *Evolution of an American Indian Prose Epic* (1954); B. Malinowski, *Magic, Science and Religion* (1948), pp. 83-84, 96 ff., *Argonauts of the Western Pacific* (1922), chap. 12, and *Myth in Primitive Psychology* (1926); H. J. Rose, "Myth and Pseudo-Myth," *Folklore* 46:10 (1935).

[2] Radin, *The Trickster*, pp. 122 ff.

[3] "The Origin and Function of the Gorgon-Head," *American Journal of Archaeology* 58:209 ff. (1954).

[4] Gustaf Stern's important study on semantic analysis is particularly recommended: *Swift, Swiftly and Their Synonyms* (1921).

[5] P. Mazon, in his edition of Hesiod's *Theogony* (Budé, 1928), is of the opinion that Hesiod concluded his work on this poem at line 964, and the remainder of the poem, lines 965-1022, is the appended work of an inferior poet. For a fuller discussion see F. Jacoby, *Hesiodi Theogonia* (1930) pp. 30 ff. The material under discussion is derived from both sections of the poem but remains unaffected by the textual problems of the dual authorship.

[6] Particular thanks are due here to the poetic insight of Eric Havelock who first pointed out to me in the course of conversation the striking similarity of

names in this passage, and who subsequently has made most helpful suggestions and corrections.

⁷ Scholion to Pindar, *Nemean Odes* 3.92; T. Gaisford, *Poetae Minores Graeci* (1823) I; Hesiodi fragmenta 32; Evelyn-White, *Hesiod* (Loeb ed.), p. 163 frag. 13. According to Pherekydes her name was Alkimēde.

⁸ *Iliad* 24.376.

⁹ As in *Odyssey* 2.231, 8.258, 22.46, 23.14; *Iliad* 24.347; Pindar, *Nemean Odes* 9.18; Plutarch, *Lives* 2774C.

¹⁰ *Odyssey* 10.135 ff.

¹¹ Liddell and Scott, *Greek-English Lexicon* (1948); É. Boisacq, *Dictionnaire étymologique de la langue grecque*, 4th ed. (1950), s.v. *iasomai; Etym. Magnum.* ed. by Sylburg (1816), s.v. *iatrike*; cf. Pindar, *Pythian Odes* 4.115 ff. On Cheiron, see Pindar, *Nemean Odes* 3.53 ff. There is also Iaso, Goddess of Healing, of the cult circle of Asklepios, see Aristophanes frag. 21K and his *Plutus* 701 and scholion; Pausanias i.34.3; Hermippus frag. 73K. For Jason as healer, see also H. Usener, *Götternamen* (1896), pp. 156 ff.; O. Gruppe, *Griechische Mythologie* (1897-1906), pp. 544-45 and n. 1.

¹² W. Jaeger, *Paideia*, III (1939), 5; Pindar, *Pythian Odes* 3.47-53; W. Jayne, *The Healing Gods of Ancient Civilizations* (1925), p. 283.

¹³ *Odyssey* 19.455 ff. For the word "spell," Homer here uses *epaoide*, literally, 'a song,' 'sung to or over' (Liddell and Scott). Also Sophokles, *Ajax* line 581: ". . . 'tis not a skilfull leech [*iatrou sophou*] / Who mumbles charms [*epoidas*] o'er ills that need the knife" (trans. by F. Storr). This implies of course that by the time of the tragedian the surgeon had superseded the witch-doctor in professional esteem, if not completely in practice, for even in the *Agamemnon* Aeschylos still says (Loeb ed., lines 1020-21) "But man's black blood, once it hath first fallen by murder to earth—who by magic spell [*epaeidon*] shall call it back?" K. Marot, *Acta Antica. Magyar Tud. Academia.* I (1951–52), 277-79.

¹⁴ *Odyssey* 4.231; *Iliad* 4.194, 11.518.

¹⁵ B. Snell, *Discovery of the Mind* (1953), p. 21.

¹⁶ *Odyssey* 17.384.

¹⁷ Malinowski, *Magic, Science and Religion*, pp. 139 ff., and *Argonauts of the Western Pacific*, chaps. 4-6.

¹⁸ G. Kirk, "Ships on Geometric Vases," *Annual of the British School at Athens*, 44:39, fig. 1; pl. 40, fig. 1 (1949). A. Roes, *Greek Geometric Art* (1933), p. 45, sees the wheel-shaped decoration as a sun-symbol. Cf. also C. Hopkins, "Oriental Elements in the Hallstatt Culture," *American Journal of Archaeology*, 61:334 ff. (1957). But there seems no reason why it should not be regarded, instead, as deriving literally from a wheel, as the symbol of a people to whom the chariot was a new and revolutionary invention. Roes also stresses the fact that the objects most closely associated with wheels in Villanovan and Hallstatt art are horses and birds. The horse would demonstrate my point, while the bird was poetic expression of the fact that the chariot now made man as fleet as a bird. We also find birds frequently in relation to chariots and ships, for the same reason, in Geometric Greek vase painting, as in the illustrations above from Kirk. This might also explain the origins of the swastika, so frequently cited by Roes in relation to the wheel, as a four-spoked wheel with sections of the rim removed at intervals.

¹⁹ The beam from Dodona is mentioned in the account of the fifth-century B.C. mythographer, Pherekydes, as preserved in Apollodorus 1.9.16, in *The Library*, ed. by J. Frazer (1921). But there is a celebrated Geometric Greek vase

painting on a bowl from Thebes in which the beam is rendered in place; see *Iournal of the Hellenic Society*, Vol. 19 (1899), pl. 8; R. Hampe, *Frühe griechische Sagenbilder in Boeotien* (1936), pl. 22b; A. Koster, *Das Antike Seewesen* (1923), pl. 19. Kirk, "Ships on Geometric Vases" #40, fig. 4. There were also the supernatural ships of the Phaeacians (*Odyssey* 8.553 ff.) that had neither rudders nor pilots, but knew "the mind and will of man."

[20] Pindar, *Pythian Odes* 4.119. Diodorus Siculus 4.15.3 also has a late glimmering of this notion when he speaks of a Diomedes who had bronze mares (cf. the brazen bulls of Medea's father) who sailed with Jason to bring away the fleece. *Scholia Vetera in Pindari Carmina* II, Pythian Odes 4.211, ed. by Drachmann. Natalis Comes (pseud. of N. Conti), *Mythologiae* (1568), in the 1596 edition gives the name as *Dolomedes*. See E. Braun, *Bulletin des Deutsches archaeologischen Institut*, 10:13 (1838); E. Gerhard, *Auserlesene griechische Vasenbilder* (1840–58) pl. 155; Vol. III, p. 23 and notes 18-21. These two vase paintings also contain an arresting instance of symbolism in classical iconography: the focal point of both scenes, which are virtually identical, is the altar with its sacrifice of a ram's head. This is normally an undesirable portion to offer the gods, but the curved horn of the beast presumably was used by the artist to suggest the ram of the Golden Fleece. It may also suggest the curved prow of the Argo.

[21] Medeus, as Mazon remarks in his edition of Hesiod's *Theogony*, is otherwise not known in any other connection. But his role does gain significance when he is viewed as the son of this healer and his magic-working wife, and as the pupil of that physician's physician, Cheiron.

[22] Liddell and Scott, *Greek-English Lexicon*, s.v. *medomai*; É. Boisacq, *Dictionnaire étymologique de la langue grecque*, s.v. *medo*. As Snell notes in *Discovery of the Mind* in his chapter on Homer, the physical and mental processes were not regarded as the sharply demarcated functions that they were later. See the *New English Dictionary* (1888), s.v. *bethink*. Something of this also is indicated in the Prologue to Chaucer's *Wife's Tale*, line 772, "He spak moore harm than herte may bithynke." Note also that Medeia's mother's name was *Idyia*, which means 'knowledge,' or 'wisdom.' Hesiod, *Theogony* 958 ff. See Liddell and Scott, *Greek-English Lexicon*, s.v. *oida*, 'to see with the mind's eye,' 'to know.' Very closely related etymologically is the verb *mĕdomai*, 'be mindful for, contrive,' etc. (Boisacq, p. 619). In poetic connotation *mēdomai* and *mĕdomai* are indistinguishable and are used so in the context of this paper.

[23] Usener, *Götternamen*, p. 163, was the first to note this connection between medicine and Greek and Roman names containing the root *mēd*. He concluded they referred to a goddess of medicine, perhaps Agamede (*Iliad* 11.740), "who knew all drugs (*pharmaka*) that the wide earth nourisheth," or Perimede (Theocritus, *Pharmaceutria* 2.15.16). Propertius 2.4.8, ed. by Paganelli (Budé, 1921). The scholiast on Theocritus (ed. by Deubner, 1849) remarks that Perimede is the same as Agamede. J. Bacon, *The Voyage of the Argonauts* (1925), p. 132. Another goddess of medicine is Hekamede (*Iliad* 11.624–41), who mixes for Nestor a *kykeon*, from *kykao*, 'to mix thoroughly,' also 'to be mixed up, or disturbed.' Kirke's drugged drink was also a *kykeon* (*Odyssey* 10.316). Polydamna may be included among these, as the phonetic reversal of *med*. (*Odyssey* 4.219 ff.). She was a "woman of Egypt" and one "who had taught Helen how to brew drugs." Her name is derived from *poly*, 'much' and *damazo*, "to tame, master, conquer: I. of animals, . . . III. the powers of nature" (Liddell and Scott). From the several uses of this verb as they occur in the *Iliad* and *Odyssey*, one also derives the notion that it meant mastery over the physical nature of man.

²⁴ *Iliad* 11.832.

²⁵ *Iliad* 19.407. The *Iliad* states that it was the goddess Hera who had given the beast this power of speech. But the Olympian etiology is unnecessary, for one could extract this line and lose nothing of the original meaning thereby. Horses, like the oaks of Dodona and other natural objects and creatures talked to pre-Greek man long before the Olympian hierarchy was conceived.

²⁶ J. Edmonds, *Lyra Graeca*, II, 105, Ibycus frag. 42 = Bergk III, Ibycus frag. 37. Simonides, Bergk frag. 213. Scholion to Apollodorus Rhodius 4.815, ed. by C. Wendel, p. 293.

²⁷ *Odyssey* 19.455 ff. Apollodorus, *The Library*, ed. by J. Frazer (Loeb ed., 1921), 1.9.16. Apollonius Rhodius in *The Argonautica*, ed. Seaton (Loeb ed., 1912) 1.233, calls her Alkimede, instead of Polymede.

²⁸ *Iliad* 2.732; 4.194.

²⁹ *Lyra Graeca* (*supra* n. 26) on the marriage of Medeia and Achilles.

³⁰ Bacon, *The Voyage of the Argonauts*, p. 131.

³¹ Malinowski, *Magic, Science and Religion*, p. 88.

³² L. Cohn-Haft, *The Public Physicians of Ancient Greece*, (Smith College Studies in History No. 42, 1956). Jaeger, *Paideia*, III, 9 ff. Both Jaeger and Cohn-Haft are of the opinion commonly held by classical scholarship that even in the Homeric period the *iatros* was quite divorced from magic and spells. In contrast, others, such as Singer in his essay "Medicine" in Livingston's *Legacy of Greece* (Oxford, 1923) and Jayne in *The Healing Gods of Ancient Civilizations*, are of the opinion that there is ample evidence that the Greeks inherited, in common with other peoples of Europe and Asia, a whole system of magical pharmacy from remoter ancestry. The trained eye of the physician, anthropologist, and scientist recognizes and evaluates data which the best of philologists and scholars may underestimate or disregard.

³³ Cohn-Haft, *Public Physicians of Ancient Greece*, p. 14 ff., 19.

³⁴ *Ibid.*, p. 16, n. 27; W. H. S. Jones, *Hippocrates*, III (1923), 291-97; Jaeger, *Paideia*, III, 11.

³⁵ Frazer stresses this point throughout the early part of *The Golden Bough*. See also J. Maddox, *Medicine Man* (1923) I, 143.

³⁶ C. Hignett, *History of the Athenian Constitution* (1952), pp. 38 ff.; Pausanias 4.5.10; U. Wilamowitz-Moellendorf, "Die Lebenslaenglichen Archonten Athens," *Hermes* 33:119 ff. (1898). See also Liddell and Scott, s.v. *mēdomai*.

³⁷ *Annali dell' Institut* (1848) Plate G; H. Heydemann, "Jason in Kolchis," *Hallisches Winckelmannsprogramm* No. 11 (1886), figs. 1-3; Maddox, *Medicine Man*, p. 95; G. Thomson, *The Prehistoric Aegean* 2d ed. (1954), p. 336.

³⁸ As R. Lattimore has said in reference to this idea in his *Aeschylus Oresteia* (1953), p. 4 n. 3: "So Shakespeare drew on history and legend for his tragedies and romances, or, when these dealt with time not specifically antique, the place would be idealized by distance and the vagueness of his audience's information: Italy, Bohemia, Illyria, Arden." The myth-maker always depends so on the "vagueness of his audience's information."

³⁹ *Odyssey* 12.3.

⁴⁰ On Medeia as Corinthian in origin, the earliest known source is Eumelos of Corinth of the early eighth century B.C., as quoted in a scholion to Pindar, Odes 13.74 (ed. by Drachmann, I, 373). See also Pausanius 2.3.10; L. Farnell, *Cults of the Greek States* (1896–1909), I, 202 ff.; Preller-Robert, *Griechische Heldensage* (1920), II 1, 185 ff.

⁴¹ The earliest reference to this is from the *Nostoi*, as quoted in the scholion

to Euripides *Kn.* 1321 (ed. by F. Deubner, 1877), "She made good Aison lusty as a youth / Wiping old age away by wise devices / With simple seethings in a pot of gold." Bacon, *The Voyage of the Argonauts*, pp. 129 ff. One is also reminded of Shakespeare's *Merchant of Venice*, V.i.14: "Medea gathered the enchanted herbs which did renew old Aeson." Another instance of that poet's "less Greek"! See also L. Séchan, *Revue des études grecques* (1927), 40:235 n. 3, and his *Études sur la tragédie grecque* (1926), p. 408, n. 2; p. 467, n. 3.

[42] Euripides *Medea*, l. 669 ff.

[43] Boisacq, *Dictionnaire étymologique de la langue grecque*, s.v. *madan*.

[44] The Theban bowl: see references given in note 19.

[45] For illustrations of Medeia see Cohn-Haft, *The Public Physicians of Ancient Greece*, p. 14 ff., 19. For Cretan examples, see A. Evans, *Palace of Minos* (1921-36), II, figs. 194, a, d, e, 483, 559; III, figs. 39, 91, pl. 18.

[46] A. S. Diamond, *Evolution of Law and Order* (1951), pp. 90 ff., 128, 178. V. G. Childe, *Man Makes Himself* (1955), p. 71. It is worth noting in this connection that even on the celebrated scene of Harvesters on the black steatite vase from Hagia Triadha three female choristers are included in the group of male threshers who march to work singing. These women are directly behind the priest, who leads them with his sistrum in hand (Evans, *Palace of Minos*, Vol. II, fig. 22, p. 47).

[47] A. Bouché-Leclerq, *Divination* (1879-82), II, 95 ff.

[48] Hesiod, *Theogony* 969 ff.

[49] Pausanias 5.7.6; Usener, *Götternamen*, pp. 152 ff.; *Odyssey* 4.231; Thomson, *The Prehistoric Aegean*, p. 292. Charles Picard, *Revue des études grecques*, 40:336 ff. (1927).

[50] Pausanias 1.34.3. J. Frazer, *Pausanias' Description of Greece* (1898), 2, p. 474, describes the temple as having one altar divided into parts, one of which was sacred to Apollo Healer and others to Aphrodite, Panacea, Iaso, Hygeia, and Athena Healer. Note Frazer's commentary on the origins of this epithet, *Paion*: "Prof. A. Bastian, like Macrobius [1.17.15 ff.] explains the word to mean 'the Striker' (from *paio*), and supposes it to refer to a primitive method of cure, which consists in beating the sick person in order to drive out the devil by whom he is supposed to be possessed (*Die Völker der östlichen Asien*, IV, 11). But this explanation of the epithet is at best extremely doubtful." There seems less reason to doubt this interpretation now, in view of the other evidence. It would seem, however, that it was not the sick person who was beaten, but rather that the witch-doctor or shaman struck his hands or feet in rhythmic beat and sang his incantation. This musical beating of time might well explain the meaning of the word *paean*, as chant or song of victory and possibly part war-dance as well. See in this connection M. Nilsson, *Griechische Festschrift* (1906), pp. 99 ff. Also K. Marot, *Acta Antica. Magyar Tud. Akademia* I (1951–52), 279. Further, Apollo's connections with Paionios might well have suggested the Olympian's dual role of God of Healing and of Music, because the two functions were, originally, inseparable. *Paeion*, the name as it appears in Homer (*Odyssey* 4.231 ff.) and Solon (frag. 13.43) etc., does not refer to an individual, but is a generic term for the divine skill of healing.

PLATO AND THE DEFINITION OF THE PRIMITIVE

By Stanley Diamond

IN THIS LITTLE PAPER, conceived, I trust, in Paul Radin's free and challenging spirit, I propose to place certain aspects of Plato's *Republic* in anthropological, and critical, perspective. The origin and nature of the state is a subject peculiarly appropriate to cultural anthropology, for states first arise through the transformation and obliteration of typically primitive institutions. Thinkers of the most diverse backgrounds and intentions have, throughout history, grasped this cardinal fact of state formation. Lao-tzu, Rousseau, Marx and Engels, Maine, Morgan, Maitland, Tonnies, and many contemporary students of society have understood that there is a qualitative distinction between the structure of primitive life and civilization. Moreover, they have, more or less explicitly, sensed the contradictions inherent in the transition from kinship, or primitive, to civilized, or political, society. This momentous transition, this great transformation in the life of man, this social and cultural trauma, if you will, has led to a passionate, and ancient, debate about the merits of primitive existence as opposed to civilization, to the state. Indeed, the debate has frequently been waged in utopian terms; some utopias face backward to a sometimes fantastic image of the primitive, others face forward to the complete triumph of the rational state. Although I have no intention of engaging in this debate, it seems to me that it is the opposition to the primitive which lies at the root of Plato's utopia,[1] and that is the theme I intend to pursue here. In opposing the primitive, Plato helps us define both it and the state.

I

The *Republic* can be considered a projection of the idealized, total city-state, conjured out of the ruins of fourth-century Athens, and

---

The author's recent field work among the Anaguta of the Nigerian Middle Belt supports many of the more intricate details of the argument set forth here, but, for obvious reasons, amplification of the article would have been inappropriate.

influenced by the Spartan oligarchy. But, in its perfection, it transcends these local boundaries and becomes a classic model of the state to which Western scholars have turned for centuries in debating the good life and its relation to political society. This tension between the local and the universal is evident in all utopian constructs, whether merely literary, or socially realized; it is preeminently true of the *Republic*. Plato maintains certain landmarks of the city-state, but he takes us as he says, on a "journey of a thousand years." This span of time is reckoned, perhaps, too modestly, for all subsequent political societies commanded by a permanent, self-proclaimed, benevolent élite, and all élitist social theory, are adumbrated in the *Republic*.

The *Republic,* of course, is more than a political tract. It is also a psychology, an aesthetics, and a philosophy, but it is all these things within a political context. There is hardly any facet of Plato's vision, however abstruse, nor any action he believed imperative which is not colored or dictated by political considerations. The *Republic* is, in short, a work of enormous scope, but it is saturated with politics, with ideology. This point deserves emphasis because Plato has traditionally been considered the very image of the pure philosopher, and the *Republic* has been extolled as the masterwork, in which most of his major ideas appear, impressively interwoven. As Emerson put it, "Plato is philosophy and philosophy Plato. . . ." The New England Platonist goes further, ceding to Plato Omar's "fanatical compliment" to the Koran: "Burn the libraries, for their value is in this book." [2] The phrase sticks, it is an appropriately Platonic sentiment, and it is a political remark.

What then are the political assumptions underlying the *Republic*? To begin with, Plato's personal political bias is clear. He was an aristocrat, who experienced the decay of the Athenian "democracy." He was a philosopher in a society that put Socrates to death. He avoided the rough-and-tumble of politics and shrank from any actual political role for which his birth and training may have qualified him. Yet he seems to have been obsessed with the idea of politics; the political problem for Plato seems to have consisted in how to abolish politics.

It is possible, therefore, to view the *Republic* as the idealization and rationalization of Plato's personal motives. His ideal state is, after all, a utopian aristocracy, ruled by philosophers who have become kings, and the political problem has ceased to exist. But this is too close an exercise in the sociology of knowledge. Plato's personal motives are unquestionably important; they help fix the precise form of the republic, but they do not determine its broader cultural-historical meaning. In Cornford's words,

> The city-state was a frame within which any type of constitution could subsist; a despotism, an oligarchy, or a democracy. Any Greek citizen of Plato's day, rich or poor, would have been completely puzzled, if he had been told that he had no interest in maintaining the structure of the city-state. The democrat, in particular, would have replied: "Do you really think that an oriental despotism, where all men but one are slaves, is a higher and happier type of society? Or would you reduce us to the level of those savages with all their queer customs described by Herodotus?" [3]

Plato's oligarchic inclinations, then, cannot be considered contradictory to the basic structure of the city-state; the exact form of his republic is less significant than its over-all statism. Returning to the theme set above, the political assumptions underlying the *Republic* are simply the assumptions of political society, of the state, writ large and idealized. We must remember that classical Greece could look back to its own archaic and primitive past; moreover, it lived on the fringe of a "barbarian" Europe. Thus, the forms and usages of primitive society, even when these were being transformed into organs of the state or abolished in favor of state institutions, were by no means strange to the Greeks, as Fustel de Coulanges, Engels, Morgan, Bury, and others, in varying contexts, have emphasized. Bury, for example, in tracing the early history of Greece, speaks of the authority of the state growing and asserting itself against the comparative independence of the family, and he remarks further that "in the heroic age . . . the state had not emerged fully from the society. No laws were enacted and maintained by the state." [4]

It seems likely, then, that Plato had ample opportunity to react against concrete primitive elements in Greek society and cultural tradition while envisioning his utopian state. Only the classical scholars, with the aid of a more fully developed classical anthropology, can establish the degree to which this was possible, but it is not essential to my argument. Plato could have been acting out of sheer political instinct, logically constructing the perfect political society, and rejecting those institutions and modes of behavior which could not be coordinated with it, that is, the primitive modes. In any case, the fact of opposition to the primitive is clear in the *Republic,* as is Plato's sure sense of the strategy of political society. And this, I believe, is the larger cultural-historical meaning of his work, conceived, as it was, in the morning of European civilization.

II

Although the themes that will concern us in the *Republic* are very subtly interwoven, and sometimes lack precise definition, I shall consider them separately, without trying to reconstruct Plato's full argument.

There is, first of all, the suggestion that Socrates makes about the initiation of the republic:

They will begin by sending out into the country all the inhabitants of the city who are more than ten years old, and will take possession of their children, who will be unaffected by the habits of their parents; these they will train in their own habits and laws, I mean in the laws which we have given them: and in this way the State and constitution of which we were speaking will soonest and most easily attain happiness, and the nation which has such a constitution will gain most.[5]

The republic is to begin, then, by severing the bonds between the generations, and by obliterating the primary kinship ties. This is, of course, an extreme statement of the general process through which states arise, that is, by releasing the individual from kinship controls and obligations and thus making him subject to the emerging civil laws. There is, however, a remarkably exact parallel to Socrates' suggestion in native Dahomean usage, as reported by Norris, one of the early chroniclers of the Slave Coast. In the Dahomean proto-state, "children are taken from their mothers at an early age, and distributed to places remote from their village of nativity, where they remain with little chance of being ever seen, or at least recognized, by their parents afterwards. The motive for this is that there may be no family connections or combinations, no associations that might prove injurious to the King's unlimited power."[6]

But we must never forget that Plato has no intention of outlining the process of state formation per se; he is, in our view, idealizing that process, hence the purpose of setting up the republic in the manner described is seen as beneficent.

I might add, parenthetically, that the attempt to weaken or sever the ties between the generations is also a typical utopian and quasi-revolutionary aim. The most recent instance is the Israeli Kibbutz, wherein the collective rearing of children is motivated by the desire to produce a generation quite different in character from the parental image of the Shtetl Jew.[7] As a matter of fact, wherever a massive shift in political power and structure is contemplated, or wherever a radical rearrangement of public loyalties is demanded, the family, the psychic transmission belt between the generations, tends to be attacked not merely in terms of any particular form, but as a primary social unit. This is evident, in rather different ways, in the work of many reformists, in early Marxist literature, and in Nazi theory and practice.

Plato's modest proposal for initiating the republic, then, can be seen in both a "revolutionary" and cultural-historical perspective. The *Republic* begins, appropriately enough, in opposition to the antecedent kin and generational ties. And we shall see below that this imperative is extended to the rearing of the guardians within the republic. That is, state and family, echoing the old antagonism between political and primitive organization, are seen to be antithetical, even after the establishment of the ideal polity.

III

Primitive societies that are not in transition to one or another archaic form of the state, that is, that are not proto-states, may function through rank and status systems, and always function through kin or transfigured kin units, the latter being associations whose members are not necessarily reckoned as kin, but which pattern themselves on kin forms. They are, however, devoid of class or caste. Further, primitive societies do not manifest the highly specialized division of labor which is one of the major determinants in the rise of class and caste systems. In these related respects, Plato's republic represents the reverse of primitive usage, and is the state brought to its highest power. To clarify, let us begin with his vision of an absolute division of labor.

In the republic, no man is to engage in more than a single task. Indeed, the ultimate definition of justice, which Socrates pursues as perhaps the major aim of the entire dialogue, consists in each person doing the work "for which he was by nature fitted," within the class to which he constitutionally belongs. And "at that [occupation] he is to continue working all his life long and at no other." [8] Later on, Socrates elaborates this point as follows: ". . . in our State, and in our State only, we shall find a shoemaker to be a shoemaker, and not a pilot also, and a soldier a soldier, and not a trader also, and the same throughout." He emphasizes: in ". . . our State . . . human nature is not twofold or manifold, for one man plays one part only." [9]

In other words, it is imagined that the identity of the individual is exhausted by the single occupation in which he engages. The occupational status, so to speak, becomes the man, just as his class position is, in a wider sense, said to be determined by his nature. In this way, the existence of the state is guaranteed, but the life of the person is constricted and diminished. I do not evaluate this, for the division of labor is, even under ideal political conditions, an expression of the available technology. The point is that Plato not only sensed the congruence of the elaborate division of labor with state organization, but carried it to its furthest reach, and then gave it the name of justice.

The contrast with primitive usage could hardly be more striking. Primitives learn a variety of skills; a single family unit, as among the Hottentot, Anaguta, or Eskimo, may make its own clothing, tools, and weapons, build its own houses, and so on. Even in a transitional society such as the Dahomean proto-state it is expected that every man, whatever his occupation, know three things well: how to cut a field, how to build a wall, and how to roof a house. [10] Moreover, the average primitive participates *directly* in a wide range of cultural activities, relative to the total available in his society, and he may move, in his lifetime, through a whole series of culturally prescribed statuses. He plays, in short, many parts, and his nature is viewed as manifold. The relevance of this to Plato's conception of the drama will be considered below, but, it is first necessary to examine the class structure of his republic, and its implications.

The republic is to be divided into three classes: the guardians, or ruling élite; the auxiliaries, including, apparently, the soldiers; and the lowest class, consisting of all those engaged in economic production, particularly the artisans and farmers. We see, at once, that the manual laborers are at the base of the social hierarchy, being considered constitutionally unfit to rule themselves. This is, of course, a quite typical attitude, however rationalized, and we find it associated with the rise of civilization almost everywhere. In early states, the intellectual gradually emerges from the class of scribes or priests; his connections with the ruling groups are primary. The artisans and farmers grow out of the submerged primitive community, which is transformed into a reservoir of workers for the state through direct conscription of labor, taxation, slavery, or related means.

But, whatever the details of the process, and they vary in different areas, the subordination of primitive artisan and cultivator is a function of state formation. An Egyptian document dating from the New Kingdom is pertinent, in that it reflects this state of affairs, long consolidated:

Put writing in your heart that you may protect yourself from hard labor of any kind and be a magistrate of high repute. The scribe is released from manual tasks; it is he who commands. . . . Do you not hold the scribe's palette? That is what makes the difference between you and the man who handles an oar.

I have seen the metal worker at his task at the mouth of his furnace with fingers like a crocodile's. He stank worse than fish spawn. Every workman who holds a chisel suffers more than the men who hack the ground; wood is his field and the chisel his mattock. At night when he is free, he toils more than his arms can do; even at night he lights [his lamp to work by]. . . . The stonecutter seeks work in every hard stone; when he has done the great part of his labor his arms are exhausted, he is tired out. . . . The weaver in a workshop is worse off than a woman; [he squats] with his knees to his belly and does not taste [fresh] air. He must give loaves to the porters to see the light.[11]

This process and the attendant attitudes are, I believe, ideally reflected in the *Republic*. They develop in Plato's cave, so to speak, in the turmoil of history, but they are presented to us in a purified, philosophic, and ultimate form.

Now the classes in the ideal state are relatively fixed; they tend to be castes, rationalized on a eugenic basis. But Plato provides for both a modicum of social mobility and the predominant freezing of the entire structure through the medium of a "royal lie," that is, through "propaganda," a term that Cornford considers more appropriate,[12] and a condition which we shall take up later in connection with the exile of the dramatist. Socrates states:

Citizens. . . . God has framed you differently. Some of you have the power of command, and in the composition of these he has mingled gold, wherefore also they have the greatest honor; others he has made of silver, to be auxiliaries; others again to be husbandmen and craftsmen he has composed of brass and iron; and the species will generally be preserved in the children. But . . . a golden parent will sometimes have a silver son, or a silver parent a golden son. And God proclaims as a first principle to the rulers, and above all else, that there is nothing which they should so anxiously guard . . . as the purity of the race . . . if the son of a golden or silver parent has an admixture of brass and iron, then nature orders a transportation of ranks and the eye of the ruler must not be pitiful towards the child because he has to descend in the scale and become a husbandman or artisan, just as there may be sons of artisans who having an admixture of gold or silver in them are raised to honor, and become guardians or auxiliaries. For an oracle says that when a man of brass or iron guards the state, it will be destroyed. Such is the tale; is there any possibility of making our citizens believe in it? [13]

The class structure of the republic is, then, based on a theory of human nature, assimilated to Plato's doctrine of essences.[14] Here we confront a perfect example of the convergence of characteristic Platonic concepts to an immediate political issue, a technique that weaves throughout the dialogue, and accounts, in part, for its great dialectic density. The final nature of the individual is viewed as unambiguous, since human nature is a matter of distinct and single higher and lower essences, subdivided further into occupational essences. That is to say, the division of labor and class in the *Republic* is reflected in the division into essences, or, vice versa, if you will. The important point is that the whole structure is guaranteed by human nature, watched over by the guardians, justified by philosophy, and sanctified by God, as the allegory states.

At the peak of the pyramid stand the guardians. They are said to have a pure intuition of the good; they live in the place of light above the cave and are, in a sense, divine; or, they have, at least, intimations of divinity. Shall we call them divine kings? It matters little, for all kings have been considered holy since the primary differentiation of the king from the local primitive chief. The holiness of the king is the sanctification of civil power, as opposed to the common traditions which are symbolized in the person of the local chief and may thus render *him* sacred. The ultimate other-worldliness of the guardians, or philosopher kings, is, I believe, a reflection of the process through which civil power was first sanctified as the primitive community was transformed into political society. We should recall that Plato was impressed by the Egyptian theocracy and actually visited Egypt, where the concept of divine rule was as old as the state itself. In any event, the élite tradition of the guardians is the opposite of the communal tradition of primitive peoples.

Yet neither the divinity of the kings, who shape the end of the republic, nor the sterling quality of their auxiliaries is sufficient to ensure their devotion to the state. This can be achieved most readily through a completely collective life and training. Socrates says: ". . . the wives of our guardians are to be common, and their children are to be common, and no parent is to know his own child, nor any child his parent." [15] The children are to be reared collectively by special nurses who "dwell in a separate quarter." The mothers will nurse them but "the greatest possible care" will be taken that no mother recognizes her own child, nor will suckling be "protracted too long." The mother will "have no getting up at night or other trouble, but will hand over all this sort of thing to the nurses and attendants." [16]

Further, the guardians and their helpers, under a regime of spartan simplicity, are to live in common houses, dine in common, and hold no property; and they are not to engage in economically productive work. The obvious aim is to disengage them from all connections and motives which might diminish their dedication to the state. As noted above, Plato clearly sensed the antagonism between state and family, and in order to guarantee total loyalty to the former, he simply abolished the latter. Moreover, his distrust of kin ties in the ideal state leads him to invoke the aid of a "royal lie," possibly the first half of the propaganda-myth quoted above. Socrates, simulating embarrassment, says:

. . . I really know not how to look you in the face, or in what words to utter the audacious fiction, which I propose to communicate gradually, first to the rulers, then to the soldiers, and lastly to the people. They are to be told that their youth was a dream, and the education and training they received from us, an appearance only; in reality during all that time they were being formed and fed in the womb of the earth, where they themselves and their arms and appurtenances were manufactured; when they were completed, the earth, their mother, sent them up; and so their country being their mother and also their nurse, they are bound to advise for her good, and to defend her against attacks, and her citizens they are to regard as children of the earth and their brothers. [17]

This is, of course, a direct statement of the conflict between kin and political principles. The territorial state is to receive the loyalty previously accorded the kin group, and this can only be done by personifying the state, an essentially impersonal structure. Plato remarks that the fiction is an old Phoenician tale of "what has often occurred before now in other places." [18] Certainly, the myth is precisely of the type we would expect in societies in transition from kin to civil structure, that is, in societies engaged in a primary kin-civil conflict.

There is a peculiar parallel with Dahomean usage here, not in the form of myth, but in actual social convention. In Dahomey, every important official in the emerging state structure had a female counterpart within the king's compound. This woman, termed his "mother," had precedence at "court," acting as a sort of buffer between the official and the king and personalizing the purely material relationship involved.[19] The bureaucrats were mustered from the local villages, the conquered and subordinate areas; they had no kin ties with the royal clan or dynastic lineage. The system of "civil mothers" thus symbolized the new connections that had begun to develop in distinction to the old kin loyalties. The idea of the motherland, or fatherland, then, although expressed in kin terms, seems coincident with the rise of the state, at the point where the *problem* of political loyalty begins. This, I believe, is the meaning of Plato's fiction, concretely revealed in Dahomean usage.

It should be noted that Plato apparently confines the fiction of the "earth-born heroes" to the guardians and auxiliaries. The ordinary people, composed of brass and iron, are to live under ordinary family circumstances. No extraordinary behavior of any kind is expected of them, certainly no unusual loyalty to the state. Their worldly concerns, their emotional ties, and their inferior natures are conceived as making such behavior impossible. The soldiers guard the city, the guardians rule it; acquiescence and temperance, a living up to their own limited possibilities, are the demands made on the mass of people. That, and the labor which supports the upper classes. The economic producers are, of course, deprived of political means; in the ideal state this was visualized as the solution to the political problem. Yet Plato seems uncertain. He speaks of the soldiers selecting a spot "whence they can best suppress insurrection, if any prove refractory within," [20] and also of their maintaining "peace among our citizens at home . . . [that they may not] have the power to harm us." [21]

One further point is worth consideration. The selectively bred, but family-less, upper classes are to refer to all peers as brothers and sisters and to the members of the older generation as father and mother, seemingly congruent with extended family or clan usage. However, the upper classes represent what can be technically termed a collective, not a community, that is, the relational forms are retained, but the substance is lacking.[22] What we confront here is a rather interesting politicization of kin terminology, as in the case of the Dahomean "civil mothers," in direct opposition to primitive behavior. The latter is always based on concrete and complex family relationships which may then be extended outward to include remote relatives, strangers, or even natural phenomena. But, as we have seen, the mothers of the upper classes are not to know their own children.[23] They are to be relieved of all domestic and maternal responsibility, and thus converted into ideal instruments of the state, fully equal, in this respect, to the men.

The above, then, is a rough outline of class structure and function in the *Republic*. In general, and in the particulars considered, it is the antithesis of what Kroeber, for one, has called "primitive democracy."[24]

IV

There is, I believe, a keystone in the soaring arch of Plato's argument, an imperative on which it must inevitably rest. In this imperative, the statism of the republic culminates, as does its opposition to the primitive.

The dramatists, the makers of tragedy and comedy, the "imitative poets," as Plato calls them, are to be exiled, and their works are to be abolished or heavily censored. Socrates says:

When any one of these pantomimic gentlemen, who are so clever that they can imitate anything, comes to us, and makes a proposal to exhibit himself and his poetry, we will fall down and worship him as a sweet and holy and wonderful being; but we must also inform him that in our State such as he are not permitted to exist; the law will not allow them.[25]

Plato has already given us a reason for this, quoted above in connection with the division of labor: ". . . [in] our State human nature is not twofold or manifold, for one man plays one part only." The "pantomimic gentlemen," Homer or Aeschylus, for example, have no place in the class and occupational structure of the republic, assimilated, as it is, to the doctrine of essences or ultimate forms. Socrates makes this clear to Adeimantus: ". . . human nature appears to have been coined into yet smaller pieces, and to be as incapable of imitating many things well, as of performing well the actions of which the imitations are copies." [26]

But before pursuing Plato's theory of art, which emerges so logically out of the dialogue, let us examine some of the simpler reasons for establishing a "censorship of the writers of fiction" [27] and the implications thereof.

The poets are perceived as impious, and corrupters of youth. They misrepresent the nature of God, which is absolutely good, by spinning tales of rage and ribaldry in heaven. If at all possible, children in the ideal state should be told that conflict is unholy, and has never existed among the gods or between citizens. The wicked must always be represented as miserable, "because they require to be punished, and are benefitted by receiving punishment from God," but God must never, in verse or prose, be considered the author of evil, for such a fiction would be suicidal in "any well-ordered commonwealth." The poets, such as Euripides, must not be permitted to say that suffering is the work of God, or if it is of God, they "must devise some explanation . . . such as we are seeking." The task of the poet, then, is to justify the ways of God to man, to buttress morality in the republic. And the ultimate impiety is to speak, with Homer, of "Zeus, who is the dispenser of good *and* evil to us." [28]

Moreover, the poets are inappropriately emotional. They portray death and the underworld in lurid terms; they lament the fallen warrior, and rail against fortune, whereas, in the republic, "the good man . . . will not sorrow for his departed friend [or son, or brother], as though he had suffered anything terrible, [since he] is sufficient for himself . . . and therefore is least in need of other men." [29] What is worse, the poets portray famous men, heroes, even the gods themselves, in undignified postures of grief or frenzy. Nor can Homeric laughter, whether indulged in by men or gods, be tolerated; in men it leads to "violent reaction[s]," and it is a falsification of the nature of God. Hence, such verses from the *Iliad* as "inextinguishable laughter arose among the blessed gods, when they saw Hephaestus bustling about the mansion," must be excised.[30]

Finally, the heresy of the poets is expressed in the conception of

God as a magician, "and of a nature to appear insidiously now in one shape, and now in another—sometimes himself changing and passing into many forms, sometimes deceiving us with the semblance of such 'transformations.'"[31] For, "the gods are not magicians who transform themselves, neither do they deceive mankind in any way."[32]

Thus far, then, there are three related reasons for Plato's antagonism to the poets. First, they ascribe a dual nature to the gods, that is, the gods are the authors of good *and* evil. Second, they portray the gods as extravagantly emotional, sometimes obscenely so, as in the case of Zeus, who, at the sight of Hera, "forgot . . . all [his plans] in a moment through his lust."[33] Third, they present the gods in a variety of shapes and deceptive appearances.

I submit that Plato's objections converge to a direct antagonism against the transformer, or trickster, image of the gods, projected by the poets, but, in fact, "one of the oldest expressions of mankind," as Paul Radin has conclusively shown.[34] The Trickster is an authentically primitive figure, appearing in his sharpest form among primitive peoples, a bestial, human, and divine being, knowing "neither good nor evil, yet . . . responsible for both." Trickster "is at the mercy of his passions and appetites," is devoid of values, "yet through his actions all values come into being." At the same time, all figures associated with Trickster, for example the "various supernatural beings" and man, possess his traits. Thus, Plato says the poets must not be permitted to "persuade our youth that the Gods are the authors of evil, and that heroes are no better than men"; for "everybody will begin to excuse his own vice when he is convinced that similar wickednesses are always being perpetrated by 'The kindred of the Gods, the relatives of Zeus.'" He gives as an example "the tale of Theseus, son of Poseidon, or of Peirithous, son of Zeus, [who went forth] to perpetrate a horrid rape."[35]

In his never ending search for himself, Trickster changes shape, and experiments with a thousand identities. He has enormous power, is enormously stupid, is "creator and destroyer, giver and negator." Trickster is the personification of human ambiguity. He is the archetype of the comic spirit, the burlesque of the problem of identity, the ancestor of the clown, the fool of the ages.

Inevitably, Trickster must be banished from the republic, wherein identity is a matter of pure, ideal, unambiguous forms, and where men are to be totally and strategically socialized. The poets who have created or inherited Trickster's image of the world are, it follows, to be silenced. Once again, Plato's opposition to the primitive is clear, if not necessarily conscious.

It would be possible to claim that Plato's negative image of the poets themselves is that of the trickster, for has he not called them "pantomimic gentlemen" and "imitators"? And may we not add that Plato sensed and distrusted the old connection between art and magic? This is a sensible, if superficial, interpretation; to deepen it we must explore Plato's theory of art and its implications.

Plato regarded the art of the tragic and comic dramatists, along with that of the painters, as essentially imitative, as dealing with appearances only. The painter, for example, paints a bed, but this image is "thrice removed" from the truth. The ideal form or essence of the bed is created by God; this is the eternal bed which the philosopher kings can intuit; it is the bed in truth and goodness, of one nature, essentially inimitable and complete. At a second remove from the truth is the tangible bed created by the artisan, the particular bed, which is a "semblance of existence," [36] but not existence entire as manifested in God's bed. But the bed of the painter is sheer imitation, being neither useful nor ideal. In no sense can it be considered a *creation*. Further, all artists, save those who echo the needs of the state by composing "hymns to the Gods and praises of famous men," [37] are deceivers who, in effect, presume to create but cannot.[38] The painter, for example, does not know how to make a bed nor does he know anything of the work of the cobbler or carpenter whom he may represent. Socrates states: ". . . the imitator has no knowledge worth mentioning of what he imitates. Imitation is only a kind of play or sport, and the tragic poets, whether they write in Iambic or Heroic verse, are imitators in the highest degree." [39] Nor can the artist-imitator have any knowledge of good or evil, "and may be expected, therefore, to imitate only what appears good to the ignorant multitude." [40] Plato seems to mean here that the intuition into pure existence aided by the study of mathematics, a basic subject for the guardians, is also the apprehension of the good, or at least a prerequisite to it. The artist reproduces appearances only, and these vary; pure essence cannot be reproduced, only intuited. Since the artist has no knowledge of the good, he can have no knowledge of evil, nor does he possess any understanding of the useful for he is once removed from the particulars that he copies, hence thrice removed from the truth.[41]

Now, whether or not we accept the terms in which it is couched, this is an argument of extraordinary power and beauty. Plato expressed completely what many who have subsequently shared his attitudes have only dimly perceived; the artist is dangerous, as life is dangerous; he sees too much, because that is all he desires to do, and he presumes to create, to erect man into the role of the creator. But his vision is incomplete, he cannot penetrate to the objective order of the universe, the handiwork of God. And to men of Plato's temperament that objective order, the pure anatomy of reason, is as essential as breathing. Yet if the artist would accept the eternal order, and thus learn humility; if he could convert his art into a public strategy in behalf of an abstract idea of the good, the state would find a place for him. Let the protagonists of Homer, and of poetry in general, prove their worth and they will be returned from exile. Moreover, there is a passionate tie between the artist and the "ignorant multitude," the artist deals, not with intellectual, but with felt and ordered emotional ideas. Emotions ebb and flow, they are an unstable medium in which to work, the artist himself may be unstable, and this is a threat to any establishment. Thus Plato is entirely consistent. He was, it seems, a man of a certain type, incapable of tolerating ambiguity, positive in his conviction of an objective, superhuman good. He believed in God with the cool passion of a mathematician, and he believed, at least abstractly, that the perfectly just city could be established, through perfectly rational and perfectly autocratic means. He began as a poet, and so he must have understood in his own being the old argument between poetry and philosophy to which he occasionally refers. In evicting the dramatist, Plato reveals himself, the nature of the republic, and the functions of art; his motives, of course, are above suspicion.

The poets, then, are to be exiled from the ideal state. There is simply no room for them; they are the first superfluous men. The philosopher kings intuit the universal, ultimate forms, God creates them, and the multitude lives among, and constructs, their particular manifestations. Hence, the class structure of the republic reflects, or is reflected in, the doctrine of forms or essences. It descends from the superior, that is, from the abstract, created by God and grasped by the guardians, to the inferior, that is, to the particular, grasped by the craftsmen, and ordinary citizens, who live in a world of ordinary, useful, sensuous things. Here we encounter platonism enthroned, a political hierarchy perfectly mated to a conceptual one. The "fleshly" Homer, who also presumes to create, is a threat to this structure, and cannot be tolerated.

The class division between the universal and particular, between the institutionalized intellectuals and the economic men reflects, as noted above, a condition that develops with ancient civilization as opposed to the primitive. This is not to say that temperamental distinctions do not exist among primitives, for they do, as Radin has brilliantly shown in his analysis of the thinker and man of action.[42] The point is that among primitives such distinctions complement each other, the concrete and the abstract interpenetrate, "thinker" and "man of action" are tied together; sometimes, as Radin points out, they meet in the same individual, and, in any case, such differences are not politicized. Just as soon as the latter occurs, in early states or as idealized in the *Republic,* there is both an impoverishment and a denial of the sources of human creativity. Further, in early states in the real world, the differential worth often ascribed to people in the various occupations within the broader classes is a political rationalization, generated from the top down. For, not only did accidents of birth and training determine social fate, but the *point of view* from which evaluations were made was that of the scribes, the priests, the nobility. In the *Republic,* in the ideal world, Plato's division of labor and conceptual capacity is said to be genetically determined, the social accident is nullified, yet the division remains artificial because it isolates the abstract from the concrete, the intellectual from the emotional, and considers the craftsman and the farmer useful but inferior beings, not from the perspective of the priest or noble, but from that of Plato's philosophy.

I submit, further, that the Platonic definition of the abstract has become so entrenched in Western thought that the frequently encountered attitude toward primitives, that they are incapable of or deficient in this capacity, is a manifestation of it. Conversely, the attempt to prove that primitives are capable of abstracting too often centers on the types of abstraction emerging out of the history of Western culture, which would seem quite irrelevant. While it is true that no primitive group is made up of Platonists in the technical sense of that term, for primitives tend to live, as Radin has put it, "in a blaze of reality," and the various politico-conceptual divisions generic to the state have not yet been established, this does not mean that they do not think abstractly. In the basic sense, every linguistic system is a system of abstractions; each sorting out of experience and conclusion from it is an abstract endeavor; every tool is a symbol of abstract thinking; indeed, all cultural convention, all custom, is testimony to the generic human capacity for abstracting. But such abstractions are indissolubly wedded to the concrete; they are nourished by the concrete, and they are, I believe, ultimately, induced, not deduced. They are not, in short, specifically Platonic abstractions, and they do not have the politicized psychological connotations of the latter.

V

Plato's opposition to the drama and dramatist is directly associated with the class and ideational structure of the *Republic*. At its root, this is also an opposition to the primitive, not merely with reference to the trickster, or the old tie between artist and magician, but, more comprehensively, in connection with the form and meaning of the primitive ritual drama.

In the ritual drama, art and life converge, life itself is seen as a drama, roles are symbolically acted out, dangers confronted and overcome, anxieties faced and resolved. Relations among the individual, society, and nature are defined, renewed, and reinterpreted. There is no theater containing these performances, ancestral to the civilized drama; the world is a stage and, at one time or another, all the people are players.

I am, of course, defining the primitive ritual drama in the broadest possible way, that is, as comprising those ceremonies which cluster around life crises or discontinuities, either of the individual or of the group at large. Generally speaking, the latter are concerned with crises arising from the group's relation to the natural environment, while the former are concerned with personal crises, that is, with the individual's relation to himself and the group. In all ritual dramas, however, despite the relative emphasis on the group or the individual, there is an apparent continuity from the individual's setting in the group to the group's setting in nature. Moreover, the problems of identity and survival are always the dominant themes, and it is for this reason that we can, I believe, term these primitive ceremonials, dramas.

To clarify, let us consider those ceremonials which devolve upon personal crises, such as death, marriage, puberty, or illness. These can be considered "existential" situations; that is, people die, marry, sicken, become sexually mature and economically responsible in all societies. In primitive societies, such ordinary human events are rendered extraordinary, that is, they are made meaningful and valuable, through the medium of the dramatic ceremonies. Here we confront man raising himself above the level of the merely biological, affirming his identity, and defining his obligations to himself and to the group. The ritual drama, then, focuses on ordinary human events and makes them, in a sense, sacramental.

At the same time, the ceremonials we are speaking of enable the individual to maintain integrity of self while changing life roles. The person is freed to act in new ways without crippling anxiety, or becoming a social automaton. That is, the person discharges the new status but the status does not become the person. This, I believe, is the central psychological meaning of the theme of death and rebirth, of constant psychic renewal, which is encountered so frequently in primitive ceremonials. It is an organic theme; what one is emerges out of what one was. There is no mechanical separation, only an organic transition, extending, characteristically, over a considerable time, often crowded with events, and never traumatic, but modulated and realistic in its effects.[43]

Hence, the ceremonies of personal crisis are prototypically dramatic in two related ways. They affirm the human struggle for values within a social setting, while confirming individual identity in the face of ordinary "existential" situations such as death or puberty. These ceremonial dramas, then, constitute a shaping, and an acting out of the raw materials of life. All primitives have their brilliant moments on this stage, each becomes the focus of attention by the mere fact of his humanity; and in the light of the ordinary-extraordinary events, his kinship to others is clarified. Moreover, these ritual dramas, based on the typical crisis situations, seem to represent the culmination of all primitive art forms; they are, perhaps, the primary form of art, around which cluster most of the aesthetic artifacts of primitive society —the masks, poems, songs, myths, above all the dance, that quintessential rhythm of life and culture.

Ritual dramas are not automatic expressions of the folk spirit. They were created, just as were the poems, dances, and songs that heighten their impact, by individuals moving in a certain cultural sequence, formed by that tradition and forming it. Whether we call these individuals "poet-thinkers," "medicine men," or "shamans," terms used by Paul Radin,[44] seems unimportant. Plainly, they were individuals who reacted with unusual sensitivity to the stresses of the life cycle and were faced, in extreme cases, with the alternative of breaking down or creating meaning out of apparent chaos. Let us call them primitive dramatists. The meanings they created, the conflicts they symbolized, and sometimes resolved in their own "pantomimic" performances, were felt by the majority of so-called ordinary individuals. There was, of course, magic here too; but, more deeply, there was a perception of human nature that tied the group together. The primitive dramatist served as the "lightning rod" for the commonly experienced anxieties, which, in concert with his peers and buttressed by tradition, the primitive individual was able to resolve. This is not to say that the primitive dramatist simply invented meanings promiscuously. It was always done within a given socio-economic and natural setting. But he shaped dramatic forms through which the participants were able to clarify their own conflicts and more readily establish their own identities.

There was an organic tie, then, between the primitive dramatist and the people at large, the tie of creation and response, which is, in itself, a type of creation. The difference was that the dramatist lived under relatively continuous stress, most people only periodically so. Thus the dramatist was in constant danger of breakdown, of ceasing to function, or functioning fantastically, in ways that were too private to elicit a popular response. In this prototypical primitive situation, we can, I think, sense the connection that binds the psychotic to the "shaman" whom we have called a dramatist and the dramatist to the people at large. The distinctions are a matter of degree. The very presence of the shaman-dramatist is a continuous reminder that life often balances on the knife edge between chaos and meaning, and that meaning is created or apprehended by man coming, as it were, naked into the world.

VI

The Greek drama is the direct heir of the primitive ritual drama, as

Cornford, Murray, and Harrison have helped establish. Indeed it retains various technical ritual elements: the chorus, the conscience of the play, was a vestige of group participation; the plays of Sophocles were watched with an air of "ritual expectancy," [45] Aristophanes was performed at the Dionysiac festivals, and the themes of Greek drama had the style of ritual.

Thus we can begin to apprehend why Plato found it necessary to exile the dramatist, as the very prototype of the artist, from the republic. The dramatist is tied to the "ignorant multitude," he presumes to create meanings and reveal conflicts, he senses in his own being the ambiguity of man, and he is concerned with the ordinary-extraordinary things, with values as a problem and the common human struggle for personal identity. Such men are dangerous precisely because they view life as problematical in the best of states; they clarify what others feel. Hence, they must either be confined to composing "hymns to the Gods and praises of famous men," or exiled.

We must remember that in the republic the problem of identity is presumably solved in terms of a political interpretation of higher and lower human natures. Such an institutionalized human identity is entirely contrary to the dramatist's perceptions; it is equally foreign to the mind of primitive man. The dramatist, as a dramatist, cannot believe in such stark and ultimate separations between men or within the individual man. When Shakespeare writes his tragedies of kings, he plays out their conflicts against a specific socio-economic background, but in the end he tells all of us about ourselves, and the "multitude" in the pit responds. And was not Shakespeare, in a sense, all the characters he constructed, what Plato would call a gross "imitator"?

Nor can the dramatist deny the sensuous, earthy things, since his plots are based on the "existential" situations: marriage, death, the coming to maturity, sickness of mind and body, the recurring issues in the inner relations among men, the very themes that served as the occasions for the primitive drama of personal crisis. Let me put it as plainly as I can. In the end, the dramatist must either become an antagonist to Plato's perfectionist God, or he must cease being a dramatist. Within his own lights, the philosopher was right.

VII

If the dramatist is a tragedian, then he is grimly concerned with the problem of identity, self-definition, integrity; for tragedy is no more than the dissolution of personal identity and social value through behavior to which the hero is compelled, and of which he is, sooner or later, aware. And by that awareness, he transcends, in one final blinding moment, as did Oedipus at Colonus, himself. *The civilized tragic drama is, then, a free elaboration on the theme of identity, celebrated in the primitive ritual.*

If the dramatist is a comedian, then he burlesques the problem of identity, he laughs it out of court, he stands aside and lets men make fools of themselves; men, he tells us, with Aristophanes, are everything but what they presume to be. *The civilized comic drama, then, is based on the trickster's primitive image of the world, on identity, as it were, turned inside out.* It is a celebration of the failure of identity.

Among primitives, the most serious rituals, those ancestral to the modern tragedy, and the ancient comic spirit of the trickster are often mingled. In Wintun, Pueblo, and Kind ceremonials, for example, "in nearly every instance it is the very thing which is regarded with greatest reverence or respect which is ridiculed," as Steward states.[46] The Dionysiac tradition of the satyr (or trickster) play following the tragic trilogy echoes this primitive usage.

It should be clear, then, that on every major count Plato's exile of comedy and tragedy was inevitable; for the dramatist, in his elemental—or, better, primitive—nature, would have worked havoc with the structure of the ideal state, and its ideology of identities.

But if one exiles or diminishes the artist, who, then, helps discover and dramatize the people to themselves; and if the people are considered incapable of attaining to real understanding, a view obviously not held here but essential to the *Republic,* how, then, are value and meaning to be transmitted to them? Plato answers this question, although he does not ask it. The royal or noble lie, the manufactured or applied myth filtering down from above, that is, official propaganda, is to provide the popular *raison d'être* of the republic. The youth are to be told, in morality tales, that they live in the best of all possible worlds. We have already quoted the fictions which justify the class structure. These "lies," these political, as opposed to primitive, myths are the means for fixing personal and social identity for the majority of people in the ideal state, in the absence of the artist, both as a specialized figure and as an inherent aspect of the personality of every man.

But if the philosopher kings can lie in the name of the public good, and in the interests of a higher truth accessible only to them, the common people cannot. Socrates says: "It seems that our rulers will have to administer a great quantity of falsehood and deceit for the benefit of the ruled." [47] And further, "for a private man to lie to them in return is to be deemed a more heinous fault than for the patient or the pupil of a gymnasium not to speak the truth about his own bodily illnesses to the physician or to the trainer, or for a sailor not to tell the captain what is happening about the ship and the rest of the crew." [48]

VIII

Plato was a sober, shrewd, sometimes witty, but hardly comic, idealist; he constructed his heavenly city, brick by brick, with great care and impeccable intentions. When he has finished—and what a craftsman he was—we confront a shining, impervious structure, a luminous monolith, a society with no problems, no conflicts, no tensions, individual or collective. As the *Republic* approaches its end of perfect justice and harmony, it becomes perfectly inhuman. It is so abstractly and ruthlessly wise, so canny and complete an exercise in statecraft, that were we to disregard Plato's temperament, we should have to consider him one of the most skilled totalitarian thinkers in history, the first state utopian, as opposed to the primitive utopians. His historic fault, that speaks to us across millennia, is not merely in his anthropology, it is certainly not his intoxication with God, abstract though that was, but rather that he, who so fastidiously shunned politics, should have insisted upon the politicization of his faith. Even Cornford, an eloquent defender of Plato,[49] sees him finally as president of the Nocturnal Council, an inquisitor. His prisoner, of course, is Socrates.

NOTES

[1] Although Plato makes a passing reference to a kind of idyllic rusticity which some of his interpreters have called "primitive" life, it bears no resemblance to the latter at all and serves merely as a foil for his developing rationale of the state. See *The Republic of Plato,* trans. by B. Jowett (Oxford, Clarendon Press, 1925), p. 53.

[2] Ralph Waldo Emerson, *Representative Men: Seven Lectures* (Boston and New York, Houghton, Mifflin and Company, 1903), pp. 39-40.

[3] F. M. Cornford, *The Unwritten Philosophy and Other Essays* (Cambridge, The University Press, 1950), p. 129.

[4] J. B. Bury, *A History of Greece to the Death of Alexander the Great* (London, Macmillan, 3d ed., 1956), p. 56.

[5] *The Dialogues of Plato,* trans. by B. Jowett (New York, Bigelow, Brown, 1914). Vol. II, *The Republic,* p. 303. All citations, unless otherwise indicated, are to this edition.

[6] Although the details of the chronicler's observations are, in all likelihood, distorted, his conclusion is sound. Stanley Diamond, *Dahomey: A Proto-State in West Africa* (Ph.D. Dissertation, Columbia University, 1951), p. 26. Microfilm. This is a study of a society in transition from kin to civil structure and involved in a kin-civil conflict that ramifies throughout the culture.

[7] Stanley Diamond, "Kibbutz and Shtetl: The History of an Idea," *Social Problems,* V (Fall, 1957), 71-99.

[8] *Republic,* p. 68.

[9] *Ibid.,* p. 102. Compare this with the famous passage from *As You Like It:* "And one man in his time plays many parts." Shakespeare would have been excluded from the republic on the double score of being both a tragedian and a comic dramatist.

[10] Melville J. Herskovits, *Dahomey, An Ancient West African Kingdom,* I (New York, J. J. Augustin, 1938), p. 30.

[11] V. Gordon Childe, *Man Makes Himself* (New York, New American Library, 1955), p. 149.

[12] Cornford, *Unwritten Philosophy,* p. 134.

[13] *Republic,* p. 129.

[14] However, Plato's philosophy could, today, be characterized as both transcendental and essentialist.

[15] *Ibid.,* p. 187.

[16] *Ibid.,* pp. 191-92.

[17] *Ibid.,* p. 129.

[18] *Ibid.,* p. 128.

[19] Diamond, *Dahomey,* p. 91.

[20] *Republic,* p. 130.

[21] *Ibid.,* p. 128.

[22] For a recent, and rich, analysis of the distinction between collective and community, see Erich Kahler, *The Tower and the Abyss* (New York, George Braziller, Inc., 1957).

[23] Plato's educational psychology is what we would probably term "mechanically behavioristic." The attenuation of immediate kin ties among the élite, and the emphasis on morality tales, would tend to diffuse emotional-intellectual growth; the tensions that provide leverage for such growth can hardly be generated by institutions and abstractions. Further, the collective rearing of élite children would probably have defeated itself in the end by not producing enough emotion to secure loyalty. See, for example, the writer's remarks on collective rearing in the Israeli Kibbutz. "Kibbutz and Shtetl," *Social Problems,* V (Fall, 1957), 88-93.

[24] A. L. Kroeber, *Anthropology: Race, Language, Culture, Psychology, Prehistory* (New York, Harcourt, Brace, rev. ed., 1948), p. 281.

[25] *Republic,* p. 102.

[26] *Ibid.,* p. 98.

[27] *Ibid.,* p. 73.

[28] *Ibid.,* pp. 75-78.

[29] *Ibid.,* p. 86.

[30] *Ibid.,* p. 88.

[31] *Ibid.,* p. 78.

[32] *Ibid.,* p. 82.

[33] *Ibid.,* p. 91.

[34] Paul Radin, *The Trickster, A Study in American Indian Mythology,* with commentaries by Karl Kerenyi and C. J. Jung (London, Routledge and Kegan Paul, 1956), p. ix.

[35] *Republic,* p. 93.

[36] *Ibid.,* p. 380.

[37] *Ibid.,* p. 396.

[38] As Joyce Kilmer confessed, "Poems are made by fools like me, but only God can make a tree."

[39] *Republic,* p. 389.

[40] *Ibid.*

[41] For a perfectly antithetical view of the artist, written by a great artist, see Goya's statement in the catalogue to *Los Caprichos:* "Painting, like poetry, selects from the universe the material she can best use for her own ends. She unites and concentrates in one fantastic figure circumstances and characters which nature has distributed among a number of individuals. Thanks to the wise and ingenious combination, the artist deserves the *name of inventor and ceases to be a mere subordinate copyist."* (Italics added.)
The absolute, reciprocal antagonism of the true artist and Platonism could not be more pertinently expressed. But this antagonism, it must be said, on the artist's side, is not necessarily directed against a belief in God or religiosity as such, only against the removal of God from the concretely human, i.e., against the turning of God into an abstraction. All religious art of any stature, and all religious artists worthy of the name, from the Byzantines and Giotto through Michelangelo to Blake and Rouault (confining the example to a fragment of the "Western" tradition), inscribe their vision in the flesh and see God either as an aspect of man's nature or as a perception to which every man is capable of attaining, usually out of his agony. Hence God may be apprehended by the artist as objectively real, yet always in the most ordinary, unexpected, various, but human guises. The institutionalized and abstract God of the church and the philosophers is never the God of the artist, though called by the same name. The human distance between Plato's God and Blake's is infinite.

[42] Paul Radin, *Primitive Man as Philosopher* (New York, Dover, 1957).

[43] I use the term "traumatic" here in the sense of deep, psychic trauma. This is not to deny the pain and suffering often involved in primitive rituals, but the personal and traditional meanings infusing them, the conventional structuring of the situation, strip these experiences of the unwitting, and pathological, ramifications of trauma.

[44] Paul Radin, *Primitive Religion, Its Nature and Origin* (New York, Dover, 1957).

[45] Francis Fergusson, *The Idea of a Theater* (New York, Doubleday, "Anchor Books," n.d.), p. 40.

[46] J. H. Steward, "The Ceremonial Buffoon of the American Indian," in *Papers of the Michigan Academy of Science, Arts, and Letters,* XIV (1930), 187-207.

[47] *The Republic of Plato,* trans. by A. D. Lindsay (New York, E. P. Dutton, "Everyman's Library," 1940), p. 148.

[48] *The Republic,* trans. by Jowett, p. 89.

[49] Cornford, *Unwritten Philosophy,* p. 67.

ANTHROPOLOGICAL PERSPECTIVES ON THE MODERN COMMUNITY

By Maurice Stein

SOCIOLOGICAL THEORIES about community development usually contain historical assumptions as to the character of earlier communities. If the theory aims at encompassing the broadest sweep of human history, the theorist has to include anthropological materials. In the best tradition of social-political theorizing starting perhaps with Hobbes and Rousseau and moving through Marx, Spencer, Comte, Maine, Tönnies, Veblen, Durkheim and Weber, there is a serious effort to come to terms with available ethnographic materials. The classical theorists have been eminently responsible in this connection; for example, Maine's status-based social order, Tönnies' Gemeinschaft, or Durkheim's mechanical solidarity all offer conceptions of primitive social structure which constitute important contributions to the development of both anthropology and sociology.

In this connection, Robert Park's sociological theory of urbanization contains many important leads for anthropologists. While his own work focused on the modern city against the background of the rural community, his analysis of city life recognized the importance of folk cultural elements as a basis for important urban sub-communities and as a source of cultural vitality. Park's essays in *Race and Culture* written throughout his long, active career reflect an enduring concern with the effects of acculturation on the folk culture of American Negroes.

Robert Redfield recently employed Park's distinction between the technical and the moral order in community life as the central structur-

This essay, originally written for this volume, appears in slightly different form in *The Eclipse of Community: An Interpretation of American Studies* (Princeton, 1960), which goes further into the themes presented here to show hoy they clarify important aspects of modern American community life. Stanley Diamond helped me to grasp the significance of the anthropological perspective set forth in this paper, and Paul Radin patiently answered questions about his own work. I want to thank them both for introducing me to a conception of anthropology that differs considerably from those to which I had previously been exposed.

al concept in his synthetic work, *The Primitive World and Its Transformations*. Redfield's later volumes, *The Little Community* and *Peasant Society and Culture*, advance our understanding of this distinction considerably and point the way toward developing concepts for analyzing intermediate types on the folk-urban continuum. The importance of these books for sociological students of communities can hardly be overestimated. They will be discussed later, since their full significance can only be grasped in light of the anthropological tradition to which they are closely related.

There are signs that modern anthropologists are beginning to find more to admire in the folk societies they study than has been fashionable over the past few decades. The recent series of BBC lectures published as *The Institutions of Primitive Society* containing contributions from several leading British social anthropologists reflects this trend. It is by no means a form of primitivism or eulogy of any "noble savages," but rather proceeds with full consciousness of the special virtues of modern civilization. It seems to be a complex reaction on the one hand to the urgency of the immediate difficulties of that civilization, coupled with awareness that these difficulties can be illuminated when studied against the background of primitive societies where they do not appear. Anthropologists now seem increasingly willing to let their research throw light on the crises of our own civilization. They no longer feel that this necessarily entails abandoning scientific objectivity or choosing between primitive and modern ways of life.

Edward Sapir in a classic essay, "Culture, Genuine and Spurious," first published in the early twenties used his familiarity with primitive society as a baseline for commenting on contemporary culture. While there is much that can and has been justly criticized in his effort, it certainly does block out some of the main considerations:

... a genuine culture refuses to consider the individual as a mere cog, as an entity whose sole raison d'être lies in his subservience to a collective purpose that he is not conscious of or that has only a remote relevancy to his interests and strivings. The major activities of the individual must directly satisfy his own creative and emotional impulses, must always be something more than means to an end. The great cultural fallacy of industrialism, as developed up to the present time, is that in harnessing machines to our uses it has not known how to avoid the harnessing of the majority of mankind to its machines. The telephone girl who lends her capacities, during the greater part of the living day, to the manipulation of a technical routine that has an eventually high efficienc value but that answers to no spiritual needs of her own is an appalling sacrifice to civiliza- tion. As a solution of the problem of culture she is a failure—the more dismal the greater her natural endowment. As with the telephone girl, so, it is to be feared, with the great majority of us, slave-stokers to fires that burn for demons we would destroy, were it not that they appear in the guise of our benefactors. The American Indian who solves the economic problem with salmon-spear and rabbit-snare operates on a relatively low level of civilization, but he represents an incomparably higher solution than our telephone girl of the questions that culture has to ask of economics. There is here no question of the immediate utility, of the effective direct- ness, of economic effort, nor of any sentimentalizing regrets as to the passing of the "natural man." The Indian's salmon-spearing is a culturally higher type of activity than that of the telephone girl or mill hand simply because there is normally no sense of spiritual frustration during its prosecu- tion, no feeling of subservience to tyrannous yet largely inchoate demands, because it works in naturally with all the rest of the Indian's activities instead of standing out as a desert patch of merely economic effort in the whole of life.[1]

This quote does not sum up Sapir's whole argument, though it reflects the strengths and weaknesses of his position. His aspiration towards individual fulfillment *through* rather than despite community roles stands as a philosophic contribution of the very civilization which denies its realization. Contemporary existentialist critiques like those of Karl Jaspers and Gabriel Marcel elaborate these same points with similar emphasis on the fragmentation and despiritualization of modern life. Unfortunately, their grasp of the phenomenology of this ex- perience remains as impressionistic as the "sense of spiritual frustration" and "subservience" that Sapir imputes to his telephone girl. Yet all three point to an important problem for the community sociologist requiring historical or anthropological perspective to conceptualize properly.

Running through this essay as well as Sapir's later articles on the interplay between culture and personality, is his profound emphasis on the requirement that any society should provide its members with meaningful life activities through which they can grow and express their full individuality. It is this emphasis that distinguishes him from most recent "objective" students of the relation between culture and personality, and which gives his writing on this subject much greater depth than this later work. Ruth Benedict, ardent exponent of cultural relativism though she may have been, frequently adopted a similar perspective. Her familiar article, "Continuities and Discontinuities in Cultural Conditioning," which is probably as widely known among sociologists as any other single piece of anthropological writing is an important case in point. Here she shows that our society forces sharply contrasting roles over the life cycle progression from child to adult as regards responsibility, authority, and sexuality without providing any significant transition rituals to bridge these discontinuities.

Her main thesis is in itself rather obvious, but it gains its special force from the brilliantly chosen illustrations of contrasting instances among non-literate cultures where these role disparities are either rendered continuous throughout the life cycle or bridged by elaborate rituals. It is hard to forget her description of the Papago grandfather's respectful patience while his three-year old granddaughter closes a heavy door, or the reciprocity expressed in primitive kinship terminology where the same term applies to father and son as our term "cousin" applies to equal participants in a paired relationship. Her comments on comparative sexual training deserve mention:

If the cultural emphasis is upon sexual pleasure the child who is continuously conditioned will be encouraged to experiment freely and pleasurably, as among the Marquesans; if emphasis is upon reproduction, as among the Zuni of New Mexico, childish sex proclivities will not be exploited, for the only important use to which sex is thought to serve in his culture is not yet possible to him. The important contrast with our child training is that although a Zuni child is impressed with the wickedness of premature sex experimentation he does not run the risk as in our culture of associating this wickedness with sex itself rather than with sex at his age. The adult in our culture has often failed to unlearn the wickedness or the dangerousness of sex, a lesson which was impressed upon him strongly in his most formative years.[2]

This commentary on the origins of sexual disturbances throws out a real challenge to conventional psychoanalytic theories dealing with the same problem.

Benedict goes on to observe that some primitive societies do make discontinuous demands, but that resultant strains are experienced collectively through the "solid phalanx of age mates" and supported by graduation into traditionally prestigeful secret societies with elaborate initiation rituals interdicting previous behavior and sanctifying new role expectations. Our own difficulties then appear in new light:

It is clear that if we were to look at our own arrangements as an outsider, we should infer directly from our family institutions and habits of child training that many individuals would not "put off childish things"; we should have to say that our adult activity demands traits that are interdicted in children, and that far from redoubling efforts to help bridge this gap, adults in our culture put all the blame on the child when he fails to manifest spontaneously the new behavior or, overstepping the mark, manifests it with untoward belligerence. It is not surprising that in such a society many individuals fear to use behavior which has up to that time been under a ban and trust instead, though at great psychic cost, to attitudes that have been exercised with approval during their formative years.[3]

So this seemingly simple thesis conceals a double criticism of a culture which both creates immense discontinuities in vital areas of life, and ignores the necessity for providing transition rituals when major strains arise. This double failure leaves the members of such a society eternally tied to their childhood regardless of chronological aging, even as the necessities of adult role-playing entail suppression of these childish "fantasies" lest they interfere with adult tasks. There are two main outcomes of this double failure: Insufficient suppression of fantasy can lead to inability to distinguish it from reality and consequent mental breakdown. Too firm suppression shrivels effective life to the point where spontaneous fantasy or perception becomes impossible. In either event, childish experience and experiential modes are not assimilated and therefore adult life remains significantly impoverished.

Far more comprehensive work has been done on the ways whereby primitive societies guarantee their members a full life. The whole corpus of Paul Radin's work is directed at this problem. His interpretation of primitive social structure and culture as summarized in *The World of Primitive Man* documents in great detail the defenses of individuation embedded in primitive social organization. It is unnecessary to trace his long dispute with the proponents of theories about the insufficiences of "the primitive mind," except to point out that this dispute was part of his larger aim in that it entailed elucidating the exceptional balance between reason and emotions which distinguish the socialized primitive from his civilized brethren. Here his convergence with Jung strengthened both their positions though no one has yet systematically explored the full implications of their common discoveries. Jung uncovered among his patients a twisted need for the same life syntheses that Radin found to be the cherished core of primitive social structure.

There is no point in trying to reproduce Radin's dense picture of this social structure. Doing so is as difficult as paraphrasing a poem and indeed, doing so would entail paraphrasing the many poetic and philosophic expressions with which his work is studded as it points at essentials of primitive life. Who can condense the saga of Trickster without doing serious injustice to it? Jung, Kerenyi, and Radin himself do try in the volume *The Trickster* but the story itself remains, like all works of art, immune to a final paraphrase. It is this literary quality in Radin's work, the acceptance of the finality of poetry and philosophy, that leads him to describe the primitive world-view by quoting examples with only slight analytic adumbrations, and that accounts for both its depth and its elusiveness. He asks us, by exercising our imaginative faculties, to see through the primitive's eyes; and if we are not ready or able to do so, both Radin and the world-view he strives to recapture remain beyond our reach.

But there is more of science in his work than this. He actually does provide an abstract conception of institutional functioning in primitive society which can stand with the best anthropological and sociological theorizing. His interpretation of primitive economics seems far closer to the facts as ethnographers have reported them than many of the interpretations of these same ethnographers. If one accepts his central thesis that primitive economies exist to insure each member of the society an irreducible minimum of adequate food, shelter, and clothing on the ground that ". . . Being alive signifies not only that blood is coursing through a man's body but that he obtains the wherewithal to keep it coursing,"[4] then his interpretations of primitive ownership, exchange, and distribution are indisputable. In this context, the inter-mixed utilitarian and non-utilitarian concerns in primitive economies can be explained in their own terms as products of a fundamental purpose utterly different from that underlying both our economy and our economics. So, his seemingly slight shift in emphasis when interpreting the flow of goods in primitive society clarifies a broad variety of specific manifestations:

In general, the tendency has been to speak of all aspects of primitive economics connected with transfer, barter and purchase, as if their main function was to serve as an outlet for the expression of specific human emotions and as if there was not a rigorous restriction of purely personal activity in such matters.

... What apparently Fortune, Malinowski and Thurnwald seem to have failed properly to understand and stress is that one of the primary roles, if indeed, it is not actually the primary, of a transfer and exchange is to visualize, dramatize and authenticate the existence of certain fixed relations subsisting between specific people and that this relationship has a "monetary" value. The actual reaffirmation of this relationship may take an exceedingly short time and the non-material emoluments flowing from it a very long time. That is, after all, true of every type of exchange and transfer. It is an unjustifiable procedure to relegate the utilitarian aspect of a transfer among primitive peoples to a secondary position because of the richness and the duration of its non-utilitarian accessories, just as unjustifiable as it would be to do the same in our own civilization.[5]

By hewing to his conception of primitive life as balanced between utility and ceremony rather than viewing it as being as lopsided in the direction of the latter as we are towards the former, he is able to comprehend the deeper "utilities" underlying property transfer and illuminate the brilliant ethnography contained in Malinowski's description of the "Kula" without imposing alien categories on it.

It is hard to leave Radin's analysis of primitive economics without reporting his neat conception of the function of "wealth" and "ceremonial property destruction" or to omit the brilliant disentangling and realignment of economics, magic and religion in Chapter Six of *The World of Primitive Man*; but space forbids this. Let it be noted, however, that he takes account of the exploitative manipulation of magic and religion when the fundamental purpose of the primitive economy has been perverted by the emergence of a surplus and a ruling class. Underlying this is a vital distinction between socially creative ceremonial magic which enhances living, and socially destructive magic which renders men subject to unnecessary exploitations.

With this distinction in mind, Radin's treatment of the crises of life and their rituals becomes immensely revealing. He starts by recognizing, as does Benedict, that growth from childhood to adulthood entails a major transition at puberty. But he recognizes that resolution of the strains accompanying this transition is always accomplished in such a fashion as to preserve the vested interests of the older people. This "subjection and domination" is only transformed into exploitation when the benefits are reaped and accumulated by individuals as such, rather than consumed immediately and ceremonially so that the persons enjoying them sanctify the rights of all to their irreducible minimum and to their private life cycle. It is hard to keep attention focused on this vital distinction, and Radin does not always help as much as his own firm capacity to do so indicated that he might have. Perhaps it is so clear to him that he never understood the difficulty others might have with the distinction. One almost has the feeling here that on these matters Radin is so sympathetic with the movement of the primitive mind as to almost forget how remote this is from the spontaneous movement of civilized minds.

For that reason perhaps, useful as his chapter on the crises of life and their rituals may be, too much is left for the untutored imagination. Here, we need the help of other students like Stanley Diamond and Meyer Fortes to clarify the mysteries of the ritual dramas that Paul Radin inducts us into. But even here his first words, though not the last, remain indispensable:

... puberty, became not simply the recognition that an individual had reached the age of sexual maturity; it became dramatized as the period of transition par excellence: the passing of an individual from the position of being an economic liability to that of an economic and social asset.... Two distinct sets of circumstances, one physiological, the other economic-social, thus conspired to make of puberty an outstanding focus which was to serve as the prototype for all other periods interpreted as transitional. It was certified and authenticated by magic and subsequently sanctified and sacramentalized by religion. Its social and economic significance and evaluation are attested by the fact that the simplest tribes, the food-gatherers and fishing-hunting peoples, have already developed intricate and complex initiation rites around it. These puberty rites are the fundamental and basic rites of mankind. They have been reorganized, remodelled and reinterpreted myriads of times and, on their analogy, have been created not only new types of societal units, such as secret societies, but new ideological systems as well.[6]

He goes on to place the puberty rites at the central and vivifying focal point from which rites and observances celebrating birth and death radiated so that the phases of human life were knit together, perhaps as the poet would have it, "bound to each other by natural piety." Separation and reintegration were accomplished through the social-biological formula involving death in one status with subsequent re-birth in another on a higher level. Underlying all of the great ritual dramas is the impulse:

... on the one hand, to validate the reality of the physical, outward world and the psychical inward world and, on the other, to dramatize the struggle for integration, that of the individual, the group and the external world. This is done in terms of a special symbolism which is expressed in actions and in words, a symbolism which represents the merging of images coming from within and from without. This validation, finally, is articulated artistically and creatively by individuals peculiarly qualified, emotionally and intellectually, that is, by the thinker and the religious formulator.[7]

So the old prestidigitator leads us to the periphery of the mystery by juggling inner and outer symbols, leaving those of us who are at least as peculiarly qualified as primitive "men of action" to pick them up ourselves when he drops them. That this is no easy task, all who have tried will testify.

Understanding these ritual dramas in the context of the part they play in protecting the primitive life cycle can be enhanced by closer inspection of the social and psychic mechanisms through which their effects are achieved. In order to show that anthropologists are still thinking about this problem, some comments by Meyer Fortes will be quoted at length:

Primitive people express the elementary emotions we describe by terms like fear and anger, love and hate, joy and grief in words and acts that are easily recognizable by us. Some anthropologists say that many non-European peoples are sensitive to the feeling of shame but not to guilt feelings. I doubt this. One of the most important functions of ritual in all societies is to provide a legitimate means of attributing guilt for one's sins and crimes to other persons or outside powers. In many primitive societies this function of ritual customs is prominent and it leads to the impression that individuals have a feeble sense of guilt, by comparison with Europeans. The truth is that our social system throws a hard and perhaps excessive burden of moral decision on the individual who has no such outlets for guilt feelings as are found in simpler societies. This is correlated with the fragmentation of social relations, and the division of allegiances and affectations in our society. I am sure it has a great deal to do with the terrifying toll of mental disease and psychoneurosis in modern industrial countries. We know very little about mental diseases in primitive communities. What evidence there is suggests that those regarded by many authorities as of constitutional origin occur in the same forms as with us. But disturbances of personality and character similar to those that cause mental conflict and social maladjustment in our society seem to be rare. I do not mean to imply that everybody is always happy, contented, and free of care in a primitive society. On the contrary, there is plenty of evidence that among them, as with us, affability may conceal hatred and jealousy, friendliness and devotion enjoined by law and morals may mask enmity, exemplary citizenship may be a way of compensating for frustration and fears. *The important thing is that in primitive societies there are customary methods of dealing with these common human problems of emotional adjustment by which they are externalized, publicly accepted, and given treatment in terms of ritual beliefs; society takes over the burden which, with us, falls entirely on the individual.* [Italics are mine.] Restored to the esteem of his fellows he is able to take up with ease the routine of existence which was thrown temporarily off its course by an emotional upheaval. Behavior that would be the maddest of fantasies in the individual, or even the worst of vices, becomes tolerable and sane, in his society, if it is transformed into custom and woven into the outward and visible fabric of a community's social life. This is easy in primitive societies where the boundary between the inner world of the self and the outer world of the community marks their line of fusion rather than of separation. Lest this may sound like a metaphysical lapse, I want to remind you that it springs from a very tangible and characteristic feature of primitive social structure, the widely extended network of kinship. The individual's identification with his immediate family is thus extended outward into the greater society, not broken off at the threshold of his home.[8]

This lengthy passage is quoted in full because its profound comparison of primitive and civilized situations contains enough leads for further exploration to keep a crew of social scientists profitably occupied for a long time to come. It points toward a breakdown of the boundaries between sociology, anthropology and psychiatry along lines designed to ensure their collective reconstitution as a genuine science of man in which the problems of healthy and pathological human functioning will emerge as central. Because of the dependence of ritual drama on the state of the arts, the humanities would necessarily play an important role in filling out this reconstituted science of man. As one indication of this, Francis Fergusson in *The Idea of A Theatre*, working in the tradition of Jane Harrison, develops an interpretation of drama that beautifully complements the anthropological contributions. His interpretation of *Oedipus Rex* as ritual encompasses the insights of Freud but avoids psychoanalytic reduction, by showing how the play functioned in the context of its place within the Greek Festival of Dionysos where it acted on the developed "histrionic sensibilities" of the audience. They were able to experience the rhythms and impulses behind tragic action without actually undergoing its disasters.

Paul Radin's synthetic view of primitive institutions includes a detailed interpretation of their political-legal structure and patterns of personal and social status. This is far too complex to be summarized here but the main links to the earlier discussion might be suggested. Primitive government consists of extended kin organizations like the clans with tribal chiefs serving to symbolize authority, while clan leaders actually wield authority over their kin when necessary. In all instances, authority carries as many duties as prerogatives. It is never personalized but must always be exercised in the name of the group. Custom hedges in persons wielding authority as much or more than it does their subordinates. Legal codes rarely appear until the kin authority system begins to give way to state forms. These are usually imposed by emerging national authorities and opposed by the tribal system. All important statuses in primitive society are kin statuses so that marriage becomes essentially the uniting of two kin groups. Individuality is status so that status ceremonies become vehicles whereby the primitive expresses his individuality at the same time that he reaffirms his social existence and the social existences of his relatives.

Primitive social order, as conceived by Radin, rests on a dramatic synthesis in which everyday life is imaginatively transformed and saturated with meaning. Individuality depends on the capacity to participate imaginatively in the experiences and satisfactions of the whole community. Men and women, old and young, weak and powerful, all have their place in the tribal order so that status guarantees the privilege of participation as well as assurance of the irreducible minimum required to sustain it. Western thought patterns interfere with sympathetic appreciation of this kind of individuation. In a sense, it is the deterioration of this same imaginative faculty so central to primitive life that renders us incapable of apprehending the fashion in which it releases human potentialities. In an essay on aesthetics, the British social anthropologist E. R. Leach comments on the symbolic powers of primitives expressed in daily life:

Whereas we are trained to think scientifically, many primitive peoples are trained to think poetically. Because we are literate, we tend to credit words with exact meanings—dictionary meanings. Our whole education is designed to make language a precise scientific instrument. The ordinary speech of an educated man is expected to conform to the canons of prose rather than of poetry; ambiguity of statement is deplored. But in primitive society the reverse may be the case; a faculty for making and understanding ambiguous statements may even be cultivated.

In many parts of Asia, for example, we find variants of a courtship game the essence of which is that the young man first recites a verse of poetry which is formally innocent but amorous by innuendo. The girl must then reply with another poem which matches the first not only in its overt theme, but also in its erotic covert meaning. People who use language in this way become highly adept at understanding symbolic statements. This applies not only to words but also to the motifs and arrangements of material designs. For us Europeans a good deal of primitive art has a kind of surrealist quality. We feel that it contains a symbolic statement, but we have no idea what the symbols mean. We ought not to infer from this that the primitive artist is intentionally obscure. He is addressing an audience which is much more practised than we are at understanding poetic statement.[9]

It is this trained imagination that allows the primitive to participate in the status dramas of daily life. Similarly, it allows him to dramatize the natural world so as to see in it regularly what only our painters and poets can see and they only sporadically.

This is a far cry from Levy Bruhl's conception of "participation mystique." In no sense does imaginative symbolization preclude logical thought or separation of self from the symbols or the objects symbolized. Our tendency to see it so is probably a cultural reflex arising from the deep split between logic and emotion in our own daily lives. Primitive life entails no such split so that duty, will, and impulse are imaginatively apprehended rather than explained logically—and imaginatively apprehended in a manner that admits the claims of all three even as the requirements of status are fulfilled. Here is where Radin's contribution to our understanding of primitive life is most important as well as least susceptible to paraphrase. *Primitive Man as Philosopher* reveals abundantly the complex perceptions of human nature and the human condition embodied in primitive folklore, mythology, and religion. These perceptions however, like the "obscure" character of primitive art referred to by Leach, require a symbolically imaginative response for comprehension. Anything less is likely to convert them to "parables" or explain them in one or another reductive frame of reference.

When Radin tells us that the Winnebago narrative about Trickster, which he so carefully preserved, contains a profound moral regarding the dangers of instinctual, non-socialized behavior, he is providing us with a clue for grasping the meaning of the story. The point here is that no Winnebago would ever have needed any such clue. The meaning of the story was directly and symbolically apprehended and its relevance to his imaginative reconstruction of his own experiences clarified as he assimilated the symbols and symbolic events in the story. Here is art functioning to modify consciousness directly, as it only occasionally does for us. Until we are able to feel its rhythms, even Radin's sensitive interpretation leaves us outside the story. Only when we let it infect our inner life, that is, experience it imaginatively, can we see how it could affect behavior. For we have to feel the Trickster in ourselves as the primitive does—quite spontaneously— before we can appreciate its tragic consequences or conquer it. Being told that the narrative ridicules Trickster's blind striving can hardly take the place of the wisdom that comes from sensing the folly in unguided instincts, both our own and those of our fellow men, any more than maturity can come from memorizing theories about human growth. The wonderful Winnebago philosophic tale, "The Seer," reproduced in *The World of Primitive Man* tells us more about human limits and the tragedies of human over-reaching than many books on ethics. But it speaks first to the ear of the heart and only when that ear listens can the ear of the head hear what is being said.

The combination of artist and philosopher in the role of the primitive thinker as distinct from the man of action is not as removed from civilized actuality as many would contend. Poetry and philosophy are intimately interrelated as diverse figures like George Santayana, T. S. Eliot and Wallace Stevens have argued and exemplified. But the conception that these activities *must* be interrelated is alien to our specialized civilization. And even more alien is the relation between primitive thinkers and men of action which rests upon the thinker's ability to sense crises of the community and cope with resulting strains by symbolic and ceremonial acts. While men of action live in a "blaze of reality," there are strains in their relation to their impulses, to the community and to the external world. Thinkers who perform properly feel these strains first and express them symbolically. Religious men, shamans and priests, cooperate in this endeavor and indeed are occasionally themselves the artist-philosophers of the tribe. Radin's complex interpretation of primitive religion denies the theories of "mystical participation" without denying that the bulk of primitives who are non-religious still have their experience illuminated by their relation to the authentic religious men of the tribe. Actually there is always a possibility that the tribal intellectuals will become exploitative, but prior to state development the larger context of tribal status should keep this tendency within limits.

In terms of a perspective on the modern community, the distinctions between men of action and thinkers or between religious and non-religious men must be seen as entailing important points of contact and even fusion between the distinctive groups. Primitive artist-philosophers articulate the symbolic-ceremonial web of the tribe, while religious men authenticate this web by inspiration and the evidence of their "seizures." Both are more sensitive to strains and tensions than ordinary members of the community and in their different ways both react to these strains in order to cushion their impacts on the less introspective members. But all remain tied to each other in the larger network of kin statuses and the experiences are shared insofar as they can be symbolically communicated. The revelations of the shaman are the property of the tribe.

Unfortunately modern counterparts of these primitive creators are hard-put to find a similar context for their own activities though many of them do indeed search for it. The turn toward magical doctrine and Celtic fables by a great poet like Yeats is one such manifestation. But the modern artist, mystic, or philosopher rarely breaks through to community experience, nor does he help to authenticate communal symbols. Modern men of thought are segregated from the everyday world and the people who live in it by barriers of sensibility and language. Our artists are therefore forced to record their private responses to the strains of civilization without any assurance that the meaning of their expression will carry much beyond a small circle of similarly inclined creators and critics.

More fundamentally, the role as celebrants of the major life transitions has been taken over perfunctorily by impersonal social agencies, the schools, churches, city halls, and newspapers of the modern city. Indeed these life transitions are often passed over in comparative silence. Adults have to a large extent lost control over their changing communities and so are neither inclined nor equipped to initiate succeeding generations. On the face of things, more distress is aroused over threats to job security than over the assumption of masculine or feminine duties. Social roles and role transitions are occasions for anxiety rather than vehicles for human fulfillment. The very lack of communal ties makes pursuit of substitutes mandatory. Insofar as the

substitutes always whet the appetite further without satisfying it significantly, the individual finds himself back on the status treadmill no
matter how badly he might have wished to get off.

There is an unfortunate inner dynamic in modern "spurious" community life wherein the very spuriousness creates anxiety which propels
the climb to new levels of status in the hope that the gnawing will
cease, yet this upward movement only leads to further anxiety aroused
by the insufficiencies at the new level. The people involved soon lose
their capacity for distinguishing status anxiety connected with important
life transitions from the myriad status threats that daily life presents.
There are no communal rituals to help discriminate the real from the
trivial nor are there any close kin capable of providing guidance through
stormy passages. The intellect is a weak crutch, since the complexity
of modern existence demands broader perspective than most people
can attain, while emotions are even more unreliable so long as childish
impulses reign.

It almost seems as if community in the anthropological sense is
necessary before human maturity or individuation can be achieved,
while this same maturity is, in turn, a prerequisite for community.
This is an over-simplification since we know that some people achieve
integrity in spite of anomic community experiences. The real problems
of life and its transitions have a way of breaking through even where
appropriate ritual occasions are absent, and some people manage to
lead fairly genuine lives in a spurious culture. Sociologists must
search out such people to study the conditions that made their achievement possible. This could lead to further understanding of community
patterns arising within our complicated civilization with potentialities
for releasing true individuality.

There is little to be gained by sentimentalizing about primitive life
or advocating a return to it in any form. We are far too deeply committed to urban-industrial civilization even to think of abandoning it
now. Nor can we artificially incorporate outposts of "folk culture"
within our own context since they quickly deteriorate into "pseudo-
folk" forms when ripped from their proper setting. Folk music written
on Tin Pan Alley or jazz produced by classical musicians, whatever
its intrinsic merits, is hardly a satisfactory solution. Instead, the image
of primitive society supplied us by Radin, Redfield, and Sapir, in
which integral human functioning through an intelligible life cycle

where major human needs are assured of satisfaction and major life transitions directly confronted helps us to formulate norms for human community life.

Anthropologists also provide a good many specific clues about the circumstances of life in a genuine culture even though these circumstances cannot be directly reproduced in a civilized community. Redfield's most recent book, *Peasant Society and Culture*, deals with peasant communities, which he regards as an intermediate type falling between folk or primitive society, on the one hand, and urban society on the other. He develops theoretical models for studying the linkages between urban and peasant social patterns co-existing within the same national framework. Sociologists are familiar with this problem. Most of the sub-cultural diversity of which Park and the Chicago sociologists during the twenties were so fond, stemmed from the presence in the city of first generation immigrants, many of whom retained peasant values and social patterns. Redfield's sensitive distinction between the great or sophisticated-urban tradition and the little or peasant tradition reformulates the time-worn division between high and low culture.

Community sociologists would be well advised to ask themselves why the most important book on methods of community study in recent years should have come from an anthropologist. This is, of course, Redfield's exemplary handbook, *The Little Community*, which contains far more than technical aids. It presents a number of alternative complementary conceptual frameworks as well as a highly sophisticated philosophy of research. It is as applicable to the study of cities or urban sub-communities as to peasant or folk societies, so that the outworn distinction between anthropological and sociological field methods is here exploded in the most convincing fashion possible. Even more striking, however, is Redfield's ability to combine methods for studying social structures from outside with techniques for exploring the inner perspectives of participants so that his battery of approaches ranges from ecology to life histories and the delineation of typical world outlooks. Here the "insight" of the humanist is combined with the "objectivity" of the scientist to present a richer conception of social science than one confined to either alternative.

Sociologists then can fruitfully turn to contemporary anthropology for perspectives on all phases of community life. Our whole interpretation of the structure of folk society, on which so many of our concepts rest, must be modified according to the theories and findings developed by Radin, Sapir, Redfield and the British anthropologists quoted earlier. These concepts and findings acquaint us with unique community systems in which important human potentialities are fulfilled in a fashion peculiarly alien to present-day America. It is exactly our collective commitment to ever-receding status goals that makes the contrasts provided by primitive peoples unusually apt. By cutting through the confusion between "success" defined in marketing terms and the achievement of integrity as a human being, these studies shed light on a dark aspect of American life.

NOTES

[1] Edward Sapir, *Selected Writings of Edward Sapir,* ed. by David G. Mandelbaum (University of California Press, Berkeley, 1949), pp. 315-16.

[2] Ruth Benedict, in *A Study of Interpersonal Relations,* ed. by Patrick Mullahy (Hermitage Press, Inc., New York, 1949), p. 305.

[3] *Ibid.,* p. 308.

[4] Paul Radin, *The World of Primitive Man* (Henry Schuman, New York, 1953), p. 106.

[5] *Ibid.,* pp. 126, 130.

[6] *Ibid.,* p. 152.

[7] *Ibid.,* p. 172.

[8] Meyer Fortes, *The Institutions of Primitive Society; A Series of Broadcast Talks by Evans-Pritchard, et al.* (The Free Press, Glencoe, Illinois, 1956), pp. 89-90.

[9] E. R. Leach, *The Institutions of Primitive Society, A Series of Broadcast Talks by Evans-Pritchard, et al.* (The Free Press, Glencoe, Illinois, 1956), pp. 29-30.